GW00393323

Volunteer Tales

Experiences of Working Abroad

Edited by

Savita Bailur and Helen Grant

The Lutterworth Press

To all the host communities that put up with us
and taught us so much.
We owe you everything that we are today.

The Lutterworth Press
P.O. Box 60
Cambridge
CB1 2NT

www.lutterworth.com
publishing@lutterworth.com

First Published in 2003

ISBN 0 7188 3030 X

British Library Cataloguing in Publication Data
A catalogue record is available from the British Library

Copyright © Savita Bailur and Helen Rana

All rights reserved. No part of this edition may be reproduced,
stored in a retrieval system, or transmitted in any form or by any means,
electronic, mechanical, photocopying, recording or otherwise, without the
prior permission in writing from the Publisher.

Printed in the United Kingdom by
Athenaeum Press

CONTENTS

NOTE FROM THE EDITORS

We hope you feel inspired, uplifted and entertained by the pieces in this book. We're already planning a second edition, with more contributions from Southern volunteers, host communities and programme/country officers, so if you'd like to send us feedback and any contributions, please email us at: info@volunteertales.org

FOREWORD

Anita Roddick OBE

Founder, Non-Executive Director
and Consultant to The Body Shop

For far too long we have been obsessed with paid work – assuming that money changing hands made it far more important. That has been the cliché. Of course it isn't like that any more. People of all ages and social class are giving their time. Some of them even have fun. And the old narrow definition of work is blurring more every year.

The Body Shop already encourages staff to volunteer in the community, and 70 percent of our shop staff do. I discovered early on that there are few motivational forces more potent than giving people an opportunity to exercise their idealism. This blurring between work and leisure, workers and volunteers, is just the beginning.

In the future, I believe we will realise there are some things that volunteers can do far better than professionals. They can provide a human face to impersonal public services. They can provide friendship. Professionals can't do that. And we will also realise that simply helping someone can sometimes be disempowering to the person being helped. That sometimes we can set somebody free just by asking them for help.

My work has enabled me to travel all over the world, learning from people who have little in the way of material possessions, but plenty of knowledge and wisdom to offer. This is the basis of volunteering – the two-way excitement of learning about different people, cultures and different ways of living.

That's what's exciting about the years ahead. In the future, volunteering and work and jobs may not look the same to us at all. As we continue to travel more, and spend time on more important things than just making money, I hope that more people will enjoy volunteering abroad – and that includes volunteers from the South bringing their skills and expertise to the so-called more 'developed' nations.

The articles and stories included in this anthology are essential reading for anyone considering volunteering in another country. Whatever your age, class or nationality, I believe that everyone should try to make time to give, to learn, and to enjoy the satisfaction of achievement.

ABOUT THE EDITORS

Savita Bailur

Savita was an AFS volunteer in Honduras, where she was a socio-economic researcher for RECAP (rebuilding Honduran infrastructure after Hurricane Mitch). Her family moved from India to England when she was eleven. She has a degree in Hispanic Studies from London University, an MPhil in European Literature from Cambridge University and has recently completed an MSc in Information Systems from the London School of Economics.

Her career has focused on project management positions at several large electronic publishing companies and she is currently a research assistant at LSE.

Savita hopes that this anthology will prove inspirational to anyone interested in volunteering overseas, but being 'Southern' by birth, she's also determined to avoid any overtones of neo-colonialism or mawkish sentimentality.

Savita has travelled in North, Central and South America, Australasia, South Asia, the Far East and across Europe (including a memorable 'drive' from London to St. Petersburg, crossing six countries).

Helen Grant

Helen was a VSO volunteer in Zambia, where she worked as Publishing Adviser in a gender research and development NGO in the capital city, Lusaka. She has a BA in Communication & Media Production, an MA in Film & Television Studies and a Postgraduate Diploma in Diplomatic Studies.

Her career and voluntary activities have focused on publishing and development. She has self-published two books: *Zambian Phrase Book* (Lusaka: Khozi-Grant, 2000) and *Tales from Zambia* (Lusaka: H. Grant Publishing, 2000), and has contributed to books, newsletters and magazines for organisations including The Atlantic Council of the UK, the Institute of Latin American Studies and VSO (Zambia). She is a PhD student at Cambridge University, exploring modern African history.

Helen has travelled extensively throughout Europe, Latin America and Africa, and enjoys keeping up to date with international relations and history. Her hobbies include reading, cinema, music, museums, cycling and swimming.

INTRODUCTION

Illustration © Karen Thomas, 2003

Only volunteers, like the people in this book, know what it's like to uproot yourself from your own life, culture, everyone you have ever met, and everything that gives your life any meaning. Because of some (perhaps half-baked) notion of 'helping people' or 'doing something more with your life', you throw caution to the wind and take leave of your senses.

In your voluntary placement, you suddenly find yourself in the middle of a new way of life. You will most probably live in a country of extremes, live as an 'insider', but always feel like an outsider. By the time you return, you will be a changed person in one way or another. You may feel you have achieved something and made the world a slightly better place, although volunteers often find themselves believing they have gained more than they have given from their experience.

Volunteering abroad is a roller-coaster of the most extreme emotions and intense experiences. Many volunteers return to the life they left behind to find it changed beyond all recognition – because their perception is totally altered and their 'recognition' culturally skewed. Many volunteers decide to change the course of their life by going to college instead of returning to work, volunteering again in a another country or doing something else they would not have considered before. The volunteer's emotional experience seems to follow this general pattern. Not everyone goes through all these stages, but most people experience most of them, more or less in this order:

- Excitement and initial curiosity. Wow, everything here is so different. Everyone here is so interesting!
- Altruism and determination, wanting to do something positive and beneficial, working and living in a co-operative way. Trying not to make a fool of yourself by saying or doing culturally inappropriate things.
- Horror and sadness – the people you work with endure such hard lives. There are such extremes of wealth and poverty in this country. The problems are immense. I don't think I can do anything to help.
- Depression and despair. What on earth am I doing here? Why is life so difficult? I'm just going to give it all up and go home.
- Humility. We are so spoilt back home, we don't appreciate what we've got. The humour and survival spirit of my new colleagues and neighbours is amazing.
- Lack of expectations and support. Nobody was expecting me! Nobody tells me what to do. The job will be what I make it.
- Irritation. Haven't these people ever seen a foreigner before? Why do they all keep staring? Leave me alone! What do they want?
- Learning about 'development'. There is a whole development and aid 'industry' in developing countries. Thousands of 'experts' are trying to eradicate poverty, corruption and illness. These experts all live in big, secure houses, drive good cars and have private medical cover.
- Having settled in, boredom of everyday mundane life. I feel so alone. I've only got acquaintances, no friends.
- Exasperation. Am I the only one doing any work around here? Nothing here makes sense. I don't think I can stand much more of this.
- Contentment, being accustomed to a new normality. I'm used to life here now – this is how things are done. I understand new ways of thinking and a different form of society. Feeling sure enough about yourself to be different from the people you've got to know, in ways that suit you.
- Return of your sense of humour. Life here is completely absurd . . . but then my life at home was also absurd.
- Relaxing and taking it easy. Enjoying life to the full, travelling and making new friends.
- Embarrassment at having gained so much and given so little. Oh no, it can't be time to leave already – I haven't done anything yet. I don't feel like I've contributed anything.
- Humility at people's gratitude and appreciation for your efforts and endeavours. Being incredibly grateful to your close friends for their companionship and help. Feeling guilty that you'll be going 'home' to a comfortable lifestyle while they continue to face minor irritations and matters of life and death.

- Making decisions about what to do after your time as a volunteer abroad ends. Realising that you may have changed considerably since you left home. Excitement at going home mixed with nervousness.
- Depression or hilarity on your return 'home'. The shock of the 'new' – what should be familiar seems strange. Your own culture, your own friends and family don't make sense. Their way of life seems bizarre, their priorities wrong.
- Calmness, realisation that you did not change the world but you made a small difference. Your time as a volunteer abroad was worthwhile.
- Nobody understands me properly. Nobody is interested in what I did as a volunteer. The only people who know what I'm talking about are other volunteers. I'm going to write a book based on my time abroad. . . .

So here it is . . . an anthology of around seventy contributions on what the volunteering abroad experience is really like: from setting out, working and living in a different culture, to coming 'home'. These contributions are from people from various nationalities, volunteering through a number of agencies or independently, in a range of countries from Canada to Zambia (the host country is next to the author's name). This anthology is the result of an effort which took two years in the making on a shoestring budget, but one we were determined to achieve. We hope you enjoy these volunteer tales.

All the best
Helen and Savita
London, December 2002

CULTURE SHOCK!

Kumbungu, Village of Banana-Eating *Dirave*s
Zibiah Alfred (Ghana)

The only '*suliminga*' (white girl) in the village finds herself greeted by fierce hissing from the market women, cries of '*Un boro me*' (I love you) from opportunistic men of full teeth and none, and by a colourful cacophony of delighted whoops and terrified howls from the very young.

In Lydia, whose tiger-striped cheekbones plainly denote her arrival to the village from another people, I find a first friend. She welcomes me with open arms, wide-open eyes and open curiosity about the place from which I have come.

It is Lydia who shows me around the market, introducing me to the purple and yellow-clad woman who sells the juiciest green oranges, and Lydia who teaches me the magic Dagbani words which multiply threefold the number of tomatoes my cedis can buy.

It is Lydia who issues the warning not to buy doughnuts from the woman with the wayside cauldron, for fear 'strong strong *juju* (local magic)' will tie me to the woman's ageing son.

It is Lydia who laughs with me when I ask why the girl selling bread has decorated her thumb nails orange – 'these village girls – they don't know what nail paint is for', and Lydia who explains that the fiercely hissing market women are only trying to attract my attention so that they can sell enough wares to pay for their children to go to school. 'In Kumbungu we say that from England it is three miles to heaven. Everyone in Kumbungu thinks white people have money to throw.'

Lydia is the one who knocks on my door with news of a chameleon crawling up a potato plant, with a pot to collect water when she learns the supply is low, with unabashed curiosity when she sees bicycles leaning against my wall and with great delight when she scents that I am frying yam.

Turning up with an apron full of bananas, the first fruits of her tree, it is Lydia who insists on washing all my clothes again, after my attempt to wring out the orange dust of road travel leaves my pale shirts blushing pinkly on the line.

Most of the time we understand each other quite well. Although she did not complete primary school, her English is good, so good that for a moment I believe I have heard correctly when, very proudly, she introduces me to her dogs 'Piss' and 'Hop'.

Such is my Dagbani that I can refer to a snake '*wohow*' as though it were a horse '*wahow*' and find, quite by accident, that this skill induces a considerably more memorable response when performed in reverse.

One afternoon, after a lesson teaching poetry to half a dozen pupils and a curious chicken, I return home in the heat of the day to find Lydia hopping about impatiently on my doorstep. Animated and ecstatic, she is waving her watch at me wildly. I am slow to catch onto the crux of her excitement. The watch, like many worn in Kumbungu, does not go, its battery worn out several owners ago. 'It's come back!' Lydia is busy exclaiming but seeing that I do not join in with her dance she eventually yields to interrogation.

She has been washing her sheets. After a six-month absence, of great distress to its owner, it would seem that the very same scratched watch that is being waved in front of me had impishly decided to reveal itself lying lazily, one eye open, under a mattress.

My puzzled face exasperates her into further explanation. 'The *diraves* carry it back,' she shouts, her shining eyes searching for my slow response. '*The diraves carry it back*!'

I dig gently and discover this word, pronounced something like 'giraffe' is the cause of her great animation. 'Dirave – you know – little little men . . . who live in the forest and eat banana. . . .'

For a moment I wonder if she is talking about monkeys, but no, a '*dirave*' according to Lydia, is an invisible banana-eating dwarf, often with only one leg and a disposition to steal. The strong pulling sensation in my own leg triggers a suspicion that perhaps I am the dwarf here, a kind of fascinatingly grotesque incomprehensible semi-human from a far-off world, but Lydia's face is earnest. Later, I find well-informed locals share Lydia's beliefs about these mischievous single-limbed creatures.

It is Lydia's claim that half a year ago a *dirave* crept into her room and made off with her watch and no amount of teasing about how the watch has subsequently reappeared will demolish this conviction. 'The *dirave* must have crept in and put it back,' she maintains and I begin to empathise with her incredulity when I tell her more about England, the bizarre country where women choose to push their children ahead of them in wheelbarrows and where girls delay having children in order to leave their village and live among strangers.

The Second Hand
David Jefferess (Malawi)

the second hand
here makes its merry-way-around
in time
with clouds
tumbling out of nothing
into clear blue sky
all afternoon
like flowers stretching
into the light of
the morning sun

the second hand
here
wiggles its bottom
around the mango tree
to the rhythm of a drum
and the pace of
bawo played all day
faster than the eye
seemingly still
strolling
around pot-holes and goats
under maize sacks
to the buses that will wait
or there'll be another
when it comes
so don't run

the second hand
here
slides into
moments to stop
and greet strangers
smiling

Keeping Me in Czech
David Barnes (Czech Republic)

Outward Journey

On 30 January 1999, I left England on a coach bound for Prague. There were seven of us taking a gap year in the Czech Republic. I think we were all excited. I know I was; more excited than nervous, certainly, as I remember that the moment we'd crossed the channel I found a dramatic song on my Portishead album and played it through my Discman.

I remember that journey very clearly (I remember my journey back far less clearly even though it was much more recent). There were very few people on the bus: one or two people on their own, a Czech family and us. The two drivers had mullet hairstyles and wore moustaches. That's quite a popular style with a certain type of Czech man.

I swayed from half-sleep to semi-consciousness through most of Germany. I liked it when I awoke to see both sides covered in snow. The thick east German pine forests were dusted with it, like icing sugar. It was freezing outside when we stopped at a service station. When we actually crossed the border, into Bohemia, it was more of the same but the forests were prettier, and I saw startled deer standing by the roadside. With the snow, the little villages and onion-domed churches, it was like arriving in the land of fairytales.

The Kindness of Strangers

Hospitality is taken seriously in Eastern Europe. When I came down to breakfast with the Czech family with whom I was staying, the Sancovi, a formidable breakfast spread, was laid out. Thin sliced ham, salami, cream cheese, paté, rye bread, bread rolls sprinkled with poppy seeds and salt, yoghurt, pastries and black tea all lay enticingly on the table. During the next week I would be attacked with an army of cheesecakes, gateaux and patisserie. The challenge of any 'gapper' faced with Czech hospitality is not to become enormously fat.

I'd give a warning to anyone considering a gap year in this part of the world: don't take this hospitality to its limits. If you accept every offer of a beer, every 'You like slivovitz?', you'll be under the table and have a terrible hangover the next morning when you're trying to teach a class about Canada. It's difficult though – the typical Czech response to 'Just the one, thanks' is, 'But a pair is only natural.'

Removal of Footwear and Other Clothing

In my *Teach Yourself Czech* book, there's a section on 'the footwear ritual'. I didn't realise how widespread this would be. Most households expect you to take your shoes off on entering. When I gave lessons to David Schiller, his family provided slippers for me, set aside. They were too small, and I would hobble about in them around the house.

My host liked to take off his trousers too. In fact, it was one of the first things he did on meeting me. I didn't feel like joining in this particular ritual, although there's obviously a lot less embarrassment about this sort of thing in the Czech Republic. In fact a journey from Zilina to Kosice in Slovakia was enlivened by a related incident. The train was pushing through the Carpathians when I decided to check out the buffet car. It was empty save a few staff: on one side a solemn-faced group counting out money round a table, and in the doorway of the kitchen a man standing in nothing but his blue underpants. He looked up. They all looked at me rather seriously. I looked from one to the other and left, inconspicuously.

Outside of Prague
Prague is wonderful, and familiar to a lot of British tourists. There's the Old Town Square with its gingerbread buildings, majestic Charles Bridge, and Prague Castle with its stylish guards. (President Havel used the costume designer from 'Amadeus' for their uniforms.)

I lived on the outskirts of Kolín, a fairly industrial town 60 km from the capital. It's a different world. People kept chickens and ducks in their gardens. A herd of goats would play outside my window, in the shadow of a huge factory, with towering chimneys that belched out smoke. Into the countryside a little, you'd sometimes see horse-drawn carts ploughing the fields. Out there, people had their little 'chatas', the Czech equivalent of a dacha.

I went to a chata near Karlovy Vary once. There were five of us, including a very petulant grandmother. She objected to being removed from the Prague flat by her granddaughter, Jana. I was treated to a real Czech domestic scene. She had to be dragged, both arms restrained, down the stairs. 'Help! Help!' she screamed. A minute's pause. 'Help! Help!' Well, she quietened down when she got into the car.

The chata was lovely though. It was a beautiful spring day, the first of May, and the little cottage was set amongst thickly-forested highlands. The cherry blossom was out, a woodcutter's axe was stuck in a log in the garden and chickens pecked around.

The Dog's Wig
Holly Twiname (China)

The other day, I saw one of my neighbours walking her little dog. Not in itself surreal . . . until I spotted that the dog was wearing a wig. (Had this occurred a year ago, when I had just arrived, I would have dismissed it as a figment of my imagination, but having been here a year, I know that what you see is in fact real, no matter how bizarre it may seem.)

A few days later, a representative from my volunteer-sending agency came on a routine visit and we were out walking when we met my neighbour with the dog. I had just been telling her what an interesting place Zhoukou can be, and what more fitting example than this? So I took the opportunity to point out the dog. We asked the lady if in fact the dog really was wearing a wig – to which my neighbour, quite openly and proudly, said 'yes'. We asked why, and she said, 'because it looks good!' (The dog is all white, and the little black wig is on its head – quite firmly attached, too. I don't quite know how she did it.)

Rats, Bats, Cats
Russell Smeaton (Maldives)

The Maldives are well known for their amazing coral reefs, and aquarium-like waters. However, plenty of other wildlife abounds, as I discovered.

One of the more common in our house was the shrew. These little cute furry things would scamper about all night, squeezing under doors and running blindly into walls, furniture and anyone that didn't move fast enough. However, they were not alone, and there were plenty of rats to eat the shrews. The rats weren't so cute. They would keep us awake at night with their all night parties on the rooftops. One day, we had a black-out, and went to shower in a Gifili – an area with a well in it, and a stick with a bucket on the end – the normal way of showering in Maldives. You can hear the people showering at night before going to the mosques to pray. Anyway, my friend and I ran out to take a shower, but found a decomposing rat in the bucket. Needless to say, we decided to pass on the shower that day.

Due to the large number of rats and the absence of dogs (dogs are forbidden in Muslim countries such as Maldives), there were a huge number of cats – domestic and wild. These cats would chase the rats (good) but then continue the party the rats had started (bad). At least we never found a dead cat in the shower.

Furry creatures were not the only type of creature you could expect to find. There were plenty of insects. We found some in most unusual places. For example, bread is not a Maldivian thing – other than the Indian paratha bread, the choices are limited. So, we decided to make our own. We bought the flour, and made some pretty good loaves. A little on the heavy side, we sifted the flour to see what a difference that would make. A big difference as it turned out – we discovered a whole host of insects in there. Grubs, weevils, and other things I can't really think about – seeing as we'd already eaten two loaves of 'meat' bread.

Geckos were everywhere. You could hear the almost bird-like chirp of them as they scampered about their nightly duty of eating flies and mosquitoes. They would run over my back when I was shaving – I liked to think they were attracted by the lizard tattoo that I have there, but maybe not.

Living on an island meant there were plenty of crabs going from one side to the other. Sometimes, they would come through our house on their quest for the sea, and we would simply move out of the way of these determined crustaceans. One set up residence in a little hole just outside our house, and he (I'm not sure if he was a 'he' really) became quite tame. I would feed him, but stopped – too many horror films as a young boy came to mind.

The most impressive of all the animals in Maldives for me were the fruit bats. You could cycle around the island at twilight – the stars would be coming out in the indigo sky, the prayer calls were being sung from the minarets, people would be coming out to chat and relax, and these huge bats would be everywhere – swooping out from their nests. I saw many things in my two years, met many friends and had many good times, but the image of these bats at night is the most lasting impression that I have of those balmy nights on an island in the middle of the Indian Ocean.

Parallel Lives
Eva Corral (Angola)

It's Friday evening. I'm on home leave in Spain. It's my last day. Tomorrow I will fly back to Angola. I'm seated on a *terraza* in Madrid waiting for a friend and having a glass of wine, Rioja.

The terraza is located in a pedestrian street surrounded by other terrazas. All of them have black plastic tables: the upper part imitation wood with matching chairs. Working in them are waiters dressed in black trousers with cummerbunds and carrying a notebook with a pencil in the pocket of their shirts and a round metallic tray in their hands.

All along the street, on both sides there are flower-boxes with pansies, miniature roses and magnolias. The colours of the pansies alternate white and red. Tall buildings edge the street. At the lower level there are shops with big luminous letters on the wall.

The sign in front of where I'm seated is in white letters on a red background: *Banco Santander*. If I look to the right there is written in blue, red and white: *Wall Street English School* and to the left in black letters on a yellow background: *Correiduria de Seguros*.

In front of the bank there is a lottery kiosk.

If you raise your eyes to the first and second floor balconies, above the bank one can read the following series of signs: *Sastre. Se elaboran trajes a medida* (Tailor. We make fitted suits), *Centro de Estetica. Depilacion a la cera fria. Manicura (uñas de porcelana). Rayos UVA* (Beauty Parlour. Cold depilation. Manicure (porcelain nails). Sunbed).

As it gets dark the heat lessens and the street fills up with people. Groups of teenagers, girls and boys apart – boys on one side, girls on the other – exchange looks and laugh. Families with small children pass by, some mothers with pushchairs among them.

A girl passes near me on a pink bicycle with a pink basket on the handlebars. Another girl passes with her parents. The mother has a pushchair with a baby in it, the girl has a toy version of her own pushchair with a doll inside.

The *terraza* is full of people now occupying all the tables. Seated to my right there is a family with two small children. The parents have some tapas as dinner while the children eat an ice cream, quarrel between themselves and play amongst the tables. To my left four women in their late fifties have coffee.

My friend finally arrives. She asks for a beer and I ask for another wine. We chat for a while until it gets dark. When we leave the terraza, the only lights we can see are the streetlights.

* * *

A thousand kilometres away lies Kuito, located in the middle of Angola. In the evening, after work, I like to sit outside the house and relax thinking my own thoughts or just watch, through the gate that fronts our little garden, the people that pass by in the street.

In front of the house there is a building. All that survives of it are the outside walls and each window is shrouded with a grille of thick metal bars. Kids normally play football inside. The good thing about this improvised soccer pitch is that the ball cannot escape out of it. To the right there is a white wall with a big metallic door in the middle. It is the warehouse of another NGO. During the day there is always a truck or a tractor loading big sacks full of food to be distributed in the refugee camps that surround the city.

To the left there is a semi-derelict house. It has all the windows permanently blocked up with wooden planks, some big and a lot of very tiny holes in the outside wall due to the impact of mortars and bullets as a result of the war that assaulted the city a couple of years ago but now continues in the countryside around. For a long time I thought nobody lived there, although a group of children always played in its garden, until one day I saw some women sitting in the open door.

Groups of kids walk along the street. Some children, when passing near my house, put their faces through the gateposts and call me by my name, 'Eva!' I don't know how they know it. I never told them, yet without fail all the children living in my street know my name and shout it each time I walk by them.

One of those kids, a girl, is particularly beautiful. She has long cornrow braided hair. The front is in a fringe over her eyes with a little silver-coloured bead at the end of each plait. She looks like Cleopatra.

The boys play with cars they have made from old oil cans supplied for humanitarian aid. They make pick-ups, trucks or planes. They tie a string to the car: attached to the string is a stick, and with this they pull the cars along behind them. Necessity develops imagination.

Some women walk down the street carrying their babies on their backs. They tie colourful material around the baby and then secure them by tying the fabric around their own pendulous chests. Some are barefoot. Other women carry plastic basins of unsold fruits and vegetables on their heads.

When it gets dark it begins to get cold. It's winter in Angola and Kuito is quite high above sea level. The street is almost deserted. There are no streetlights. I raise my head and look at the sky. It is crowded with stars . . . stars that see parallel lives.

Hamna Shida
Jean Cooper (Tanzania)

Yesterday a lorry carrying eighty-odd people to a football match overturned. Three were killed and a fair number brought here.

Wadi Moja (Ward One) , which already has more than its fair share of problems, resembled a battlefield. There were over sixty patients, four nurses, me, and one clean sheet.

Hamna shida (no problem).

Waiting patiently in the corridor for admission were ten men, most of whom were bleeding from somewhere. All the usual chores, operation cases, etc., plus relatives milling around, did not alter the admitting nurse's usual polite greetings in any way.

Each individual was greeted in the same manner as they would have been if there had been only one of them and the whole afternoon stretching ahead.

'Habari za leo?' (what is the news of the day?)

'Nzuri' (good).

'Habari za nyambani?' (what is the news of your home?)

Even – 'Habari za afya?' (what is the news of your health?)

'Nzuri kidogo. Nzuri kidogo' (good, quite good). This is to a man with blood pouring from his chin, and his leg in plaster of Paris from toe to groin.

Each of the ten got the same treatment.

No hurry or panic on Wadi Moja.

When everyone had been admitted, some two to a bed, some on the floor of the corridor, the nurses tied on their *kangas* and wandered off. One day is much like another here.

Allergic!
Bronwyn Hudson (Vanuatu)

I have been in the wars recently. To start with I had a severe allergic reaction to kava, only a week after recovering from a virus. I have never been allergic to anything in my life before (except for a psychological allergy to mushrooms). I figure that if one had to choose at least one thing to be allergic to (apart from boys when you're seven years old) kava would have to be top of the list. I'll explain why.

One of the ni-Vanuatu cultural institutions is the *nakamal* or kava bar. It is a place where people go to sit and share their day with their friends and drink kava. All of the nakamals I have been to are nothing more than a tin shed or bamboo construction that have a small lamp hanging outside to indicate that the nakamal is open and has kava. The lamp goes out once the kava runs out and everyone goes home. There are some two hundred nakamals in Port Vila alone and only three pubs, which kind of gives you an idea as to the magnitude of this custom.

Kava is made from the ground root of a local pepper tree and the connoisseur of kava can tell which island the kava has come from according to the taste and consistency of the kava. The root is ground in what looks like a big mortar and pestle and is then mixed with water and swished around in a big tub. Traditional kava is made by the virginal village boys chewing the root, mixing it with their saliva and then spitting it into the tub, a true delicacy by anyone's standards and taboo for women.

Kava looks and tastes like mud. What's the attraction (and why would one be disappointed to be allergic to the stuff)? Well, after a shell of kava (served in communal half coconut shells), your mouth goes a little numb and you feel all tingly. After a few shells the world slows down and you feel something akin to being stoned (so I am told).

One of the best things about kava is the opportunity to mix with the locals. While tourists partake in the odd shell of kava, they very rarely go to the 'out of the way' ones that we have been frequenting. The nakamal provides a great location to sit and talk with the local people and hear their stories. Ni-Vans are the best storytellers and one of their favourite pastimes is telling their stories to anyone who will listen. It is an honour to be invited to someone else's local nakamal, it is a sign of acceptance and an offer of friendship. This, plus the after effects, made me determined to get over the horrendous taste of the stuff. I had mastered the art of drinking kava without tasting it when disaster struck.

On Friday night after work Nat, Ben and I sauntered down to Ronnies (one of the more famous nakamals) for a few shells. After a really quiet 'post kava' night, I woke up at 4am with the distinct feeling that something was not right. I looked in the mirror and was greeted by this human blowfish of a face that I didn't recognise. Off to the hospital, diagnosis . . . kava allergy. So it's no more kava for me. I am yet to figure out what I will do when I am invited for kava again. What's the Bislama word for allergic or perhaps blowfish?

On the Road
Eva and Bernard Batchelor (Cameroon)

After our previous fiasco travelling by air, we had the unexpected opportunity to return to Yaoundé by road. The British High Commission personnel were visiting Chad and their driver was returning to Yaoundé alone on the weekend of our return. The British High Commission personnel were flying back and so we hitched a lift with the driver. What better way to travel – top of the range Toyota Land Cruiser, air conditioned, satellite radio, long range fuel tanks, two spare wheels (fortunately we only used one on the way) and diplomatic plates so there was no police harassment at the check points. The journey took three days over some very rugged mountain roads which carried the threat of banditry.

For three days we became part of those innumerable vignettes of life which travellers encounter. Shortly after we left Maroua we caught up a convoy of cattle trucks and UN Red Cross refugee vehicles. In the trucks were tired desperate-looking people surrounded by basic goods, beds, cooking pots and bundles of clothing. We had time to understand a little of their plight while we drove with them. They were refugees from the war zone in Chad being resettled in Cameroon, just another group of desperate people not important enough to be mentioned on the world news.

We passed fully-laden trucks, which had crashed off the road. The trucks only travel at night and the drivers frequently fall asleep. On a particularly steep mountain road we drove around half a truck-load of cotton bales neatly stacked in the road. At the top of the climb we came across the lorry with the driver unloading the other half of his load before going back to collect the bales of cotton that he had abandoned. His truck was so overloaded that it could not climb the hill. There must have been fifty tons of cotton being loaded and unloaded by hand. He must have been exhausted at the end of the activity, considering the heat.

We often passed broken-down vehicles whose drivers waved for help but you don't dare stop since this is often a decoy for an armed ambush. As soon as drivers stop, armed bandits appear out of the bush to hijack the vehicle, steal money and probably shoot them. Our colleagues at Plan International lost their new Toyota truck like this and the driver was shot in the shoulder. It is for this reason that we did not travel after dark. The usual procedure in the event of a breakdown is to wait for a lorry to stop as they carry a driver and a 'motor boy', who is the mechanic. The mechanics earn extra money by 'fixing' broken-down vehicles in this way.

We passed over the central range of mountains and on this section we only met about four vehicles an hour. High in these mountains we met our first troop of monkeys. We stopped when we saw a big male cross the road but the rest would not follow and ran parallel to the road and rushed across about twenty metres behind our vehicle. After that we saw other troops, either in the bush or crossing the road.

There was so much to see as we travelled through major climatic and scenic variations. There were different methods of constructing houses and the ways in which the villages were built, some with compounds, others scattered over a wider area with their farms close by. The vegetation changed constantly, as we travelled from eight in the morning until six in the evening. In the rainy season this journey would take six to eight weeks – when the roads become quagmires and landslides block the way.

'Language Out'
Stuart Marriott (Tanzania)

All this 'language out' work was in preparation for the weekend when, to many people's trepidation, we were due to stay from Friday evening to Monday morning with local families. To soften the blow, we all met our hosts in a local container bar on Thursday evening. The beer flowed and inhibitions broke down, but this left us with very little unused Swahili to employ during the forthcoming weekend.

Barbara and I were guests of Moses and Hilda Msami who are perhaps not absolutely typical of a Tanzanian family in that they are comparatively 'middle class'. Moses owns a business buying and selling woodcarvings. He also employs a number of craftsmen who make and sell carvings for him. He has a workshop and showroom attached to his house in a suburb of Dar es Salaam (Dar) and another in Arusha where he spends alternate fortnights. Hilda works as a senior secretary in a computer salesroom.

As well as speaking pretty good English (officially forbidden during the forthcoming weekend), they were both fluent in Italian. We found out later that this was because they both had lived in Italy for some years and had brothers and sisters in Italy, some married to Italians. It's a mark of our own insularity that we should be surprised that Tanzanians should speak a European language other than English.

The family represent a very good model for the religious tolerance that is to be found in Tanzania. This tolerance is very much the product of the efforts of Julius Nyerere, the first president after independence, widely known as the Father of the Nation, who swiftly recognised the importance of tribal harmony if the nation was to survive. He successfully persuaded the hundred or so different tribes in the country to adopt Swahili as their first language so as to recognise themselves as Tanzanians first and members of tribes second. As a result, inter-tribal and even inter-religious marriage is commonplace in Tanzania, which must be quite unique in Africa.

Even by Tanzanian standards, Hilda and Moses must be remarkable cases. Hilda's grandfather was the first Anglican African priest in Tanga province near the Kenyan border and all her side of the family have remained Anglican. Moses was born a Muslim and had the name Musa. He later converted to Catholicism and indeed he and Hilda were married in a Catholic ceremony. Moses' father is still a Muslim but is also a respected 'witch doctor' (his words) in a Dar suburb. One of Moses' sisters had pictures of Mecca hanging side by side with ones of the Holy Family.

By our standards, Hilda and Moses' middle-class dwelling was a miserable hovel, which probably would be condemned by even the most un-enlightened of councils. However, there were some pretensions to wealth to discover – a black-and-white TV, an electric cooking ring and an electric iron. The crowning glory was the bathroom – fully appointed with a washbasin, hot and cold taps, a shower with shower-head and fittings and a flush toilet. Unfortunately, this grand effect was ruined by the fact that the only source of water in the whole house was from one small tap in the corner of the bathroom, so all the water had to be hosed from this to all parts of the house and also over the wall to the dingy shack where six of Moses' workers lived with their families.

Saturday night was something of an ordeal. The community centre next door finished its all-night drumming session at dawn to coincide neatly with the beginning of the amplified sermon by the Muslim priest at the mosque on the other side of the house.

Hilda and Moses are extremely nice people but by Sunday morning it was an uphill struggle, particularly in our sleep-deprived state, finding new things to say with our couple of hundred words of Swahili. Relief came on Sunday afternoon in the shape of a visit to one of Hilda's sisters to attend the confirmation party of her son. This family live in the village of Pugu about twenty miles and two *dalla-dalla* (minibus) rides out of Dar, probably the nearest bit of proper countryside to the big city, thus giving us our first taste of rural Tanzania.

Their *shamba* (farm) is about an acre in extent and has lots of fruit trees, a big vegetable garden, a fish pond (for food) but also a decorative flower border around the house – just for decoration. The only source of water for all household uses appeared to be a muddy pool in the middle of the vegetable garden. In my Swahili lessons I had been a little confused as to why the word *jiko* could mean both kitchen and stove. I now found my answer.

When we arrived, the women of the extended family – about ten of them –

were busy cooking the celebratory feast. They simply plonked down charcoal stoves wherever suited them in the bare earth in front of the house, found a convenient corner to chop vegetables and pulled off a leaf from a handy tree to use as an oven cloth while at the same time shooing off any chickens, which might be pecking at the bits of discarded food. In other words, the real translation of jiko is simply 'somewhere where you prepare food'.

Whenever a new guest approached the compound she would ululate shrilly and break into a dance to be greeted in similar fashion by the women in the kitchen. Then, of course, she would join the kitchen staff. From time to time the women would get up, do a song and dance number and then return to their cooking. Meanwhile, of course, the men were nowhere to be seen – probably down the garden somewhere, drinking. I suppose officially I should have been with them but as an ignorant foreigner I claimed the right to break tradition. Tanzanian women certainly have a tough time in many ways but they also know how to have fun. I'd rather be with the ladies.

They had cordoned off a pleasant area in the shamba for the party proper and decorated it with bits of tinsel and any other colourful bits they could lay their hands on – rather limp balloons advertising Fanta Orange being prominent. The local DJ had set up his clapped-out sound system and was entertaining us with very tinny Congolese music when, at about 2pm, we heard ululating in the distance indicating that the confirmation party was approaching. They had walked 5 km from the church (where, I believe, two hundred young people had been confirmed that afternoon). This party was led by the confirmee himself, a very proud young man, wearing a beautifully white shirt and home-made tinsel garland around his neck. He was followed by a train of ecstatic relatives shimmying and chanting their hero into the party.

At the party we were embarrassed to find that we had been placed well up the pecking order (much of Tanzanian life, including parties, seems to involve some sort of hierarchy), so were ushered to easy chairs near the front and got our food directly after the young man's immediate family. The celebration itself was great fun, a mixture of solemnity and joy, generally orchestrated by the exuberance of the women. Before the dancing and boozing began everyone at the party had to be introduced. When Hilda announced us as volunteers an old lady yelled 'Halleluyah'. I fear her expectations might be rather high.

Confirmation ceremony at Pugu

As parties go, it would be easy to be critical; the decorations were tacky, the music tinny and often unintentionally inappropriate (obscene American 'rap' playing behind the solemn speeches); the confirmation cake was lopsided, the food undistinguished, the beer warm, the guests unfashionably dressed, the seats, even the comfortable ones, uncomfortable. But, quite simply, none of this matters – the simple philosophy seems to be – if there is a good time to be had, have it. And we did.

We only had to get through Sunday evening and we had cracked the ordeal of the weekend. Spending three days with a local family was far from easy. Conversation dries up very quickly and you are constantly on show in a society which doesn't really recognise privacy as I know it. But we survived and returned to base on Monday morning armed with lots of tales to tell our colleagues.

First Views of Ahmedabad
Asif Pradhan (India)

After spending a couple of days in Mumbai (aka Bombay), my colleagues and I arrived in Ahmedabad where we had a ten-day orientation that included visits to a variety of Non-Governmental Organisations (NGOs), a visit to the field and handicraft stores, language training and a sampling of the finest cuisine in India.

The flat that we now call home is comfortable and located in a very busy part of the city close to everything. The neighbours, especially the children, are charming. As they're accustomed to seeing different Canadians every year, they are quite used to us and readily try to speak in English. There is a strong sense of community, which is a refreshing change.

Traffic is crazy and more of a threat than the malaria mosquito. While traffic lights do exist, they are lacking in number and there is no order. The sheer number of vehicles – motorcycles, bikes, scooters, rickshaws, cars, buses, trucks – not to mention the cows that are sprawled all over the streets – make crossing the road impossible and walking on the roadside an incredible chore. When walking during the night, I am constantly on the alert to ensure that I don't step on any of the cows, camels, goats or dogs.

Riding a rickshaw has become part of my daily routine and is something I often look forward to. Despite the bumpy roads, the deadly traffic and the loud and

Typical traffic scene in Ahmedabad, Gujarat

continuous sounds of horns, the breeze while driving has a nice cooling effect on what is regularly a very hot and humid day.

I have also ventured into taking the bus, and what an experience that has been. Not being able to read Gujarati script has resulted in me getting on the wrong bus a couple of times and my poor pronunciation of the language and limited vocabulary has amused the other passengers. Even though language is often a frustrating barrier, the people have been extremely supportive. There is always someone looking out for me and assisting me. Some people even go as far as reminding me when to get off.

The sights, smells and sounds here are very real. Poverty is a reality. I am often overcome with emotion seeing people without limbs, people looking for things in the garbage and children without clothes. Material wealth as we know it is, for the most part, unheard-of here. Yet even with so little, the people here seem content and exemplify a wonderful spirit of generosity and kindness. I am grateful to be here and feel so blessed. The warmth of the people here is incredible.

My experience with the organisation I have been placed with has been very positive so far. They are extremely innovative and have been instrumental in changing government policy on watershed, irrigation and forest management practices in the state of Gujarat. Having worked for only the last couple of weeks, I have already been to the field and observed a three-day training workshop for Watershed Committee members. I've also learnt to take a bath with half a bucket of water. My supervisor, with the other staff, is very friendly and keen to provide me with a good orientation to all components of the organisation before I settle into a focused study that I hope will be mutually beneficial.

Images of Ghana
Zibiah Alfred (Ghana)

Tamale. A big bustling city, motorcyclists squirling noisily around bowls of wares balanced on women's heads. Bright cloths lend the women invisibility. It is the children who are the visible ones, running everywhere, chasing goats and shrieking greetings at the tourists.

With the business of bright colours and the immediacy of the traffic, it is easy to push through without noticing minutiae – an old man sitting by the roadside under a splayed conical hat, drinking water out of the spout of a plastic tiger-striped kettle; a small boy sitting with a needle and cotton sewing up the split in the sole of a man's flip-flop; small children wandering the streets crying 'ice-water, ice-water', no fairground goldfish in these bags – just typhoid on the cheap. Muslims in flowing colours picking their way to the mosque across the piles of stones and dusty rubble. Women straddling the open drains to wash up their plastic tea-party sets; other women selling leathered meats from hot glass boxes on their heads; men lolling against broken stalls eyeing up the day; giddy cyclists struggling along with benches and bed-frames strapped to their backs; pedlars and street hawkers circling and swooping, beggars and sweet talkers calling and crooning; the mating calls of taxis and angry berating of the driver's opportunistic fare prices, and in no particular hurry, wandering through the middle of it all a few families of goats and some harassed-looking chickens.

Lydia and I walk to the market. Many, many women, all wrapped in layer upon layer of patterned cloth; yellow for an apron, pink for a head-scarf, purple and green for a skirt, a tie-dyed shawl to hump a baby to her back. So many colours seething, seething. Reds and oranges stewing in the sun, the colours make me giddy. 'Suliminga, suliminga!' (white girl, white girl) until I am tired of responding. I just want to get out with my *kamatosie* (tomatoes).

Lydia wants fish. Shrivels of tarnished silver, dulled in the sun, like rusty bits of metal. The woman wraps her four screws, economically tearing out dabs of brown paper; her hands are sweaty with fish oil. We squeeze through the people, treading carefully between small children asleep on sacks, and make our way to the slaughterhouse. The cow tied up by the car station is now cut up inside.

Kumbungu market scene

* * *

From Tamale in the rain, travelling with eight people in a four-seater car, the road flashing up through the holes in the floor, we break down and the driver spends an hour fiddling with wires, whilst spiky-hatted children, with no shoes or shirts, stand in the puddles and laugh at us. Every time the driver tries to start the engine he has to hold together two ragged bits of wire and make a spark between his thumbs. Power here is haphazard.

Kumbungu cars are hazards, held together by rope, rust and their drivers' determination to make a living. Most children in the village will never make the hour's journey out to Tamale. At twelve hundred cedis, the price of thirteen oranges, this bumpy adventure is too dear.

* * *

Outside the communication centre under the leafy shade of the mango tree. The electricity is off and the phone has been silent all day. On the radio Nigeria are beating Ghana at football. A rooster with a double chin walks up to us, picking its way through the sandy red earth, past the stripy plastic kettles used for washing feet as well as drinking from the spout. A black and white goat strains upwards to tug out the moisture from the sweetcorn leaves. I imagine what a good place this would be for a café or ice-cream shop; instead only the radio, a few plastic chairs, an old bench and the plastic kettles. A straw prayer mat sleeps at the side of the wall. Men cycle over to say hello. One man wants to know if I have children – his friend translates for him. 'Two hundred', I retort, 'at the school'. His friend thinks my answers are funny. The man continues to question me in Dagbani. I ask if he can speak English. His friend explains the man has not been to school. But he wants to go. I predict his next line before it has been translated.

Nothing left to say, the man sits with us on the bench, picking up the Ghanaian newspaper printed in English, at first upside-down and later guided by the pictures, rotated to its more customary position. His friends mock him. Eventually he gets up and cycles off. Two small boys come and stand behind us giggling. 'He says he wants to marry you,' one man explains, pointing at the smaller one.

Still waiting for the lights to come on, an hour passes by and the heat rises out of the day. Four small girls go out of their way to walk round in front of us so that they can get a better look at the '*suliminga*'. They giggle nervously when they see I am also looking at them. The men on the benches admonish them; they run past and the tin bowl falls from the tallest one's head; two empty tins, some chilli peppers and a bag of red *kpam* (palm oil) roll on the ground. Much giggling, more admonishment. Eventually, holding each other's arms, hiding behind each other, they come forward and greet me.

'*Antire*' (good afternoon)
'*Naa*' (and to you)
'*Antire*'
'*Naa*'
'*Antire*'
'*Naa*'
'*Antire*'
'*Naa*'.

They run off giggling.

On the way back to my house I go through the ritual of greeting people all over again. '*Antire*', '*Anoola*' (good evening), '*Abira*' (how are you?), '*Na gwarm*' (how goes your walking?); I am being tested.

A fire spits by the side of the road; a goat on its back, its legs stiffly in the air, is being roasted, still in its coat, poked by small children with sticks. Other fires and cooking pots and crouching children. Women who look at me through closed eyes, resting against the trees. Young men whose egos all expect a personal greeting; '*Ya ka ayinah*?' – where are you going, where have you been?

'*Madam, antire*' from the men I have failed to greet. Nods from the old men gathered in their hats, under the trees.

As I reach home the sun falls from the sky. Inusah is waiting with her books on my doorstep.

Up the Mosquito Coast with a Gun at My Head
Savita Bailur (Honduras)

Four months into my research on Honduran infrastructure devastated by Hurricane Mitch, I was tackling the country's wild north-east.

Remote even before Mitch flattened the area, it is now purely jungle and beach. Bonito Oriental was made famous by Paul Theroux's disturbing book *Mosquito Coast*, and it was appropriately where the village madman jumped into the pickup in pre-dawn darkness. He didn't mind where we went, he said, he just liked riding in the back. Madness in itself – who'd want to be jolted around in the fierce heat as the 4x4 vainly gripped the treacle that passed as a road? It was too dark then to notice the bulge in his torn jeans. Only after the sun had risen did my American colleague hiss: 'He's packing.'

It could've been my lack of gun vocabulary or that I was fed up with Mike after four months on the road together.

'Who's packing what?' I said through uncharitably clenched teeth.

Damage after Hurricane Mitch

'The loco ... is packing a gun ... he is loading a gun.' And with an ease that can only come from having lived a lifetime in New York, 'or perhaps he's just pleased to see you, har har har.'

Heart thudding, I turned around to look at Loco ('They call me Loco,' he'd said, pleasantly enough). He flashed a charming (disturbed? murderous?) smile, eyes fixed on my face, right hand burrowed into his pocket. None of us were armed. We carried a rusty machete but no-one wanted to use it for fear of tetanus. Mike and Jorge the driver were arguing about buying an armadillo for dinner. But whenever I turned around, Loco stared intently at me.

In the Garifuna settlements we heard tragic stories of Mitch – swollen rivers roaring through towns, people killed within minutes, main streets now innocent Caribbean inlets. We constantly met doctors, engineers and health workers. The Garifuna – descendants of escaped slaves from nearby islands, and a minority in Honduras – were furious that they were once more sidelined by authorities. We continued further east, driving along the beach when the track surrendered completely to the jungle. The poverty at Iriona appeared all the more harsh against blindingly white beaches and turquoise seas. More than once, my naïve volunteer eyes would smart with tears. Meanwhile, Loco shadowed me closely all the time, with hands in his pockets.

Iriona was literally the end of the road. From here it was a day's walk along the beach to Batalla, where canoes go upriver into the Mosquitia. We turned back reluctantly. I spent the interminable journey swatting creepy-crawlies and keeping an eye on Loco. He dozed in the back, surrounded by the poor trussed-up armadillo and gifts of plantains and coconuts. The gun was outlined against denim. Oh well, I thought, I'm not dead yet.

We finally screeched to a dusty halt by Jorge's thatched home. His sleepy kids crowded around, barefoot, orange-haired with malnutrition, but excited at the armadillo. With a dazzling smile, Loco delved into his pocket. His fingers closed in on the weapon. He drew it out carefully and pointed it at his head.

'Bang,' he yelled and all the kids howled with laughter.

It was a toy gun.

THERE ARE MANY KINDS OF

VOLUNTEER

The 'Typical Volunteer'
Fergus Power (Angola)

If you were asked to picture a volunteer, what would come to mind?

Having spoken to a few people about this, a consistent image emerges – notwithstanding that this is distilled from descriptions of people of both sexes with ages ranging from the early twenties to mid-seventies. The image is that of a person who isn't overly concerned about appearance, with a tendency to dress for comfort and durability rather than style.

I think that this is partly due to mindset, but it also comes of working in places where clothing is good because it lasts, or is light, or has many pockets, rather than because it's fashionable or bears a particular label. It is also the case, I think, because volunteers typically work with people who have very, very little, in situations where ostentation is obvious and may attract attention of the type that it is better to avoid.

Consider then the reaction that one would get, when visiting the HQ of an NGO for an informal interview, if one were to present oneself much more formally attired.

When I first went to talk to Concern about working as a volunteer in Angola I held the lofty position of Senior Consultant with Ernst & Young Management Consultancy Services: at the time one of the five largest financial services firms in the world and an apparent bastion of conservative respectability. As one would expect, the job required me to own a number of suits, this number being greater than one.

For some reason on the day of that first interview I was wearing the 'good' suit, the one that had cost twice that of any of the rest, the one usually reserved for the first day of a new project and other occasions when I'd need all the support I could get. Combine this with the good shirt, tie and shoes and you have the stereotypical young, upwardly-mobile professional, dressed to the nines and career in mind. I have never found out whether my interviewer was influenced by my appearance, however his focus when speaking of the positive element of working as a volunteer was not what I was expecting.

He spoke of embassy parties, NGO parties, company parties – quite fondly, it seemed – of Sundays at the beach and no winters. He spoke of housekeepers, guards and drivers, of a life free of such mundane inconveniences as grocery shopping, cooking, cleaning, laundering and driving oneself. To be fair to the man, he also told me that I would probably have to work hard, but the overall picture was of an easy lifestyle, one that in Europe is enjoyed by only a tiny few.

The suit had a different effect on the next interviewer. She questioned my motives and spoke of the difficulties I'd encounter. After the previous tales of a pampered existence this was more akin to what I'd anticipated. With Luanda in mind, she spoke of heat and humidity, sweating and sleep loss. She spoke of a city of noise and dirt, of crowds and bad sanitation. She warned me of decrepit infrastructure, sporadic electricity, undrinkable water, bland food and limited entertainment. She outlined the potential personal health problems, focusing on the bigger killers of volunteers: Road Traffic Accidents; Malaria; and Other People, whether wielding weapons or disease. Though she did add that there were quite a number of other more or less exotic-sounding threats, lest I be getting complacent.

A thorough woman, she went on to discuss possible psychological problems, such as alienation, trauma and homesickness, the last alone being enough to make some people's lives quite miserable. Having presented quite a convincing case against doing something as apparently bloody stupid as becoming a volunteer, she changed her tack and gave the case for. It was simply but powerfully put: there are few jobs in this life that will give you the same level of satisfaction as those where you are helping others, and to work as a volunteer is to help those who are among the most needy, and possibly to make a difference in one's short time on this planet.

Almost two years later I can confirm that both interviewers were absolutely right. All that they mentioned has been a part of my experience to a greater or lesser degree. However, the positive and the negative sets, as described to me above, are not complete. The same element is missing from both. Friendship. Can this be a negative? Strangely, yes.

I've been blessed to have met, befriended and been befriended by some truly special people. People with rare commitment, integrity and feeling for others, some of the most human saints one is ever likely to encounter. By the very nature of this work the time you share together is brief, and this is the negative. People reach the end of their contracts and move on, to other fields, other organisations, other lives, so that one is continually saying goodbye to good friends. This is hard, but, as my second interviewer suggested, we are amply compensated.

Totally Prepared
Jimmy Hendry (Namibia)

I decided to volunteer after yet another heavy session one Saturday night in August last year. Whilst lying in the house in a rather hungover condition after sitting through another side-splitting omnibus of EastEnders (me and Dad love it, as we often consider moving to London then watch an episode of this tripe and realise what a mistake it would be), a programme called Lifeline came on and VSO was first up. 'Do you want to work in Africa?' said the man on telly. *Aye*, thought I, *that sounds alright.* So I called and after sending everything away – papers and such – I was given a date for the assessment day.

On arrival in the big smoke I phoned my dad to tell him it wasn't as bad as we had previously thought on EastEnders. I stayed on Holloway Road with my mate Sean's folks who thankfully put me up. 'Relax,' Sean had told me as I boarded the plane at Edinburgh, 'London is just like Auchterarder but a wee bit bigger so you'll be fine.'

To my surprise he was right. I had no problem navigating London with my trusted guidebook. The only problem I encountered was when, without my knowledge, I had gone past my permitted stop and the guard in the tube station demanded I give him ten pounds as a fine. I told him he should have a mask on as he was such a robber, then I asked him where he'd left Black Bess, but he didn't get that one.

The most nervous part was waiting once we had arrived at the assessment centre. The woman sat next to me (who's now in Namibia as well) told me that she'd heard only 25% of people on assessment day get selected. Well, I thought, that was a wasted trip down, but to my amazement I was eventually selected and here I am learning so much.

Ordinary or Extraordinary
Stuart Marriott (Tanzania)

I own a charming stone-built cottage on the edge of the Peak District in Derbyshire. I am in my mid-fifties; the family has grown up; the mortgage is paid off; I don't have particularly expensive tastes and there is enough part-time work around for me to live quite comfortably for the foreseeable future in rural circumstances, which many would envy. Perhaps it comes as a bit of a surprise, therefore, that in September 1999 my wife and I set off to work as volunteers for two years in one of the remotest corners of Tanzania about which we knew very little. The only fact that we were sure of was that two genocidal civil wars were raging close by in Burundi and Congo.

The deal we had let ourselves in for would entail living and working in a society totally unfamiliar to us. We had no idea what sort of accommodation we would have, what kind of food would be available and what exactly the jobs would entail. To cap all this we would, at our comparatively advanced age, have to learn a new language, Swahili, from scratch.

Exactly what it was that tipped us into the decision to give up the well-earned comfort I can't really analyse. All the motivations that you trot out in interviews – sense of adventure, doing your bit for a fairer world, itchy feet, putting something back into the system – had their place and to be fair, we are not exactly unfamiliar with working abroad, having spent spells in Singapore and Hong Kong. But underlying all these I guess there was

'We had no idea what sort of accommodation we would have'... at work with a charcoal iron

a kind of cussedness which surfaces when life is easy and tells you that you ought to be 'suffering' a bit more. . . . . .

Looking back on the Tanzanian experience, nothing world-shattering happened to us. We were never chased by elephants; never had to flee a civil war (although two major ones were raging nearby); never suffered the absolute extremes of weather or environment. Instead, day by day, we found ourselves in circumstances in which, on the one hand, we were stretched and challenged in all sorts of ways while on the other hand we were sufficiently in control of life to make a positive impact in our jobs.

The result of this is that there was never a week when I couldn't record something new in my diary. This would certainly not have been true had we stayed put in our rural idyll in Derbyshire.

Uncle Mikey and the Famed Winged-Bean
Paul Karrer (Western Samoa)

Peace Corps Volunteer Michael stood a muscular 5 feet ten inches, and most volunteers in Teachers' Group 27 liked him. Furthermore, his polite 'Yes ma'am and no ma'am' mannerism ratcheted his likeable quotient up a twist more.

But he possessed one thing that he wished he didn't – 'The Turmoil Factor'.

Uncle Mikey, as we affectionately called him, was pretty sharp and his long-range goal was to become a doctor. Consequently, there were a few things Uncle Mikey needed to prove to himself. At the core of his needs was the desire to have a *true Peace Corps experience*.

Now a *true Peace Corps experience* entailed roughing it. Roughing it meant casting off all semblances of western civilisation and 'going native'. Uncle Mikey's option planted him squarely on the island of Savaii, Western Samoa. Once there, he found himself in what he considered to be the last village on the edge of the end of the world.

Uncle Mikey's tender care was placed in the hands of the local chieftain, who also happened to be the headmaster of Uncle Mikey's school. Uncle Mikey's world became smaller and smaller. Throw in the added element that he didn't get the kind of female attention he desired for *many* moons. Things began to occur. To state it plainly, Uncle Mikey got cranky. It didn't take too long for 'The Turmoil Factor' to rear its ugly head. Usually it would manifest itself quite clearly. Wherever Uncle Mikey was, things would screw up. Plans would go awry. Simple things became complex and the unifying factor in all this was . . . Uncle Mikey.

Now this is where the much-famed winged-bean enters the scene. It should first be explained that in our teacher training, we had been exposed to basic gardening. The ideal was to grow thriving gardens and set a positive example of proper industrious nutrition in our respective villages.

Uncle Mikey tried to introduce the winged-bean. This was a delicious, nutritious green bean which could grow in sand, shade and sun . . . anywhere. It couldn't easily be under-watered or over-watered. It was idiot-proof. It just grew and Uncle Mikey liked it. In order to save his sanity he put his entire being into a garden of mammoth proportions. Everyday after school he spent hours toiling over his soil. Good little gardener that he was, he ringed his garden with marigolds. We had been taught this kept away a wide variety of evil garden digesting insects and added an aesthetic touch.

Apparently some of the village children thought so too. In the very same village there resided a mangy, scraggly old hag of a horse. Bones, sores and hair held it together. Each day one child tethered the horse after they hauled bags of copra. On this particular day the child had become so seduced by Uncle Mikey's flowers, the child staked the horse's long tether at the edge of the garden.

In the morning the sleepy village of Faga awoke to a piercing shriek, which may or may not have been a welcome change from the usual pig grunts and rooster crowings. It appeared that the village's one and only Peace Corps volunteer had gone completely berserk. He ran amuck in the village, kicking an ancient horse in the hindquarters. Uncle Mikey spewed forth, as he ran, a rich Samoan vocabulary that both impressed and shocked his chief. Next, Uncle Mikey was seen pursuing a small child. The child, who had so far survived to the age of six, rapidly decided that he wanted to live to the ripe age of seven. Wisely, he ran and he screamed. The village poured out, guffawing and chuckling until their sides hurt.

Eventually the horse ran off and the child found refuge in the anonymity of the crowd. Uncle Mikey sat in the complete ruins of his garden. The horse had consumed everything; all the winged-beans, tomatoes, peppers and pumpkins. Uncle Mikey said, 'When I got up in the mornin', I saw that there damnable horse in the middle of ma' garden chewen', crapen' and burpen'. It was the burpen' that got me all fired up.'

After that, people in the village gave him a little more distance. The child received a tongue-lashing and there was much joking to the effect that the horse looked better than it had in a long time.

Uncle Mikey is now a proctologist in Richmond. Group 27 figured he'd never make it as a vet.

Hobbies of a Ha Tinh Hermit
What it's Really Like to be a VSO Volunteer
Bryony Fuller (Vietnam)

In June 1998, I was delighted to be informed that I had been selected to join VSO. I was in London choosing from a handful of placements and one of the descriptions particularly caught my eye. It advised: 'Volunteer must be content with simple pleasures and be able to make their own entertainment.' I failed to foresee the implications of this (under-)statement.

Perhaps I should be involved in writing the next one, which might read as follows: Come to Ha Tinh and develop skills you never knew you had! On a Saturday night, you could find yourself discovering any number of the following entertainments:

Mosquito-killing. Try it one-handed, by clutching at the air then examining your hand for bits of leg or wing. Keep a tally of your success rate to monitor your progress. Reach for a piece of paper, swat said creature, then discover bits of leg, wing, body and internal juices splattered all over your carefully-prepared, about-to-be-photocopied-for-80-students text.

Failing that, you could clap two hands together, probably not achieving much, but at least reassuring the concerned college director opposite that you're having a great time on your own after all. Searching high and low for the origin of a sporadic and really irritating buzzing sound, then grinning as you finally spot a fly dying slowly on its back under your bed.

Looking up 'sporadic' to check if that's the correct use of the word. Maybe 'erratic' would be better. . . . No, sounds too much like 'erotic', which the long fingernails of the sophisticated Vietnamese male definitely aren't.

Counting your money to see how many times you can get to Hanoi and back in the space of a month. Wondering whether you could muster up the energy to travel all the way (350 km) from Ha Tinh to Hanoi anyway . . . by a combination of motorbike taxi (ten minutes), local bus (two hours), second motorbike taxi (ten minutes), night train (ten hours) and final motorbike taxi at 4:30am (five to ten minutes).

Washing up a stray teaspoon (before the spiders, cockroaches, ants and rats get it), making a cup of green tea, washing up the cup and spoon, making a cup of green tea, washing up etc . . . etc. . . .

Writing another letter, but simultaneously recognising the futility of such an exercise. After all, no letters for 15 days from the UK must mean they've all got lost, or yours aren't getting to England, or maybe you're just on your own in your Vietnamese ivory tower forever.

Thinking back to two Saturdays ago when, new to your placement, you were 'rescued' by two colleagues.

'We say een Viet Nam very sad to be alone on Saduddy night so we come see zyou' and 'Chelsea's playing Villa on the telly so if you don't mind letting us in . . . .'

Wondering whether the above colleagues were using 'sad' in its original sense.

Rationale and Rightness – A Programme Officer's View
Diana Tottle (Nigeria)

For the potential volunteer reading through the description of the job that the postings department of VSO are proposing, the rationale and rightness of it can seem so sound. There's a map, a history of the organisation to be assisted, a description of the needs that must urgently be addressed, and explanation of how this fits into the macro-development context of the country. The logic that these needs call for a volunteer to address them and that volunteer is you seems indisputable. All roads in your life and in those of people overseas lead to this point and the way forward is clear.

But in truth, like Gabriel García Márquez's garden of forking paths, the route to this point will have been influenced by a myriad of factors, not all of them straight from textbook development manuals. The logic of it emerges only with hindsight.

My own induction to the realities of programme development took place in Nigeria in the '90s when I took up the post of Programme Officer with responsibility for identifying new volunteer posts, preparing the way for volunteers' arrival and overseeing their professional and personal support during the posting. When I arrived in August 1992 the programme faced a recruitment crisis. In previous years, encouraged by the military government, the whole VSO programme had become heavily skewed towards technical education. Experienced plumbers, builders, carpenters and electricians in the UK were given a brief crash course in teaching and then flown out to secondary schools to champion the new syllabus in Introductory Technology that other expatriate consultants had developed for the whole school system in order to churn out young Nigerians capable of contributing to the construction industry that wishful thinking politicians dreamt of.

Fine in theory. But over the years the government had failed to deliver on its promises of well-equipped workshops, counterpart Nigerian teachers, appropriate textbooks and motivated kids. Technical teachers were leaving early in disgust, the postings department was reluctant to deliver more to the slaughter and our volunteer numbers were nose-diving. And, no matter what they say, at the end of the day the numbers game is a factor in volunteer programmes. If volunteers are too few we can't justify employing staff, keeping offices open, vehicles on the road. And if there are too few staff, the current volunteers get poorer support and leave early, new posts are inadequately developed and fail to attract applicants. The downward blip becomes a terminal decline.

So the push was on to get new jobs. 'Go forth and diversify!' urged our director. We had to break free of the rut of technical education that was rapidly developing grave-like resemblance; we had to get out there and find new jobs!

But where? And how? Nigeria is a massive country divided into thirty states, each the size of Lancashire. We were four programme staff with approximately five states each, a Peugeot 405 and a notoriously unreliable map. Imagine being given a region the size of Scotland and being told to go out and find fifteen posts that will address that region's most severe needs. For, oh yes, 'need' was definitely the driving force. After all we were a development organisation; our mission was saving the world, eradicating poverty: this must be our guiding light in all that we did. Just as long as the urgent need we identified could be sorted in two, maximum three, years, by a complete outsider who would need fully-furnished accommodation with good health and sanitation, reasonable access to Pringles and Heinz beans and within striking distance of other complete outsiders for co-counselling and beer consumption on a regular basis.

It was quite a tall order and invariably an element of pragmatism and arbitrariness crept into the process. The idiosyncrasies of individual programme officers were inevitably a strong factor. My own style was to gravitate towards the bottom-up. At the sweat-soaked wheel of the tank-like Peugeot, I spluttered forth into the interior, at every junction perversely choosing the most potholed alternative, branching at run-down looking schools, clinics, local government offices, introducing myself and my organisation to bewildered heads, doctors, social workers. I once calculated that I did forty-five visits to fifteen institutions, taking a total of twenty-six working days. And how many volunteer posts did I get out of it? Two. And one of those fell through when the staff at the top were yet again swept away just as the volunteer was poised to arrive.

Gradually I became more strategic. I homed in on current success stories as my starting point. I looked at communities where the volunteers had stayed the course and had even extended; where the needs were severe and diverse as they are in many places, but where local people were familiar with the concept of VSO and knew what they were getting into. Often it might be a case of replacing a volunteer once they had left. After all, it is rare that a genuine and long-felt need has been satisfactorily addressed in two or three years. The accommodation would already have been sorted out, the systems in place to pay them, local children familiar enough with *Oyibo*, as the, usually white, Europeans were called, not to trail them everywhere for the first three months yelling 'Oyibo! Oyibo!' and scurrying for cover as soon as their target turned. And, of course the departing volunteer could leave behind reams of notes to the new arrival with survival tips on the local bars, chop-houses, shack-like shops and sources of entertainment or escape.

So such posts often got off to a good start, met real needs satisfactorily and were genuinely a good experience from all perspectives.

If there was no further need for a particular post there might be another in the area. In south-west Nigeria VSO had come across one small village where there was a hugely dynamic self-help ethic. A few local people had made it good down in Lagos and were willing to channel funds back home for 'village improvement'. Some of the projects were ludicrously ostentatious: the construction of a church of cathedral-like proportions and ornamentation; the replacement of the dirt track that linked the village to the main road with a tarred runway-like road that carved through the centre of mud-bricked houses and continued for two miles before halting abruptly in front of the gorgeous mansion of the philanthropist who had funded it. But there were also some genuinely valuable developments – in particular the construction of a small cottage hospital and the expansion of a primary school into a secondary school specialising in science education for girls from rural poor backgrounds.

These were the projects I targeted my volunteer posts on. The first request was for a doctor for the hospital. A tricky one for VSO, as doctors willing to step off the career ladder for two years for an experience which arguably bears little relevance in the high-tech health industry of the UK are a rare species. But in fact we found one – an Italian who, interestingly, found the culture shock less extreme than he had expected and whose posting was relatively successful. He got the hospital up and running, set up stock control systems, staff management systems, raised funds for drugs and equipment, provided training in primary health care, cured illnesses, saved several lives.

As his posting came to an end, the community clamoured for another, but it was apparent to me that, although we might secure another volunteer, the community was never going to persuade a Nigerian doctor to narrow his or her sights to the bushy horizons of this remote village. So I persuaded them instead to channel energies into securing an experienced Nigerian staff nurse for our VSO to train to take over as he left. And, if the community wanted another VSO, to come up with suggestions.

Which was how the girls' community secondary school came into view. A science school with no qualified science teacher: here was an obvious gap that VSO could fill. The post was duly developed and worked out very well. The volunteer rose admirably to the challenge of being treated as God's gift to education and the school capitalised well on all sort of unexpected spin-offs. They found that the novelty of having a British teacher in their otherwise low-status school caused it to shoot up the priority list of the Lagos-based philanthropists and naira consistently materialised to equip the lab, help fund books for the library and find suitable dignitaries for the annual speech days and so on. This in turn enhanced the school's reputation locally, attracting more students and eventually giving it the credibility to persuade the British High Commission to pay for a fully-fledged laboratory.

Also, from the volunteer perspective it proved a challenging but satisfying role: a necessary job, an appreciative community, a fascinating culture. So, encouraged by this success story, I was inspired to seek out other potential posts in the area. The local teacher training college needed a French lecturer; when we found one it turned out he had a French wife, who could teach either English or French. She was duly posted to the community school. Meanwhile, the chair of the hospital management committee was also striving to set up a community bank that could make loans to encourage small-scale enterprise at community level. VSO eventually found a volunteer with accounting and training skills to help set it up. Via the French connection we established links with the Alliance Française in the state capital and they eventually landed a volunteer to spread the teacher training support throughout the state.

Thus one post lead to another, gradually mushrooming out from a propitious centre. Culturally, over the years, a mutual understanding developed between VSO as an organisation and the communities it sought to benefit. The cultures were very different but they could meet each other halfway and each found value in the encounter. From every one of those posts there were genuine practical benefits that emerged, even if they were not the benefits that volunteer or community had predicted, and in most cases cross-cultural friendships were struck up that survived the test of time and the intrusion of continents. Even where people have lost touch, memories live on at both ends of the volunteer community continuum and continue to resonate in unpredictable and immeasurable ways.

So, at the end of the day, what seemed to me the best strategy for identifying the perfect volunteer placement? Of course there is no right answer. There are far too many factors entering the equation to come up with simple solutions. As programme officers in Nigeria we wrestled with the issue quite seriously, each person having a different take on what would work and why. We also developed a few initiatives that helped across the board: increasing the period of consultation with potential employers as the post was developed, streamlining the processes, organising workshops for employers to be prepared for the volunteer in the same way as the volunteer is prepared for the exposure to new cultures at the UK end. All these mechanisms definitely improved the prospects of the post working out to mutual benefit.

Yet, in the final analysis, whether the post had been developed from the top down or the bottom up, the ultimate key to its success finally lies with the volunteers. Theirs is the challenge of rendering the friction of their difference one of synergy, not fire.

'La Bes'
Valerie Broadwell (Morocco)

It's ironic and sad that on 21 September 2002 returned Peace Corps volunteers from around the USA were planning to gather in Washington, D.C. to celebrate that organisation's fortieth anniversary when the terrorist attacks in New York, Washington and Pennsylvania meant the event had to be postponed.

Forty years. That seems old but I'm two years older than the Peace Corps and I feel young. In fact, inside I still feel like the twenty-one-year-old I was when I became a volunteer and taught English in Morocco.

In light of the terrorist attacks, one might conclude that the Peace Corps has been one colossal failure. The theory of the organisation was that America's best and brightest would go where they were most needed, to work, learn the language and blend in with the locals. Unlike diplomats, they wouldn't be paid a lot and were expected, in many cases, to live with a family. They would build bridges, vaccinate babies, teach schoolchildren. Volunteers, thus all of America, would be embraced by the world.

It didn't always work that way. The two years that I spent in Morocco were some of my loneliest times. My students' giggles and classroom antics both charmed and humiliated me. I don't know if they learned much English under my instruction.

Valerie (centre) with students,
Khenifra, Morocco, 1982

I have heard others say, and from my experience I must agree, that it can be years before a volunteer realises how profoundly they were affected. Like all returned volunteers, I have spent many hours pondering my experience and what it all meant.

What is the ultimate goal of the Peace Corps? Who really benefits? Americans? Host-country nationals? Or others unknown to either of us?

I don't know if my students ever used English after I left. I don't know if many of them went on to college and escaped the poverty in which most Moroccans live. I would like to think that they learned the most important lesson of all: that Americans, despite the press that we get, weren't that different from them.

During the two years that I was in Morocco my students saw me laugh, cry, sing, make jokes, be embarrassed, get angry and work very hard at my job. In short, they witnessed me being human like them. I believe that these unspoken exchanges are what give hope to the prospect of world peace – however remote that may seem at the moment. And that belief makes me feel tremendously proud of having served as a volunteer.

Although the twenty-one idealistic years with which I departed for Morocco had me confident in my ability to change the world, I realise increasingly that it is I who received much more in return. But I also believe, despite recent events, that I did something good to disperse stereotypes and misunderstandings – factors that so often fuel the fires of war.

It is nearly twenty years since I returned from Morocco. My daughter, oblivious to world politics, sits in her first grade classroom next to a new student. Her name is Maleeka and she is from Morocco. I introduce the two and teach Kate how to say 'La bes?' – 'How are you?' in Moroccan Arabic. Kate says, 'La bes?' Maleeka smiles. The seeds of a friendship are sown and I think to myself, *Happy birthday, Peace Corps*. You're not too old. On the contrary, maybe you're still too young.

Brave, Self-Sacrificing – Me?
Claire Healing (Kazakstan)

'What on earth possessed you?'
    'Where on earth is that?'
    'Is that Africa?'
    'Minus forty degrees?'

This is what most people said on learning that we were giving up well-paid jobs and going to live in Central Kazakstan, on a minimal allowance, for at least a year.

What possesses people to volunteer overseas? I guess for everyone it's different. I can only speak for myself. There comes a time in life when you start to think 'what is this all about?'

I worked for a national charity, but working in the support functions I didn't actually have any contact with the people it exists to help. In fact, as a middle manager I saw all the things that made me wonder how we helped anyone at all. I earned a decent wage; I bought things for my house, I had foreign holidays. I found myself wondering though, what is the purpose of this life? What difference am I making to individual lives, is this what I want to do for the next thirty years? I decided probably not. My husband Tim was also ready to move on from the place he had worked for ten years. So, for me, the main motivation was: I wanted to work with people in the community, maybe to make a difference somewhere, and money really wasn't important.

Okay, you say, so work with people in the community, but why go off half way around the world to do it? Well, what a great experience. A new country, a new language, an opportunity to live in another culture. If that isn't a thousand times better than any travelling holiday, I don't know what is.

So combine those two and it's a powerful mix. No, I didn't want to 'do good' or 'help poor people' as such; it was more about my personal value base. One of my overriding philosophies has been that everyone has potential and if I can help people to learn and reach their potential then I am satisfied, whether that is in my paid work or my volunteering in the UK or overseas. I also believe that I can always learn and develop.

The people who said we were so 'brave' and 'self-sacrificing' really didn't understand. This was an opportunity to gain valuable experience, doing something completely different and was at least as much about what skills *I* could gain and how *my* life would be changed as the other way around.

Why VSO? Interesting question. Well, one of the reasons was that neither of us have 'traditional' skills or qualifications for overseas development work. We are not engineers, health professionals or teachers. Many of the agencies seemed to be looking for these skills. VSO was willing to talk, to consider transferable skills and actually seemed pretty professional into the bargain. And most importantly, they selected us. Of course they impressed upon us how difficult it might be to find placements for us . . . and then gave us Kazakstan within two months.

I received an email at work about a placement description in Kazakstan, and to be entirely honest it wasn't until I spoke to Tim on the phone that I found out where it was. (He was always better at geography than me.) He arrived home from work that night with a Central Asian Lonely Planet tucked under his arm, the page for Astana already turned down, and with a twinkle of excitement in his eye. Clearly, Kazakstan was an interesting place. (Although how he came to that conclusion I don't know. If you have ever seen a guidebook for Kazakstan, you would probably give the country a wide berth.) Basically, there wasn't much discussion. Ten years of independence, Soviet culture intermixed with Kazak, horsemen on the wild and vast steppe, and the placement was working with a women's NGO. . . . If we had realised the enormity of learning Russian, though, we might have had second thoughts. . . .

By the time we were offered this placement, family, friends and work colleagues knew we had 'signed up' with VSO. It was about this time that their incredulity kicked in, though. I think they had visions of us lounging around on a pacific island, or living in African deserts, not spending more than six months of the year in a snow-bound freezer. To be fair, close friends and family understood. They knew why we were doing it, they understood our motivations and were very excited for us. After the initial shock they were gathering hot-water bottles, thermal underwear and supplies of Branston Pickle for our departure. (Little did they know that we would arrive in June in the middle of the summer when it hits forty degrees at the other end of the thermometer.)

There followed a frenzy of preparations. We sold our house, packed up all our belongings, spent what felt like forever trying to decide what to take in our 25 kg each (which turned out to be 35 kg each two days before departure), pre-departure training and saying goodbye to everyone.

VSO's pre-departure training is almost exclusively delivered at Harbourne Hall in the Midlands. You pitch up there, flung together with other excited volunteers, and get to spend several days (or in my case two weeks), having a lot of fun, and learning some things too. I remember we introduced ourselves and as it went round the room I heard 'Zambia, Zimbabwe, Solomon Islands, the Philippines, St Lucia' and I was beginning to think that maybe Kazakstan wasn't so great after all. . . . And then I was saved by Macedonia and South Africa and began to feel a whole lot better. The reaction of fellow volunteers to Kazakstan was equally interesting – from great interest to 'Oh yes, they offered me that but I wouldn't dream of living there for a year.' Needless to say, the latter group was not the group that I was drinking in the bar with each night.

One of the downfalls of being in the first group of volunteers to go to Kazakstan was that the training could never prepare you for it. None of the trainers had any idea about CIS countries, none of the material took it into account and it felt like the focus was on rural villages of people with little access to formal education, rather than a new capital of 350,000 with 98% literacy rates. It was all very interesting, but even the course on 'adapting work practices' gave me little insight into how to adapt, or what to. . . .

Into my second week the most exciting moment of the pre-departure training came. We were starting a new programme and introducing ourselves again. As we went around the room another voice piped up 'Kazakstan'. The relief of finding someone else who was heading off to Central Asia, and was excited about it! Of all the things we covered in the pre-departure training, nothing was as valuable as that time spent with fellow Kazak volunteer Viv. Our friendship began that day, and I can say that every minute we have been here it is a valuable source of both professional and personal support, despite a twenty-one-hour train ride between our placements.

So, still here in Kazakstan, having stayed longer already than I had originally intended. We don't regret our decision to be 'brave'. Volunteering in Kazakstan has been in turns frustrating, exciting, satisfying, confusing and downright awful, but I wouldn't change the decision for the world. It's been a fantastic experience, I have gained new skills and my life has changed – in ways that I could never have anticipated.

'Minus forty degrees?' they asked before we left home

Have I made a difference? People here seem to think so. Would I do it again? Probably, although next time maybe it would be nice to be lounging on a desert island. . . .

How to Solicit . . . Stuff
George Chinnery (Romania)

For anyone who does not feel that simply requesting material gifts from their significant others would prove to be a lucrative endeavour, here are some suggestions:

1. Develop a gift list (e.g. guidebooks, coffee-house gift packs, etc.), and pick the most likely family member or friend to provide each gift.
2. Compose a specifically-tailored letter to each recipient, accounting an anecdote which illustrates your need for the respective item. For instance, if I want a subscription to *Playboy*, I could send a carefully-crafted letter to my (hypothetical) girlfriend detailing just how lonely I get here, especially with all the beautiful women I see everyday, etc. Hardships, accidents resulting in a lost article, and lack of foresight before leaving the country are appropriate themes. Embellish, exaggerate, and just plain fabricate as necessary. **Example:** 'I swear I didn't see any warning label on the radiator when I laid my favourite Gap sweater on it. . . . My counterpart told me it was fifty degrees below zero here last year . . . blah, blah, blah'.
3. Use humour. If your recipient laughs, he or she is more likely to remember the letter after having read it. Also, people do not like to hear constant whining and may ignore it as it's too negative and uncomfortable for them; humour may offset this. **Example:** 'Can you believe I snapped my *Murder Ballads* and *Judgement Night* CDs scraping the frost off my bathroom mirror yesterday?'

4. Show the recipient that you have been thinking about him or her. This can instil guilt if they do not reciprocate. **Example:** 'I dropped my camera into a well while trying to get this really cool shot. I was going to create an avant-garde layout for you for Christmas.'

5. Inquire into the recipient's welfare. People love to be asked about themselves. **Example:** 'So was the procedure painful, man. . . ? Anyway, I'm sure Tawny is pleased you can have kids again?'

6. Inquire into the status of mutual others you will not or cannot contact yourself. The recipient may network, increasing your overall return. **Example:** 'I haven't heard from Cinnamon in a while. Is she still on a quest for the tenth insight?'

7. Ask about current events at home. It makes the recipient feel useful, better about him or herself, and potentially grateful and more generous. **Example:** 'Is it true that John Glenn will be returning to space in search of Timothy Leary's head?'

8. Demonstrate your altruism. Your recipient may consequently regard you as a higher life form than they once did. **Example:** 'I plucked the down from my sleeping bag to help my students decorate the school like a winter wonderland.'

9. Focus on practical utility and dire necessity. This may elicit sympathy or pity from your recipient. **Example:** 'I tossed my Nietzsche collection and my phrase books into my furnace in a futile attempt to keep warm.'

10. Ease your recipient's shopping burden. The less effort your recipient must expend, the more likely it is they will provide. **Example:** 'My colleague Dexter said his mother ordered the latest Stephen Hawking for him over the internet.'

11. Utilise terms of endearment and/or a sentimental pet or nickname (e.g. 'Pumpkin', 'Stinky'), but do not overuse them as your recipient may suspect your ulterior motives.

12. Send the letter(s) soon. Remember that they might take a very long time to ever reach home.

13. Do not ignore number 2. If your recipient feels you took the time to write to him or her, they will feel flattered. If, however, you are too lazy to covertly canvass each person you know with a personalised letter, here are some suggestions for bulk mailings:

   a. Write a message describing, as believably as possible, your 'average' day. You must create an intricate amalgam of how you became in need of a multitude of objects in the time-frame you are spanning in your message. Good luck!

   b. Send a copy to as many people (with financial means) as you know by any means possible (e.g. email, snail-mail, message in a bottle).

   c. However, do not send your message to more than one person in each of your associations (e.g. family, group of friends, colleagues). By ignoring this caveat, you risk recipients sharing notes and foiling your scheme; you also risk receiving duplicate gifts.

The Class Outing
Charlotte Wilson (Rwanda)

Kigali, April 2000

Hi folks

I now feel like a fully-fledged teacher because I have taken a class on a daytrip!

We set off for the Nyungwe forest at dawn (about 6am). I had told the kids that they had to wear sensible shoes and the girls had to wear trousers and bring a raincoat. I also said that if they weren't there at six I'd leave without them. I was very proud of them because they were all there at six, properly equipped. I wish I could say the same for the teachers! Not a raincoat among them and most turned up in suits and short skirts.

We made it to the forest after over three hours drive and were given a talk by the head of research in the forest. I didn't realise that it takes work to maintain it in its 'natural' state. He showed us a plant that they'd pulled up and said that in Rwandan legend when it flowers there is war. The last time it flowered was six years ago and it flowers every ten to fifteen years. I'll have to be out of here in the next four then!

Then we all set off to look at the colobus monkey colony, even those in skirts and heels. After only about 45 mins trek, we found them. The students asked loads of questions in Kinyarwanda from the guide, which is why I had brought them there, really, so they could learn about their heritage from an expert.

My other reason for bringing the students is that the present generation has to understand why the forest is worth preserving if it's to be there for future generations – and they won't if it is only tourists who see it.

We were out of the forest by around 12 noon, but then, much to my astonishment we continued on to Cyangugu, to see Lake Kivu.

Most of the kids hadn't been out of the county of Gitarama before, and were dying to see the lake. It started to rain so we took shelter in a café and ran in from the minibus. I think that the proprietors were quite surprised when I burst through the cord curtain, but they didn't say anything.

When we went down to the shore it was obviously quite a touristy place and I got a lot of hassle, which was embarrassing in front of the kids. I don't think that they'd realised quite how much attention I got, because the people round Shyogwe are used to us by now. The local kids kept coming up and begging, calling me 'msungu' and touching me to see if I felt the same and if the colour came off (sometimes if I am covered in chalk it does!).

After a while I lost my cool and started pulling faces at them – if I'm going to be a spectacle I might as well give them something to look at.

The journey back goes through some truly beautiful bits of the world. We drove through the mountains at dusk, so the hills were slate blue and the sky pewter, just the clouds in the valleys below us standing out stark, bright white in contrast.

The students kept saying things like 'We will never forget this day,' and 'You are an unforgettable teacher.' They had never been on a school trip before, not even to a place that wouldn't cost anything to get to. I don't think I'll forget that day in a hurry, either.

When I suggested writing a letter of thanks, the 'prefet des études' said immediately, 'Good idea, then we've got more of a chance of going back next year.' I am hoping that I have set something up that's renewable, that'll continue when I am gone.

This term has been fairly quiet, but I did make it up to Byumba last weekend for a friend's combined 60th birthday party and football match. The scenery there is really gorgeous, you can see the volcanoes from the volunteers' back garden. It was good to be able to get out of Shyogwe and let my hair down – I was getting fed up of constantly wearing my teacher-and-responsible-member-of-the-community hat.

The football was an experience; I'd borrowed a pair of shorts from another girl that were tight and short. I felt practically naked – I haven't shown anything much above my ankles for the last seven months, but luckily it was several miles away from Shyogwe, so it shouldn't matter too much. The match started quite late but the light reflected off my bright white legs was enough for us to finish the game. Anyway, the time is nearly up here, so I'll stop. Hope all is well with you.

Lots of love,

Charlotte

A few months after she wrote this email, Charlotte Wilson was killed in an attack by the terror group Palipehutu-FNL on a civilian bus, close to the Burundian capital. Her fiancé Richard Ndereyimana, and 19 others, died alongside her. The killers, and their leader Agathon Rwasa, are still at large. Charlotte's family and friends have set up a memorial fund in her name, to help the school to which she had shown such commitment. For more details see: www.charlotte-wilson.co.uk

IT'S NOT EASY GETTING

THE WORK DONE

The Teaching Day
David Barnes (Czech Republic)

It's not wise to worry too much about teaching. My students were an extremely interesting bunch with very informed opinions about most things. Get them talking about their country as they like to moan, especially about politicians (justifiably so).

In my staffroom, lessons would often be allowed to run late for the benefit of hot wine, becherovka, slivovitz, peach vodka, open sandwiches (*chlebicky*), fruit teas and Turkish coffee. I don't condone this behaviour, but I didn't object to it strongly at the time.

If one finds oneself teaching grammar a good book full of games is invaluable. It's really rewarding when a class likes what you're doing and enjoys a game. Private teaching is a good way to meet people. I taught a wide range of people, from bank employees to engineers to fifteen-year-old schoolgirls. For the bank employees, a 5:15am start was necessary; and in the winter, a long trudge through the snow.

Pack Some Patience
Liselotte Wolters (Uganda)

Here in Uganda, you certainly learn how to do everything two gears slower. Why hurry? If you come two hours late to work, work will still be there.

Scolar, one of the lab staff, comes back a week late from a month's leave.

'Why are you a week late, Scolar?' I ask.

'I had some problems.' (The standard answer here.)

'What kind of problems?'

. . . Silence. . . .

'Can I have three days off next week?' Scolar asks.

'Why do you want three days off after five weeks of leave?'

'Well, I have some things to do.'

'What kind of things?' I ask.

... Silence. ....

Before I left home, a friend advised me to take a suitcase full of patience with me. I did, unfortunately the suitcase was empty very quickly. But well, with time you get used to everything, even to having patience.

Travelling by public transport requires a lot of patience. You get in a *matatu* (minibus) – officially there is space for fourteen passengers but, don't worry – it will easily fit twenty-six. You drive around for about an hour until the matatu is full (*really* full). Halfway you have to get into another matatu and drive around another hour till that matatu is full full. You stop several times because people want to do their shopping, and nothing is so easy as just asking the matatu driver to stop in front of the shop, do your shopping and continue the journey. Don't worry about the fact that twenty-five other passengers are waiting for you, because they will ask the driver to stop one mile further on to do their shopping.

But, in the end you will reach your destination.

Rural Students
Rob Palmer (Ghana)

There I was, five days after leaving London in cold January, standing in a dusty African village surrounded by a crowd of small faces beaming up at me screaming 'obruni' (white-man), while I silently questioned my sanity for asking BUNAC to find me 'somewhere rural, remote and by myself'.

However, when I was met by two of the girls with, 'Hello, my name is Happy, this is my friend Comfort, you are welcome to Ghana,' it was difficult to feel anything but optimistic about my stay in this tiny village despite having no water, electricity, being one and a half hours from the nearest hint of civilisation and the proud owner/user of my very own maggot-pit, cockroach-infested toilet. It would be a long eleven months. Or so I thought.

I ended up working for a Ghanaian government poverty reduction initiative, called ICCES (Integrated Community Centres for Employable Skills), which had the aim of empowering the rural youth with employable skills to make them small-scale entrepreneurs in their own communities.

Yet I soon found there to be some sort of gross miscommunication, as I found myself being introduced as a 'rural micro-project development co-ordinator', with the whole community having great expectations about my presence. So it was that I started to take on this role, spending the first week visiting surrounding communities, meeting the chiefs, elders and fetish priests of these settlements. At first it was all a bit daunting, until I was introduced to the custom of taking one 'tot' of neat moonshine spirit, *akperteshie*, with each village chief.

It was such a valuable project, I knew I had to do everything I could to live up to their expectations. About half the youth attending the training centre had previously dropped out of junior secondary school (before the age of sixteen) and many were totally illiterate. Without this centre they would have no chance to gain skills with which to construct a better life for themselves. During the time I was there we managed to build up the trainee number from just seven in January to eighty-five by the time I left in November,

Village in Ghana

raising over £11,000 in funding from Ghana and the UK.

My job essentially involved managing the centre – accounts, planning, some teaching, fundraising, marketing and selling products that we made (such as coffins), raising awareness of the scheme, visiting local NGOs, government officials and traditional leaders. You have to be willing to turn your hand to anything, but really anything is possible as long as you believe it is. One day I found myself teaching fifty girls dressmaking theory, another I was talking to one of the Cabinet Ministers about the project's potential for Ghana.

At first there was a big problem with attendance of the trainees, as many either had to help their family to farm or were not used to attending every day, not having been in education for many years. I found a cunning way to make sure the students attended all the classes. The villagers believe that the forest is inhabited by the 'little people' (the *mmoatia*), who are apparently like red, hairy dwarfs. All the villagers are afraid of them. So, perhaps unethically or unkindly, I realised I could use this local belief to my advantage. I told my students that the *mmoatia* had told me they would take away any students not in class. Attendance rates increased after that time.

However, you really do have to make allowances for the students being late or absent. The difference between English kids and Ghanaian kids is immense. When I was their age I came home from school, put my feet up and watched *The Three Muskahounds* while eating Sunpat peanut butter sandwiches before I ate a large dinner. They end school, go back to their mud-stick hut, weed the farms, fetch water, wash clothes, pound *fufu*, collect firewood and do any household chores. Some will go out hawking to earn some small money. Many work as shoe-shiners for 30p a day and can be heard coming from afar by the tap-tap they make with a stick on their wooden shoebox. They often try to shine your shoes not understanding why you don't want black shoe polish on your trainers. Others start to pick bits off your shoes, then look hopefully up at you and say, 'I have glue.'

Becoming a 'Responsible Adult'
Heidi Fitch (Canada)

I knew that I wanted to do something constructive and beneficial during my transitional year. I didn't let my severe deafness affect the things I wanted to do. I wanted to explore and discover a new country at the same time, and I accomplished that by volunteering in Canada.

I went on a six-month caring placement and didn't really have any expectations. Upon my arrival at the small university town of Antigonish, Nova Scotia, I was overwhelmed by the prospect of being away from home for so long. It was a bonus that everyone at l'Arche community project made efforts to make me feel welcome, although it was hard knowing that everyone I knew was continuing their lives on the other side of the pond. I knew I would be taking care of six mentally-disabled adults and I told myself that I would be willing to take what would be thrown at me.

Before long, I got pretty accustomed to the routines. There's me thinking, 'Whoah, I've never had to feel so responsible before!'

My role as an assistant involved preparing and serving meals, helping with morning and evening routines, refilling medications, and cleaning. I thought, 'learning the basics of managing a home sure will be useful!'

But most important of all was spending time with the core members of the community. They have Down's Syndrome to different extents, so all have different needs. They are not capable of getting along by themselves, so need assistance in their daily activities, as well as help learning to be a little independent – it was quite challenging at times. Some of the core members have psychological problems and that tended to be quite draining.

We always seemed to be celebrating something – anniversaries, birthdays, going aways – you name it. L'Arche encouraged me to learn about different things, about the people and myself through them, and it helped me feel comfortable with my identity. Looking back, it's pretty amazing to think how things like that can change your perspective on life totally. Despite my hearing loss, I coped really well and had a fantastic time. I feel that I came back to Britain with more self-confidence and 'different eyes'.

VIP Treatment
Eva and Bernard Batchelor (Cameroon)

Our flight to the Far North Province was the most bizarre farce you could ever imagine. Two football teams from the south were playing two teams from the north in Ngaoundere and Garuoa. The football teams were allowed to get on the plane first, leaving forty-two people (half the capacity of the Boeing 737) unable to get a seat. This caused a mini riot at the airport – people were shouting, pushing and climbing over barriers and along the conveyor belts. The packed plane was on the runway and all the airport officials had disappeared.

After a while the Cam Air staff reappeared with a solution – the plane would fly north to Ngaoundere and Garuoa and then return to Yaoundé to pick up the travellers to Chad and Maruoa (where we were going) and fly north again. However, there were passengers sitting on the plane from Douala who were expecting to go to Chad and Maruoa. They were told to get off and wait in the departure lounge and the people without seats going to Garuoa and Ngaoundere were told to get on the plane. This left seventy very disgruntled passengers, including us, to wait three hours for the plane to return. When it did eventually return all the passengers who boarded at Ngaoundere and were expecting to travel to Douala in the south had to get off and wait in the departure lounge in Yaoundé while the plane took all the rest of us north.

There was no food or drink on the flight as the first group of passengers had consumed it all, and the three-hour internal flight turned into an eleven-hour journey at a temperature of nearly 100°F.

Once we arrived in Maruoa we settled down to enjoy the purpose of our visit, to work with the people in the villages. The Paramount Chief of one of the villages had arranged for his Fantasia of Horses for us (a horse spectacular). He had arranged this once before for us on one of our visits but due to the death of one of the government officials it had to be cancelled. This time we had the full display.

We were seated in the VIP area in front of the Chief's Palace with two rows of local chiefs and dignitaries seated in front of us on mats and the Paramount Chief's many wives behind us. A small group of musicians and drummers set a noisy atmosphere. In the distance at the far end of the village square came a phalanx of fifteen charging horsemen, their Arab clothing billowing behind. Their eight-foot spears were lowered for the charge and they only stopped about two feet from the front row of chiefs. The noise and dust from the horses, the crowds shouting and ululating wives made the whole atmosphere electric.

The whole village population came out to watch – even the children had run out of school to come to watch as well. There followed a variety of displays – individual charges, horses dancing to the music, in fact anything we asked for. By the end the horses were very hot and lathered up. This was yet another wonderful experience for us to remember, especially the opening charge, which was so emotional and dramatic as the horses appeared out of a cloud of dust.

We revisited a small, very destitute village which had no clean water and spent some time there with our Plan International colleagues. We took a sample of water from their calabash and there were worms swimming around in it. They took us into their house and they were delighted that we were taking an interest in their acute problems. None of the children in the village go to school and the adults are illiterate. As this was our second visit we took the camera and were able to take pictures of the inside of the houses and general views of the village.

It was clean but unbelievably basic – no water, one straw hut for the whole family and animals, no medical services, no personal hygiene facilities, a staple diet of millet and minimal clothing. Life at this level is a daily struggle for survival. To have been able to share for a short time these people's lives highlighted for us the greed and selfishness of our western culture – poverty is an insidious trap from which there sometimes seems there is no escape.

While we were there we were guests of honour at an inter-village football match organised by the trainers of our project. Cameroonians take their sport seriously and unfortunately the referee was misguided enough to award a penalty in the second half. At this point a riot broke out, fists were flying and knives appeared. The local pastor kept apologising to us, our driver and vehicle quickly disappeared to collect up the visiting team to take them to safety in their own village. When it came back we had to take one of the players with a knife wound to the local hospital. We never knew whether the penalty was awarded to the home or away team. The return match is when we go back at Christmas.

Learning to Teach
Holly Twiname (China)

The work is going well, as I feel more and more like a teacher. My students are still not coming out with any profound questions, and it gets a little tedious when a student turns around and asks me whether I like Chinese food for the 174th time.

The other day I bought a tape entitled *English Excellent Songs* (which I hoped I could use to teach my students some easy to sing along to songs). Aside from the spelling, the contents of the tape are a far cry from what the cover says. According to the cover, there is supposed to be a selection of songs by various artists – Bryan Adams, Lionel Richie, Stevie Wonder, Whitney Houston, etc. Instead, there are two people – a man for all the male artists, and a woman for all the female artists, the accompanying instruments being reduced to a synthesiser. Obviously two karaoke-happy people taking it a bit too far. (I should have known that something was amiss when I saw the words to *Yesterday Once More* under the title *Sealed with a Kiss*.)

After months of trying to set up a reading room/self-access centre at college (where students can come and read, work and chat in English), today I was finally given the key to a room. Success! Or so I thought. I went and saw the room, and it was just great – exactly what I wanted. The Dean of the English Department took me to have a look, and then dropped into the conversation that they were going to tear down the building. So, within the first minute of seeing this room, I was already having to deal with the fact that soon it wasn't even going to be there. But, having been in China for some time now, I have developed a bit of a die-hard spirit, and ten minutes later, the Dean and I were in the Vice-President's office trying to dissuade him of this ludicrous idea, based mostly on the premise that it obstructs the view of a grander building.

Life continues at a slightly slower pace, following the ridiculous amounts of teaching I was doing up until last week for various reasons. The other foreign teacher had to leave suddenly about three weeks ago due to her father falling very seriously ill. So now it's just my little foreign face in these parts.

The teaching continues, in a somewhat hectic manner, with seventy students on average in a class. It's not too bad, especially after I found a small classroom which the students can squeeze into with no desks. This is better in terms of classroom dynamics (and much easier on my voice). Now that my hours have been so dramatically reduced, I am being invited by high schools around Zhoukou (in the countryside) to give lectures to their students. This started following a visit I made to a high school last term where I gave a so-called 'lecture' – to all 2,000 students in one go. It seems other schools now want me to visit them too.

Holly teaching

On Friday I went to another school, (about thirty minutes from Zhoukou) and gave a similar lecture to the entire school – which, much to my surprise turned out to be over 4,000. (The last school was only half that.) I was given a microphone and my voice was projected over loudspeakers. I stood in the middle of this crowd of students and talked about why English was important and how they could improve it. It was so much fun asking them a question and hearing the roar produced by the chorus of their response. Then, to finish off we sang a song. The most significant thing about the whole experience, for most of them, will have been seeing a foreigner for the first time. Apparently, even some passers-by had also joined the crowd to have a look, and I even had to sign autographs at the end – my only claim to fame being that I am a foreigner.

Birth in Bangladesh
Nancy MacKeith (Bangladesh)

I worked in Bangladesh for two years as a volunteer in the Jahural Islam Medical College Hospital (JIMCH) three hours north-east from Dhaka. I chose the placement out of the selection offered me because I read that when my future boss set up the nursing school at JIMCH she arranged that the female nursing students wore shalwar kameez (loose top and trousers) instead of saris as uniform. I thought that indicated a progressive frame of mind. This was a good guess, she was humorous and supportive about cultural differences and she helped me define a role for myself. I have never met a volunteer who actually did the job they came out to do and I was no exception.

I prepared myself as much as possible for my new working situation by reading about maternal health in Bangladesh but it still was very shocking when

I got there. Bangladesh has one of the highest maternal mortality rates in the world – 4.4 per thousand live births. Women are disadvantaged from childhood in their share of household food and access to medical care. An additional hazard when they become pregnant is their high risk of suicide or homicide,

Clinic in Bangladesh

particularly if they are young and unmarried. I found Therese Blanchet's anthropological writings on childbearing in Bangladesh very relevant.

Soon after I arrived some medical students and their lecturer in community medicine wanted to do a community survey on maternal health, and I thought this would be a better setting for midwifery teaching. The system that eventually became the routine was that there were clinics in people's houses arranged by field workers. I would go out in one rickshaw and the safe motherhood project doctor in another, each of us with a student. We did the same job of examination advice and referral if called for and had a midwifery student each. On one day a week we would have a safe motherhood meeting where we would discuss any problems and I would teach the field workers about antenatal care. We began to say at the clinics that we would come out to people in labour and this slowly began to happen. We found we were usually called when there was a problem but this might become less likely. On a couple of occasions the mother just needed to be catheterised. If she needed more than we could provide we could negotiate on behalf of the women for permission from her husband and the 'guardian' (decision-maker of the community) and get her to hospital.

It was a real privilege to go into people's houses, observe their ways of having a baby and to be of some use, and the students could experience decision-making in reality.

* * *

Six years after I first flew out to Bangladesh and four years after I left, I returned as part of my current work on breast-feeding. There was the same worrying descent in the aeroplane as the rainy season was at its height. The whole country seemed to be flooded and I could not imagine where we were going to land.

Although my work visit was short, I managed to get in a visit to JIMCH for twenty-four hours. I found my boss and the other staff very well. They in turn were delighted with my appearance. 'Nancy, you are so fat!'

The students from my time had jobs in the hospital, and others had got work in other good NGO hospitals or gone on to do nursing BSc degrees.

My boss showed me the record that has been kept since I started the scheme of visiting people at home in labour. They have information on who went to the house, what they found and the decisions made, as well as outcomes for mother and baby.

It was amazing to see that things I had had a part in were still going on, and I felt very privileged to have had such a good experience.

24-Hour Peace Corps Preparation
Roderick Jones (Nicaragua)

They tell you during pre-service training that you're a Peace Corps Volunteer twenty-four hours a day. What that means to me is that I don't get any bonus points for dragging myself out of bed at 5:51 in the morning so I can catch the six o'clock IFAT out to Las Sabanas. I've gotten my time down – for getting up, cramming my legs into a pair of jeans, and heading out the door – to about 120 seconds. The trick, I've learned, is preparation.

I take my cold-water shower under the stars the night before. I lay out my clothes, too: no fewer than ten córdobas in my jeans pocket, belt threaded through the belt loops, Leatherman tool fitted into its holster. Getting my backpack ready is a bit more involved because as I lay there in between asleep and awake, my mind won't stop trying to figure out what I'm forgetting. So even if I'm tucked into my sleeping bag at ten, it's not unlikely that I'll have roused myself two or three times by eleven.

I'll remember, for instance, that tomorrow I need the fake breast made out of panty hose and rubber bands for a talk that I'm giving on mother's milk, or a bag of onion seeds I promised to a family of an undernourished child. I'd prefer to be able to touch my head to the pillow and be dreaming until my wristwatch bleep-bleeps at 5:51, but I know that if I leave anything for morning, I'll forget it and be kicking myself once I'm up in Las Sabanas. Believe me, it's no treat to realise, just as you stand up in front of twenty bored campesina women who are waiting for you to knock their flip-flops off with that exciting health talk you promised, that you don't have the fake breast in your backpack.

The backpack I use is big in a sneaky sort of way. It's plain black. It doesn't have any features. I mean, there aren't special nooks for accessories, and there aren't any straps for wrapping around your gut, your chest or your forehead. And it's not long and tall, like those purple and green monsters you see attached to the hunched-over, furry-faced souls seen ambling through the bus stations of Central America. No, mine is short and fat. There are four zippered compartments, the biggest one closest to my back. Over the past eight months, I've figured out how to get the most out of a sneaky, fat backpack. There are a few things you can't do without.

In the outermost pocket, I've got:
- Toilet paper, unrolled from the cardboard spool and folded into an empty plastic candy bag (for protection from downpours).
- A 35 mm film canister filled with Bennies. I like to have Benadryl close by in case an army of ants bite my rear as I'm sitting on the latrine, causing my entire body to swell and turn red (like they did last Christmas Eve).
- A bottle of white-out. For me, it's the one thing I can never find when I need it. Now I know where to find it.
- The next pocket has thirty-two ounces of good Somoto water (minimal sediment) and two fully-charged AA batteries.

Undo zipper number three and you'll find:

- A rain poncho. It seems to get used just about everyday I'm up in Las Sabanas, whether to cover my body as I'm hiking, or to cover a load of beans in the back of a pickup during a thunderstorm. If I were to keep track of the things that my campesino friends ask me to leave behind for them when I return to the United States someday, the poncho ranks right up there with my Leatherman, my acoustic guitar, and my size thirteen boots.
- A loaded point-and-shoot camera that I use to take portraits of anyone who asks, plus a back-up roll of film.
- Six pieces of *pan simple* – hearth-baked white bread – in a plastic bag and a jar of peanut butter brought back from a recent trip to the capital. I've had many a soggy tortilla, charcoal-glazed plantain chip, and muddy-flavoured bean entrée, and then I've lived with the squirts for weeks at a time. I like to have the peanut butter sandwich option to pull out of my backpack when I find myself in a dangerous kitchen.
- A laminated 40' x 20' map of the world.
- Three baseball cards of Denis Martínez – the most famous Nicaraguan to play in the Major Leagues – to give to the children who steal my heart the first time I meet them.

Flat against my back I have:

- A rectangular aluminium box that doubles as a receptacle for the papers I accumulate and as a clipboard.
- A copy of *Where there is No Doctor* in Spanish, with its cover held on by clear packing tape and the edges of its pages blackened by sweat and mildew. I don't use this book to pretend I'm a doctor – there is a health post within a few hours of any community I would find myself in. But what sometimes happens is that I'll come across a baby who has a rash or laboured breathing, and I want to encourage the mother to go to the health post. 'I'm not sure what this is,' I'll say, 'Why don't you get it checked out?' It helps to have a reference to quote and some pictures to show whenever I'm having a conversation like this.
- *Facts for Life*, also in Spanish, which is in better shape. My goal is to get this book – a collection of basic, essential health messages – in as ragged shape as *Where there is No Doctor* is in.

* * *

The daytime skies in Nicaragua are bluer than the skies in the US, and this is especially true at dawn. As I'm waiting in the market for the IFAT to arrive, it seems to my eyes as though the silhouette of the church is black velvet painted on a canvas of rich indigo. By a few minutes after six, the choking sound of the IFAT grinding its gears drifts south toward the market.

The make of this covered-wagon-style army truck that takes me out to Las Sabanas is IFA (pronounce EE-fah). I've been told that these trucks are manufactured in an Eastern European country. During the civil war here in the 1980s, the Sandinista army used these trucks. Over the years, they became known by another name, IFAT, which stands for *Imposible Frenar A Tiempo*, (impossible to brake on time). Apparently, some service men and women had never driven an automobile prior to joining the military, and more than a few pigs, dogs, and chickens met their maker under the wheels of these vehicles that were truly IFAT.

With the change in government, so the story goes, the IFATs made their way from soldiers to friends to other friends and on into the civilian transportation system. The crew in charge of the bright green rig that takes me back and forth between Somoto and Las Sabanas consists of three young men. Chino is the *ayudante*, or helper, the one who takes my five córdobas and holds the old ladies' bags as they hoist themselves into the back of the truck. When there's a pig that needs to be transported, Chino is the one who wrestles it to the ground, clamps its squealing mouth shut, and ties it down to the back of the truck, right where the passengers are forced to use it as a step when they get on.

Some days Chino has an *ayudante* of his own, a good-natured fellow called Geraldito. Every time I've seen Geraldito on the IFAT, he is dressed in filthy clothes, with his buttons mismatched and his pants zipper undone. Geraldito is cross-eyed. He also has six fingers on his left hand, and the dangling pinkie fingernail is polished hot pink. When Geraldito helps an old lady onto the truck, he usually trips her by mistake. One time I saw him stoop to pick a shovel up from the truck bed, but he stepped on the spade end and the handle came up and smashed him in the face. It's Geraldito, not Chino, who greets me with a 'Buenos días!' when I get on in the morning.

Medardo is the driver. People say he got the job because his father owns this IFAT and two others. On occasion I've seen him throwing down a couple of beers in the cab before the return trip to Somoto in the afternoon. This doesn't bother me; I sit back, relax, and enjoy the hour-and-a-half trip through the mountains. So far, Medardo has always been able to brake on time.

We take a dirt road – the only road – with lots of rocks, bumps, and mud. Some mornings Chino whistles for Medardo to stop so chains can be strapped onto the tyres. No matter what the condition of the road, the passengers can be seen bouncing around on the benches as though they were dolls with arms and heads attached to their torsos with wire coils. The benches along either side of the truck bed are hard and narrow. My tailbone aches a bit after a week of commuting, but now that I've lost thirty pounds (and my Gringo-sized behind), I can keep from slipping off the bench like I used to. I have even managed to fall

Giving a health talk to a mothers' group in a rural community schoolhouse, Nicaragua

asleep a few times.

I don't regret being awake for the ride up the mountain, though. The IFAT is where I make connections, place names with faces, and cultivate friendships. It's where I met *El Gordo* Neftalí, the well-fed businessman who makes the trip to his plantation each morning and keeps me amused when I'm able to eavesdrop on his conversations with Chino that are sprinkled with colourful and crude slang sayings. It's where I met Juancito, the rural handyman who calls me 'Boss' or 'Comandante' or 'Doctor' even though I am none of these, and likes to remind me that during the war he was kidnapped into military service thirteen times. It's where I finally got up the nerve to ask Yanét, the lovely young school-teacher who gets off the truck in San Lucas, what her name was. Next time we ride together, maybe I'll try to find out if she's married.

* * *

By 7:30 we've arrived in Las Sabanas and the air is whipping around us, so cold that I can see my breath. The passengers hop down off the back of the truck. If one of them asks, I'll tell them I'm headed for the community of Quebrada Honda, or Deep Ravine, a 45-minute hike further on down the road. There are adobe houses along the road. The friends who live there offer me coffee, made with beans from the back yard, or freshly-boiled milk. The walk to Quebrada Honda can take as long as an hour, or half a day, depending on the stops I'm fortunate enough to make. On those walks, I think to myself how glad I am that there's no timecard to punch when I get off the IFAT in Las Sabanas, or when I finally make it to Quebrada Honda.

Then I remember: I'm a Peace Corps Volunteer twenty-four hours a day.

Meeting with a Mutilada
Colin Murphy (Angola)

It was the third time she'd waited for me, this mutilada. She was gnarled like a tree-stump, and her presence outside the office, waiting for me – to do what? – was a little unnerving. Yes, I wanted to talk to her, to do an interview of sorts. But preferably once I'd some idea of how I was going to talk to her, and how I was going to extract some information of value from her, through the layers of cultural and linguistic barriers that separated us; not least of all that my command of the national language, Portuguese, was at best hesitant; hers was non-existent.

I turned to the guards. 'Does anybody speak Kimbundo? Ask her if she'd like a glass of water.' A long and animated exchange followed, after which one of the guards turned to me and said, 'That'd be fine.' I went into the house to get her a glass of water and pondered my next move. One driver spoke good Kimbundo, and had a friendly, gentle manner, but he was out on a job. I'd have to stall her until he came back, and then we could do the interview, and drop her home, and that'd be that. The guard managed to communicate this to her, although he gave the impression that he didn't see the need to bother, that she could just wait, and I went back into the office.

When Lazari, the driver, came back – after it had started to rain and I'd lifted her chair onto the veranda and she'd dragged herself up the few steps and back onto it – we sat ourselves down in a cosy threesome, and started. I'd explained the nature of my brief to her before: I was doing a report on the circumstances of female amputees – victims of landmines, invariably – in the Malanje area. There was no money in it, at least not at this stage, and it was purely an information-gathering exercise.

She gave the impression that she didn't care either way, and that she was just here for the *craic* (experience, fun) anyway. In fact, she opened the conversation, berating me for not coming to visit her.

I have no knowledge yet of Kimbundo, and I couldn't tell what were words and what were exclamations – whichever they were, the first ejaculation of each sentence was a long, rising, wailing sound that was a cross between a comic-book expression of glee and a gargling at the back of the throat. I took to imitating these lightly, depending on her emphasis. This seemed to go down quite well. It was certainly entertaining our guards.

Name, address, place of origin all came through the translation quite efficiently. I asked Lazari if he could ask her her age.

'Aaiiihhhhhhh,' she said, followed by some other similar sounds.

'She doesn't know,' said Lazari.

'Ehhh gwahh,' she said, laughing, and I said something that sounded maybe similar and laughed too.

She was crumpled and shrunken, but there was a spark in her and her voice was as strong as an opera singer's.

I asked about her family. The details were sketchy. Her husband died – 'a lonnggg time agoo' was what her answer sounded like. Of her children, one was a soldier, and she'd heard nothing of him in maybe four years, didn't know where he was or whether he was alive. She lived with her daughter, whose husband had left her after she kept on losing her children – five died in total, although as she still had five, the husband's logic wasn't too obvious. They lived in an adobe house, with a table, chair, bed for the daughter and mat for herself.

I asked about how she lost her leg.

'Nee dayy too kimayyy! Whooshhh!' and she threw her hands up over the stub of her leg to indicate the explosion.

Returning home after a day in the fields, there was no firewood in the house and she had to go back out to find some to make the fire to cook the dinner. Walking along the path towards the wood, she stepped on an anti-personnel mine. This happened in the region of Caculama, an area which if it wasn't for the war would be a tourist resort and boasts one of the finest waterfalls on the continent. The mine blew her foot off. By the time they got to the hospital in Malanje, the next day, they had to amputate her leg from the upper thigh.

'Did she know when it happened?'

'It was during the Third War.'

That narrowed it down, then, to sometime between late '92 and '94, the so-called third stage of the war that has ripped apart Angola over the past thirty-odd years.

It appeared her husband had died soon after the accident. Her daughter lived by the archetypal woman's subsistence activity here, 'selling bits and pieces in the market'. The mother depended on her daughter for what she could spare, a bit of food, an old cloth for a wrap, a bit of soap, and after that made her way around the missions and begged. Today, after walking the mile or so to the local Catholic mission where they'd only been able to give her a small bit of the local staple dish, *funje*, she'd decided to call on me.

I was supposed to be finding out how my organisation could help women like this. I asked about her crutches. She chuckled.

'They're old. They sometimes come apart, but I'm used to them.'

I examined the crutches. Once well-cut, they were cracked and worn, and were being held together with old and bent nails and makeshift repairs. Her one un-shoed foot looked as if it was made of the same material as the crutches, only tougher.

'If I had money,' she said suddenly, 'I'd buy one of those bicycle things,' and she indicated pedalling furiously with her hands. She was referring to a type of hand-pedal wheelchair designed quite like a bicycle (and probably made out of old ones) that amputees here use quite commonly. It would obviously be more comfortable than crutches, but I wanted to see what practical use this bicycle would be. After all, sustainability is the catch-phrase. If the money came through for this project, how would I justify buying her a bicycle-chair?

'With a bicycle, I could go and beg in the bairros, as well as just in the centre of town.'

There wasn't much more to say. I put together a basic bag of food for her, and we gave her a lift back to her house.

'If I had a bicycle, you wouldn't have to drop me home,' she said.

At the door of the house, we exchanged some words in Portuguese with her daughter, a pretty, strong-looking woman of about thirty-five. They taught me to say thank you in Kimbundo, and the old woman laughed uproariously at my attempts to repeat it. I left her leaning against the doorway (I didn't actually see if there was a door or not) of an almost completely dark, windowless adobe house, with the barest of furnishings just visible inside, her battered crutches under her arm and a space hanging down under her ragged wrap where the left leg should have been.

Supply Teacher
Christopher Osborn (Thailand)

DEPDC, the Development and Education Programme for Daughters and Communities in Thailand, was started to offer free education and limited basic needs assistance to anyone who needed it, focusing particularly on recruiting and offering free education to young girls as an alternative to being sold into the sex trade. The DEPDC supports about 300 children a year, aged between six and twenty. We had agreed to help out somehow – but what could we do?

On our first day in Mae Sai – a town nestled between the river plain (with

Myanmar on the other side) and some big mountains – we head down to the admin offices. It seems most of the teaching staff got tied up in meetings south in the nearest major town, so, 'Would we mind taking on a couple of sections of the classes for the day? Only from 9am to 3pm?' Oh yeah, and they don't know any English, but don't worry about it, you can just wing it. So with about twenty minutes' warning, we are now officially 'at work' in Thailand.

We stroll into class, thirty kids grinning at us, expecting a full day's supply of scholarly instruction. I clutch in my hand a limp piece of damp, recycled paper – a list of one-word curriculum ideas scratched uselessly: Art, Gym, Language, Arts? Math, Recess? Teach Alpha, Sing song?. . . Around us: screaming, water (it is raining heavily outside) and mass pandemonium.

Our heads are still full of our three weeks of chaotic introduction to the land, language and sound. A Thai teacher comes in and barks a few pre-emptory remarks, the kids sit down quietly and respectfully and give us an official 'Hello teacher' bow of respect. The woman then turns to us with a kind smile and says, 'Okay,' and walks out.

With a last look at the drooping piece of paper we smile at the class and begin the process of writing the English alphabet on the board. This is going to be a day of English and math, the only subjects we can have any chance of teaching.

English goes okay. We sing some songs (itzy bitzy spider) teach some phrases (Hello! My name is . . . Phoang, Lon Pao, Nok, Ngigh Si . . .) Math is fine, except my great idea to do a multiplication table is stymied since the kids have never heard of multiplication and they think I am nuts to suggest $2 \times 3 = 6$. They roll their eyes at one another, nod politely at my insistence that this is true and write down on their papers the *correct* answer: $2 + 3 = 5$. (I am apparently so sloppy as to have even written the + symbol wrong too.) Perhaps out of the class of thirty, maybe three suddenly grasped the idea that 2×3 was $2 + 2 + 2$. I am glad I didn't have to clean up that mess the next day as the 'real' teacher.

Come to think of it, in a month of eating lunch in the staff kitchen, I have never actually spoken to the 'real' teacher. Maybe she is avoiding me?

Earthquake Relief
Anand Punja (India)

My Immediate Reactions to the Earthquake
I was half asleep when the earthquake struck on January 26, Republic Day in India. I was in one of those dazes when things that actually happen occur in a dream. Even after the tremors shook the earth and people were gathering outside I ignored the noise of chitter-chatter. It being Republic Day, I knew that people would be heading out early to show their patriotism for India. As it turned out, showing up for your country in some places decreased the number of dead and in others increased it. Four hundred children were killed in Anjar because they were on parade. On the other hand, at a privately-run boarding school the death toll was only one (an eight-month old baby) out of a total of 200 children plus

staff, because the kids were on the road on their way to a parade.

The first I heard of the destruction of the quake was when I reached an Internet café. They told me of the news, but at that time there was not much information. All that was known was that the epicentre (a place called Lodhal), was in Kutch district somewhere north-east of Bhuj, the district capital. Any information that was available at that time was on Ahmedabad, the largest city in Gujarat. The media had not reached Kutch at that time; there was no communication with the area at all. All I could think of was that if Ahmedabad was so bad, with it being at least 400 km from the epicentre, Kutch must be flattened.

I had been to Kutch in October and, as many people do, fell in love with the place. What I was most amazed about was the resilience of the people, living in such harsh conditions. I had been in Bhuj only one day, but had met a few people through my research colleague. I could not get their faces out of my mind, wondering where and how they were. The same thoughts rushed through my head about the people I'd met in Ahmedabad (many of them living in high-rises), which had been a stop for me only a week before the quake. I spent a long time trying to contact people I knew, and was amazed by the speed at which information travels, even when communications are down. Within a week of the quake I knew, somehow or other, that most of the people I knew were alive.

My Observations of Relief Work from Afar
During the first two weeks all I wanted to do was to drop everything that I was doing and head straight to Kutch to volunteer at one of the relief camps. I decided against it and eventually left for Kutch two weeks after the disaster, hoping to fill in gaps where people had left. The main reason for this was that I wanted to help to rebuild lives and homes. Besides, reports stated that so much help was pouring into Kutch that the place had been overwhelmed. The media emphasised that relief was reaching that district, but due to the bad organisation it was heading straight for the city of Bhuj, ironically the place the media had focused on. What surprises me is that one of the worst affected towns to be hit, Bachau is bang on the highway to Bhuj. How could people just have bypassed the town without noticing the devastation there? Maybe they thought that Bhuj was worse? In many articles and papers that I read at that time said that places like Anjar and Bachau were just being bypassed, and were reached only on the third day of the rescue operations. For me this is explained by the Gujarati mentality towards Kutch, both the general public and policy makers. Throughout its history as a district (since 1961), Kutch has been seen very much as a backward area in Gujarat, and indeed for most people Bhuj, the capital has represented the entire Kutch district.

The problem behind the whole operation was the bad organisation by the state government. Eventually heads did roll and Kutch district had new staff at the very top changed. The collector (the head at the district level in India), was the one who was supposed to be gathering information from various parts of the district, and then directing rescue and relief teams to where they were most needed. But many rescue teams that had come in from abroad had to hang around so much that they decided to do away with waiting for the government and just acted on hunches or where local people were directing them. This also caused havoc as some of these people were asking teams not to rescue people that were alive, but relatives that were dead, so that they could give them the respectable farewell that they deserved.

Relief co-ordination was also in a state. Bhuj was inundated with so many supplies and drivers were getting so frustrated at the waiting around and traffic queues that they began to dump along the roadsides so that certain areas began to look like dump yards. Of course in an emergency situation all relief material is generally welcomed and indeed needed and a lot of it was being used. However dumping it or just throwing it to people, almost as if they are like dogs is not the way to distribute and causes more troubles than it's worth. Eventually, as co-ordination improved through better communications between the increasing numbers of relief camps these incidents occurred less. Individual camps set up their own systems of distribution, with NGOs leading the way.

My Experiences as a Volunteer
In the camp where I started my voluntary work in Balasar, the north-west area of Kutch, a participatory approach was taken. Village committees were set up, with representatives of different castes and in some cases women too. It was hoped that these committees would be of a lasting nature, and I have heard mixed stories on this issue since. The committee decided the list of families that would receive relief material (rather than deciding the type of relief material), taking into account sons who had recently married but not perhaps yet moved out and widows, and in some excellent cases unmarried daughters. Distribution was therefore a two-stage process, with the first stage, a quick food distribution to make sure families had basic amenities for a week or so, and the second stage providing further amenities that would see a family through at least a month, by when it was hoped that the government would provide more, or that families could return to their homes to dig out last year's harvests. Indeed, most families could salvage a lot from their homes. However, due to the fear of another earthquake, many left possessions and food in their houses, until they were confident enough to retrieve them.

In the camp and general area where I was based, I found excellent co-ordination with other relief camps. For instance although I was based at the Narmada Bachao Andolan Camp, I was also helping out at the Government of Haryana camp. This lead to greater effectiveness and efficiency of overall relief operations. As a volunteer I had no problems with this and indeed enjoyed working with various different people.

In other camps, however I heard stories that distribution was unfair and not sensitive to the socio-cultural environment. For example I heard of unfair treatment and distribution by the RSS (a pro Hindu organisation) in districts where there are strong Muslim communities (towards the Pakistan border).

There was a mixture of appropriate and inappropriate materials that came into Kutch. Good materials that came in were the medical supplies, tarpaulins (even as much as I hate plastic, especially in India!), blankets, lanterns, cooking utensils and water containers. Manpower also flooded in, especially in the first month, with many doctors shutting surgeries in other parts of the country and heading there, along with truck drivers with their own vehicles. The trucks became very handy as they could be loaded with huge plastic water tanks and used as makeshift water tankers. This must have eased the pressure on the government water tankers, and thus thankfully I did not hear many struggles revolving around water, which is relatively common in this drought prone area.

Other things were being sent in without much thought, especially clothes and salt (in a region renowned for its salt marshes). Even mineral water was being sent from the other side of the country. However, it was not so much the lack of water that was the problem, but containers to store water. Some volunteers therefore helped in rebuilding check-dams, village tanks/wells, which was an important task before the onset of the monsoons.

Some of the clothes that were being sent were so culturally inappropriate that when I left Kutch in April there were still bundles lying around, where people would just not wear them. Maybe you can get away with sending anything for kids, but for women in particular, they needed good saris: just because they have no access to most of their belongings, it doesn't mean that they are ready to wear anything and in any condition. In an area where traditions have not changed much in the past hundred years (particularly within villages), suddenly a sack full of clothes turns up where half of them are old frilly nightshirts or ripped and torn shirts. Why does one think that people become paupers overnight? If new clothes are sent, than people at least still have a sense of self-esteem, whereas old clothes are likely to only degrade a person's self-esteem. Most of these were sent by urbanites, and it shows that there was a lot of goodwill, but goodwill without thinking about the consequences can sometimes create more problems than it solves. Eventually people have ingeniously converted old clothes into *godras* (futon-like mattresses).

Overall the most inspiring experience about volunteering was the people's resilience and their will to carry on with their lives, adapting quickly to their harsher conditions. This was truer in the rural areas rather than the urban ones. This is where I feel the legacy of drought cycles has hardened the rural villager. Their hospitality too was just as warm and welcoming, if not more, during this hard time. Indeed, on my way to the relief camp, I was stranded on the outskirts of Rapar, about 30 km short of Balasar. I had travelled thus far with a mother and her son returning from a trip to Samakiali, where they went to get news. On hearing that I would not make it to Balasar that night, they kindly offered me food and shelter for the night. They fed me very well, and provided me with good bedding in the winter desert cold, especially as we slept in their timber yard.

After my time in the relief camp I headed to the village that I had visited in October, Merka. The time in Balasar had helped me learn about relief work, and thus in conjunction with a local NGO I organised one of the few fair relief distributions in Merka. I eventually concentrated on conducting rehabilitation work, mainly to obtain temporary shelter for the villagers. This was done through another NGO that I knew had already worked in the village on a watershed project. The project started by preparing the village and organising a village committee, representing all castes, with equal representation from women. I tried to give ownership to the committee and only intervened to cool things down if they got too heated. Within my role, I learnt a lot of mediation techniques, especially in the highly politicised nature of the Indian relief system. I left Merka with a feeling that what I had achieved was on the whole good for many of the villagers. However, I was asking myself whether I interfered in village politics.

These thoughts make me realise that volunteering is an enriching experience overall, but can be very tough. It cannot be only done out of goodwill. Volunteering always gives something to the volunteer; the important thing is to give something back. This is much easier in an institutionalised format, especially when you work with other volunteers, as I did in Balasar.

My Return to Merka

I have just recently returned to Merka, a year and a half later. It was a short trip, mainly to see how lives, families and the village have been rebuilt. It was very emotional, with mixed feelings of joy, sadness and frustration at the government . . . or the lack of it as the case may be. I was also glad to know that my work there had been greatly appreciated and that after staying there during those hard times, I and indeed most villagers now see me as an adopted son: I know it is somewhere where I will always return. It was great to see new houses up (some built with the materials that had come from the NGO that we approached), and people starting to live life as normally as they could. People have married and babies been born. However, many, especially the poorer still live in makeshift houses that were constructed in the open lands. In a few areas, rubble is still lying there, and in some way I feel, that people are still waiting and have adopted a culture of dependency on the government, who are very slow to provide the little that they are giving. However, these are few, and in most cases people have moved on and rebuilt their lives. Much of this was helped by a better monsoon in 2001, where although not great, harvests were decent. What will test these people, however, is the complete failure of the rains in 2002 (only 4-5 hours have fallen all year, and now the season is over).

For me however, one positive aspect of returning was to see my friend, Chottabhai, in his new role. For me, he did the most for the village during relief and rehabilitation work. He has now joined the NGO that I conducted the fair distribution with in Merka. He is an excellent example of how people have made a success at rebuilding their lives and homes. I hope that many more will follow his example; not in the sense of working for an NGO, but in the sense of taking control of their own lives.

Pride and Prejudices
Charlotte Spinks (South Africa)

It's been just over two months since I arrived in this strange and far-off land, and discovered that water exits the plug-hole in the opposite direction to England. It is strange to be coping without decent tea, pubs and EastEnders, but the weather sort of makes up for it I guess.

I'm living and working at 'Hope House' (not its real name), a residential home for young men aged 16-21. We currently have twenty-two 'boys', most of whom are ex-street youths, from abusive families, or in some sort of trouble. Most of the boys are at school/college or out at jobs during the day, though there are a few who are unemployed and so are around the home. There aren't really any structured activities for them, and I have struggled with defining my role here and determining the best way to spend my time. Most of the boys are here because they have a problem that means they need care and help, but they don't want to admit this, are resentful, and don't want any help. Where do I start?

When I arrived I soon discovered that my role here is very much on my own initiative, and that no-one has ever held this position before. Although there is a great need with the boys, I just don't know what to do and feel totally overwhelmed by the enormity of the task, alongside my personal feelings of isolation and frustration. I haven't received much support – after being collected from the airport I was just left here in the middle of nowhere, with no transport or connections to go anywhere or do anything.

Being left to do as I please is pretty daunting considering that I know no-one and nothing about this city or country. So I suppose it is not surprising that there have been lots of tears and 'I wanna go homes', but I so much want to do something to make a difference, and not have to go home with my tail between my legs.

I don't really know what I am supposed to be doing at work, and it isn't easy to make friends outside the project as I live and work at the same place, and I am the only volunteer (in fact, virtually the only white person in the neighbourhood).

It has also been tough establishing relationships with the boys, particularly as they are all of a similar age to me and I'm the only female. I'm sure you can imagine the romantic advances, but seeing as I don't even know what my role here is it is hard to set them straight about what I do here. Yet the other response to my gender, from the project manager, is that as a single young woman I'm at the bottom of the ranking order, slightly above the insects that reside alongside us. So long as I can cook and make a nice cup of coffee all will be fine for him.

Rather than just continue to struggle on, I organised a meeting with the project manager to discuss my role here (or lack thereof). His initial response that I could 'do whatever you want around the project' was not particularly encouraging as there doesn't seem to be anything structured to do, no-one else seems to do anything, and I wouldn't know where to start anyway. In his eyes, I am just an eccentric Brit. When I told him how difficult I find the pace of life here, finally I thought I had hit the mark as his eyes lit up and he nodded emphatically in agreement. 'Yes,' he said, 'in Cape Town everyone is in such a hurry.' Back to the drawing board.

If talking doesn't help, how about some action? It seems to me that many

Working with the young men from Hope House (in background)

of the boys use Hope House as a hostel for accommodation rather than a rehabilitating social development project (which is what it is supposed to be). So I'm going all out on making some changes. I don't want to go it totally alone because any changes need to be sustainable and to last after my departure. Therefore I've made friends with the project manager's wife (by gaining her baby daughter's love), and she is a great source of advice and support. Now down to action: I've bought a file for each 'boy' and am writing a 'care plan' procedure for each of them to chart their progress.

Amazingly the project manager agrees, and later (when I hear him telling his supervisor about the changes), it all seems to be his idea. So now we're jointly running fortnightly assessment meetings for each young man in our care, to discuss their progress and decide upon goals for their time here. Ultimately they will move back into society after their stay here, so each client needs a tailored programme of rehabilitation to meet their specific needs. Although some boys are keen to avoid their meetings, others are just so happy that someone is finally taking an interest in them. And now that I'm charting their progress, and helping them develop a programme for their stay here, they no longer see me as a play-object, but more of a guardian or social worker.

Every day is still tough, but now I have a vision myself too. When a new boy arrives fresh from the streets there is a programme for him to enter to meet his individual needs and help him develop as a young independent man, rather than an institutionalised tearaway. And the best thing of all is that I feel we've changed things *slowly* and as a team so that the long-term local workers are essential to the project too.

Riots
John Bradley (Sierra Leone)

In Kabala, Sierra Leone, the school year for me started, in theory at least, at 08:45 on Tuesday 7 September, 1976. I had been warned by those starting their second year as voluntary teachers at Kabala Secondary School, that I shouldn't expect KSS to resemble any school I had ever known. The first inkling that working in Kabala may indeed be different from what I'd initially expected was the distinct lack of pupils on that Tuesday morning, supposedly the first day of the new school year. Some did eventually turn up, several hours late, and when the numbers had grown to a respectable size an assembly was held. The principal welcomed the students and introduced the new teachers – I soon became known as Mr John. I learned that class sizes were generally between 35 and 50, the vast majority of the students being keen to learn. While the class sizes were no real surprise, the discovery that some of the students were actually older than me was a little unnerving at first. The school day consisted of five lessons, of which staff generally taught four. Teaching finished at 2pm, by which time the temperature had climbed to the point where both students and staff needed a siesta in the shade.

During the first week students were expected to purchase their books from the bookshop which had travelled up from Freetown. The expense of the books and writing materials, together with the school fees of Le 10.20 per term, meant that many were asking for financial help from anyone who would listen. I was approached by several students and finally sponsored Alusine Turay, technically a fourth year pupil, although a couple of years older than me. He was keen to do a degree in physics, often coming to the bungalow after school for some extra help. By the end of the second week, those who had failed to find the fees were turned away, their short-lived attempt at trying to obtain an education coming to an abrupt and premature end. The staff celebrated the conclusion of the first full school week by throwing a party, albeit held mid-morning, so that the later classes were cancelled.

These cancellations continued throughout term for a variety of reasons including joint Christian/Muslim prayer meetings, local bank holidays and religious holy days, visits by local and national dignitaries; and on more occasions than I care to remember, for no apparent reason; the students just deciding to pack up and go home.

* * *

So I wasn't too surprised when hardly any students turned up on the first day of the second term. The rest of the week continued in much the same vein, most classes having to be cancelled due to a distinct lack of students. All of us were beginning to get quite despondent with the whole situation that we now found ourselves in. Just when we thought things couldn't get any worse we heard rumours that there had been student unrest in Freetown, culminating in riots on Saturday 29 January. The following Monday it was clear that our students had heard of the problems in Freetown and were discussing it amongst themselves and with some of the local members of staff.

The following day we found armed police on the compound. All the fourth and fifth year students were taken to the community centre in town where they were warned not to become involved with any unlawful activity. The remaining students were also dismissed, being strongly advised to go straight home. Meanwhile, we were called to an emergency staff meeting. Here we learnt that the problems in Freetown were becoming far more serious and that unrest was starting to spread up-country; rumours amongst the locals suggested that it had already reached Makeni, just a hundred miles away. This made us realise that Kabala itself could soon be involved. In the hope of averting this worsening situation and spreading civil unrest, the president at the time, Siaka Stevens, decided to declare a nationwide state of emergency. This closed all schools until further notice and it also imposed a rigorously enforced dawn to dusk curfew. The next few weeks were extremely tense. We kept a very low profile and took refuge in our bungalow, on the west-facing veranda, eating our groundnut stew supper against the backdrop of the Koinadugu mountain range.

In an attempt to return things to normality, up-country schools tried to reopen on Thursday 10 February. In our case it was fairly pointless as only twenty students turned up. On Monday two of the local teachers were attacked by a group of fourth year students. Police were called and took several students away, so 'they could be taught some respect', we were told. For the next few days we had a constant police presence on the school compound.

In order to try to halt any further deterioration in the country as a whole, a general election had been called for 4, 5 and 6 May. Volunteers were reaching saturation point and often talked of terminating. There appeared to be little chance of completing courses in time for the examinations and we were all coming to the conclusion that our role as teachers was being seriously undermined, often to the point that there seemed little reason to continue. As one succinctly put it, 'Teaching here occasionally ascends to the level of a farce.'

Summer term had started on Tuesday 12 April with a grand total of twenty-five students in school. By Thursday this had dropped to five and on the Friday no students at all turned up, despite over six hundred being registered. This was further compounded by several members of staff taking time off as well.

The elections were duly held and returned the ruling All Peoples Congress Party virtually unopposed. SB Kawusa Konte was the sitting member for our area. He was also the Minister for Lands and Mines and had a house on the other side of the valley from our bungalow. One evening prior to the elections a gun battle raged outside his compound for several hours, and although he was not injured he withdrew his nomination. In consequence, the opposing candidate SB Marah was declared the winner and, although he had stood as an Independent candidate, he declared for the APC party upon his election.

Towards the end of May, a sense of normality finally started to return. Around fifty percent of them turned up to sit their final examinations, thus completing their somewhat disrupted year's education. Some had returned to their villages during the disruptions caused by State of Emergency and its aftermath, and hadn't felt secure enough to return to Kabala and the school. Alusine Turay, the student I had sponsored during the year, returned from his home village to take the end of year examinations, all of which he subsequently passed.

On the surface, having only managed three weeks' uninterrupted teaching during the whole academic year, our role there as teachers did not appear to have been that constructive. Despite this, and the occasional questioning of our sanity, we all felt that the experience had been worthwhile.

However, this unrest was to pale into insignificance a few short years later. By 1991 Sierra Leone was in the midst of a brutal civil war lasting nine long years. Some of the bloodiest fighting took place in the Northern Province and the Kabala we had come to know just fourteen years earlier changed dramatically. Our school was closed and requisitioned by rebel forces belonging to the Revolutionary United Front, its spacious buildings and compound making it an ideal base camp for their soldiers. Following the signing of a peace agreement, hostilities between the rebel forces and the Sierra Leonean army subsided. The school and its surrounding compound, including our bungalow, were left booby-trapped with mines. Inevitably and sadly, it is almost certainly true that some of the students we taught will have perished in the long and bitter civil war. Alusine Turay was amongst those who lost their lives. As to our role as volunteers and teachers; well, at least we tried.

LIFE IS HARD, YOU LEARN HUMILITY

On the Buses
Frances Platt (Nepal)

Buses are Nepal's transport backbone. Very few can afford a car or even a motorbike, most short journeys are by bicycle or on foot, so where there's a road, and even where there's not, the bus is the only choice for most.

When we travel by country bus in the West, we are used (for the most part) to clean, well regulated services with timetables, tickets and enough seats for all passengers. In Nepal, the bus leaves when it's full, you pay on the bus but no ticket is given in exchange, you have a seat if you board the bus at the start of the journey, or you have to stand or sit on a sack of rice or potatoes, or on the spare tyre. The seats are torn, dirty and loose.

The safety record of out-of-town buses is appalling – the newspapers report accidents daily. Buses leave the road and fall down precipices, run over cyclists, children, the elderly, goats, ducks and chickens. The law is difficult to enforce, so people take the law into their own hands, sometimes setting fire to the bus or blockading the road, the driver having run off as soon as the accident happens. He (never she) knows what will occur if he's caught. He is personally liable for any injured passengers, many drivers have not passed any official test (or have forged papers) and are not insured. A dead victim is a better option than a seriously injured one, and it has been known for bus drivers to run the bus over accident victims rather than pay for their hospital treatment and maintain their families while they cannot work.

In remote areas, night buses are sometimes held up by bandits who demand cash and jewellery from passengers. If you're a woman travelling alone, expect to be harassed. The best strategy is to sit next to another woman.

Several of 'my' schools are in the rural areas of Kavre district, in the next valley east of Kathmandu. Proximity to the capital means nothing, as soon as you're away from the one main road heading east, you could be 100 km away. Most of my journeys to work are a combination of country bus and a walk. I'm used to the bus network and in its own way, it is efficient. There are no bus stops, the buses are not numbered, but everyone knows which bus goes where, because the conductor shouts out the destination along the route, and the bus points in a particular direction when it's parked.

You board the bus – usually a steep scramble up steps – and find a seat. I have long legs so can only comfortably sit near the front where there's a space for farm produce, or in the middle of the back row where I can stretch out. I wait for the bus to fill up, this can take up to 45 minutes, so I always carry a book or the newspaper. I watch while sari-clad women clamber on with infants tied to their backs in shawls, or heave sacks of potatoes or rice into the space at the front. Men of all ages, mostly unemployed, sit and chat and however poor, all wear the brightly woven cotton topi on their heads and some kind of western male dress, usually a long sleeved shirt and trousers, with rubber flip-flops.

No-one seems in a hurry. The driver isn't in his seat. The nearby teashop is doing a good trade in hot, milky tea for the remaining passengers. Suddenly the engine is turned on, the stragglers take the last seats, the unlucky ones have to hang on to the handrails above. Young men don't give up their seats but a nursing mother will pout and chivvy until someone rises. We sway around corners, in and out of potholes, stop and start seemingly on a whim to unload or take on passengers. The conductor will suddenly climb on to the roof to haul up sheets of corrugated iron for a passenger's tin roof, or to hand down empty milk churns. Loud engine noise means that conversations have to be shouted even between those sitting next to each other. Not all are human passengers – goats, chickens and ducks, sometimes loose, sometimes in a wicker basket or on a string come on board with their minders.

The bus driver joins in the conversation, turning around to argue a point, gesticulating with one hand. Sometimes a friend will share his seat, distracting him with an arm around the shoulders and an intimate chat. Clouds of dust follow the bus as soon as it leaves the bitumen and hits deep ruts in dried mud. Reading becomes impossible as the bus sways from side to side. All that's left to do is to look at the view, often quite breathtaking, terraced hills hundreds of metres high with the ever present Himalayas on the horizon.

Getting Your Hair Done in Addis Ababa
Libby Selman (Ethiopia)

Of course the volunteer experience is about more important things than hairdos! Well, yes and no. Volunteers now are not all twenty-somethings with glossy locks that spring back into shape after four weeks camping in a swamp. So here's my bad hair story.

Addis Ababa, the capital of Ethiopia, is 318 kilometres from the small town of Yirgalem where I worked, a long way to go for a hairdo. But the only local hairdresser had accidentally removed most of my American friend's hair in one afternoon. The young Ethiopian women on our campus did each other's hair in beautiful patterns of small tight plaits, and women my age just wrapped their hair up in black cloth. The novelty of my 'wavy' hair at first tempted people in shops and buses to touch it but after six months the waviness was gone, and pride required a cut and perm.

Could I afford it? Just about. It would cost the equivalent of £20 in a major hotel, where one hairdresser had trained abroad for foreign hair. Could I get there? There's a daily bus, taking ten hours, costing under £3 each way. The trip would take three days, two travelling and one in Addis Ababa.

I had a stroke of luck because a pick-up truck from our institute was to go nearly to Addis to collect *t'ef* flour (the soft golden grain that is fermented and cooked into *injera,* the national staple food). So I joined the t'ef run at 6am, leaving my companions near Addis selecting the highest quality grain as I leapt on a passing bus. My day ended with counting the flea bites from the bus – fourteen.

The Hairdo Day started badly – my shoes split off, uppers from lowers, so I arrived at the posh hotel with flapping feet, walking so oddly that the beggars even gave up following me. I had a sense of doom and it was no surprise when at the end the hairdresser said, 'Oh, madam, I am not pleased with this perm, the fluid was not very good'. I'd been watching Ethiopian clients having their hair straightened and hadn't paid much attention to my own. It was horribly short and looked as if it had been straightened, not permed. Not a happy moment . . . .

The third day of my Hairdressing Trip was worse. By that stage of my work in Ethiopia I'd done the early morning trip from the Addis Mercato bus station several times and was more relaxed than a lot of the Ethiopian passengers. My first time had been scary but now I knew you just listened hard for someone yelling 'Yirgalem!', bought a ticket from them and stuck close to their side until you could fight your way onto the bus. I wasn't lumbered with three grand-children and a sack of greens like my immediate neighbour, nor travelling with an uncooperative cockerel like the man behind.

It was a very, very slow journey, with choking clouds of exhaust, but the bus did just keep moving. It was full of soldiers as well as families. At the halfway stop in Ziway, we were over an hour late, but stopped as usual to visit one of the world's worst toilets. Buses stop there for half an hour, which is about twenty five minutes too long in the hot little hell-hole of Ziway bus station.

The bus disappeared. I knew where it should be but it wasn't. Panicking, I was reassured by a passenger that the bus had just gone to the garage for repairs for half an hour. Fine. No problem.

Two and a half hours later we were still there, gathered in the little shade beside a stall. A schoolboy and some soldiers went off to find the bus garage. On their return I grasped that the passengers were very angry and we were to 'walk together and take our money!' The group set off and I gradually picked up what was happening. Our bus was dead, finished, past it, no wheels. But instead of organising a replacement, the driver and conductor were abandoning us. They had our money – and we were only halfway through the journey. I calculated my finances – having a hairdo had left me with too little to buy another ticket.

We marched along, fast and far, but no-one flagged. Finally, beyond the town was an enclosure, with our wheel-less bus inside. The soldiers and students ran in, shouting, and there were loud cries from the conductor, a small white-haired man backing away from them. Then bank notes flew up in the air – the conductor, in tears, was throwing the money at the passengers.

With the cash in their hands, our leaders were able to commandeer another bus to continue the journey – though the operation was not totally smooth, as we'd managed to lose one or two passengers on the road, and a couple of opportunists from the bus station slipped onto our new bus in their places until the original passengers turned up . . . . However, no-one got thrown off as there was a high level of camaraderie, right through to Awassa, the regional capital. From there I took another bus, which I could afford.

I reached our campus with more flea bites, desperate for a shower. Crashing into my room, I turned on the tap. No water. Of course. A friend from across the corridor came to warn me the water was off, but couldn't help beginning: 'Oh, did you *want* your hair like that?' I'd actually forgotten about my hair for several hours. Now I would have to face everyone's comments.

But no! I was to be spared for a while, because just then the electricity went off too, leaving my hair in merciful darkness . . . .

A Helping Hand
Anne Rawling (Philippines)

It all began in May. I arrived back at the orphanage after being out for the afternoon to find people gathered at the gate. My friend informed me that someone had been stabbed. I looked up to see a man hunched over. He was in a blood-soaked shirt and in a lot of pain. People from the community gathered around and stared. I had to do what I could to assist this man, even though I only had basic first aid.

I raced to the staff house and grabbed my first aid kit to help. I put my gloves on and carefully lifted his shirt to see that he had lost a lot of blood. I was able to wrap a large bandage around his waist. Someone from the orphanage was organising the bus to take him to the rural hospital. I looked down at his wrist to see that he was also stabbed there and I could see all the bone and layers of skin. This would normally make me feel ill, but I had to continue helping him. I took another bandage and wrapped it around his wrist, I used a stick as a splint to try and keep his hand still.

I went with him on the bumpy road to the local hospital. In the emergency room he was put on two drips and told that he had to be sent to Cebu, one and a half hours away. The family had no money and there was no ambulance to take him. The local Barangay Captain (local Mayor) was at the hospital. I told him I would cover the cost of the transport, just find a vehicle. The doctor said I must travel in the vehicle with the patient and monitor both the drips. I told her that I wasn't a doctor and could not do this. She told me the patient might die if I did not go with him. After a five-minute explanation on the drips and extra supplies, we all got into a van and headed to Cebu. I was holding the drips and keeping pressure on his wound, while sitting on top of the motor.

It was a difficult couple of hours. Alfredo kept moving in pain, cramping and in shock. It was difficult monitoring the drips and ensuring that the fluids were going through to him as he twisted and turned in pain. We finally arrived at the hospital and he went straight into surgery. The family had no money for medicine, so I said I would cover some of the cost. I was outside the hospital in blood-stained pants feeling quite queasy. Alfredo died four hours later in the hospital. His kidney was sliced in half and they couldn't save him.

Anne Rawling with Anheles and her two children

Back in Bunga, Anheles, Alfredo's wife gave birth to a baby girl four days after she lost her husband. I climbed the mountain to the native hut. Her husband's coffin was surrounded by candles in one room and Anheles and her new baby were lying on the floor in the other room, both covered by a rag.

I sat down next to them and gave food and clothes for Anheles and the baby. It was a very difficult time for the mother, having just given birth and having her husband's funeral two days later. They asked me to name the baby as thanks for my help. I called her Alfreda after her father Alfredo.

I was able to help pay for the funeral, food and gas for the bus, and I went to the funeral to be with the family. A few days later, the Barangay Captain told me he was very honoured to have me in their community.

Working at the orphanage, going through extreme emotions – trying for the first time in my life to try to save someone, giving all I had by way of funds (with the support of AusAid and my family), food, emotional support, being there when someone died, Anheles giving birth, grieving with the family – it was all too much. I had many coping mechanisms in place. I was writing in a journal, talking to my family and friends and I cried a lot for the pain that the family were going through and kept on going.

It was only when I ate chicken with the children a few days later that events really caught up with me. The chicken leg looked just like the joints from Alfredo's hand. I suddenly felt queasy and light-headed. I excused myself from the table and went to the staff house. Running straight into the director at the ranch, I started weeping and told her about the chicken. I knew at that time I needed to leave the orphanage for a few days and have a short break.

* * *

Alfredo's stabbing made me realise how valuable life is and made me determined to work harder. I've been concerned with the poverty that people are facing and problems in the community like the stabbing. I really wanted to do something to help, so I've set up a handbag business that is doing well and will be able to provide the women with an income. Anheles will also be attending the next training day, so she can earn some extra money.

I'm so excited with the success of the business. We are able to pay the women a wage for their work and have hired a full-time manager to run it when I return to Australia. I will return home in January with a great sense of achievement and satisfaction, knowing that I did what I could to support the orphanage and community and that I have made a positive difference to the lives of these amazing people.

A Taste of Local Life
Rob Palmer (Ghana)

In Kumasi there was a 'vulture-kebab scare', really big, in all the papers. People were warned not to eat at roadside stalls (chop bars) as the police had uncovered some enterprising sellers who had been killing vultures and serving them up as chicken to the unsuspecting public.

Having said that, most roadside snacks were very good, even though some had disturbing names, 'Chilly Willy' (*kelewele*) for example. 'Have you ever had chilly willy?' was one such awkward question. 'Well . . . yes, there was this time when I was in Canada, minus 40 with wind-chill and . . . ahem, anyway . . . .'

One night I was settling down happily eating my coco-yam leaf soup that one of the villagers had lovingly prepared. While eating, I absently wondered what the curious black oblongs were that were floating around amongst the leaves. Thinking they must be some form of the usual 'miscellaneous meat', I ate on. When I'd nearly finished, and a particularly large oblong came into view in the flickering of the oil lamp, I picked it up and looked closely at it. It was actually meat, but not the sort I was hoping for. Some caterpillars must have snuck in under the leaves the soup was made from.

We decided to start a farm at the back of the centre, so I had to learn about agriculture. We made some yam mounds before planting yam heads in the ground. Yams really are a big thing here. When I visited the Boabeng-Fiema monkey sanctuary I was fortunate enough to be allowed to visit a sacred yam. They keep it in a sacred grove deep in the monkey forest tied to a tree with string. Every year the fetish priest and a few old farmers go to the sacred grove with the first yams of the harvest. They take a pot with them and cook some yams in the grove (but don't put *pepey* (pepper) or *shito* (strong *pepey*) in with it, as the gods do not like the taste). They then break the pot and hang up the yam. Only men are allowed to visit the yam otherwise superstition believes that the river will dry up and the harvest spoiled, having been polluted with unclean menstrual blood.

It got to the stage where I started to ask my friends to send out some recognisable food to supplement my yam and *shito* existence. However, some of my friends didn't quite grasp how hot it was, with one sending fudge which arrived in a totally melted state. I got a note from the head postmaster general in Kumasi saying I had received a 'damaged' parcel from England and that I should go to see him at once. When he got the parcel out of his personal safe that looked as though it had been digested he gave profuse apologies on behalf of the Republic of Ghana. I opened it to discover some Thornton's 'Chicken-Run' special fudge. I then had to fill in a long form about the condition of my fudge and await compensation.

Evenings in the village were a low-key affair: being governed by the sun we tended to get up very early and go to bed early. With no electricity, street-lighting was an eclectic collection of hurricane lamps, candles and little burning wicks sticking out of old Nescafé tins. These lined the main road through the village giving a deceptively festive appearance all year round.

Village entertainment was largely a do-it-yourself thing. Except that sometimes one of the more enterprising villagers used to hook up an old TV to a generator, show a video and charge 10p entrance. It was in this way I got to see *Total Recall* in Spanish. But they didn't seem to notice this, cheered everytime Arnold hit someone, and kept asking me if the characters or background was what it was like in the West. Considering that *Total Recall* is set on Mars and contains some alien-type humans, what could I say?

We had two 'bars' in the village, really just someone's mud hut where they sold (warm) beer and the moonshine spirit, *akperteshie*. If you wanted a drink they'd pull all the chairs out of their front room, stop pounding their *fufu* dinner, serve you and then get back to preparing yams with large machetes. However, you could never get a moment for a quiet drink. Small children followed your every move. *Obruni* (white man) is having a drink. *Obruni* is urinating.

My accommodation was probably one of the safest in the village, being one of the few concrete-block buildings. However, despite the conception of mud-block huts being inherently fragile, they actually appear quite stable. Saying that, I was told that they do get washed away in the rainy season and have to be rebuilt. Later on I found this to be true. The first massive rain storm came in June, during which the mango tree in my yard started propelling mangoes off in the hurricane wind and smashing them into my corrugated iron roof, each time hitting it like a bullet and making shotgun sounds. The bamboo-fence around my house got blown away and we had to find the bits the next morning and try to reconstruct it. As you can imagine, the mud huts in the village itself came off worse. Every year it rains really heavily and the mud gets soaked and walls collapse, and every year they just rebuild them again. It's normal to have your ceiling collapse on to you in the night when it rains. That's what happens if you're lucky, otherwise the wind can carry your roof off totally.

Aside from worrying about the heavy rain and wind taking off my roof, getting to sleep and staying asleep was often a problem. For a start it was frequently so hot with no fan or aircon that even sleeping in the buff I lay in a pool of sweat. Some nights I'd be awoken hearing terrible screams, a cross between a woman being stabbed to death violently and one experiencing a multiple-orgasm. Later I learned that it was just some old bird that lived in the mango tree.

Tuesdays was my anti-malaria-tablet-day, so Tuesday nights were often accompanied by bizarre, unrepeatable Lariam dreams and scary nightmares. I'd have slept with the light on if I could, except that I didn't have electricity. The hurricane lamp just made things worse, casting huge ghostly shapes through my mosquito net. Some nights I had the combination of Lariam dreams, thunder and lightning, and that orgasmic bird all at once. One night I was awoken by the sound of drumming, music and dancing coming from the next village. Apparently they were having an all-night funeral; normal in the case of death during childbirth as it is believed that *juju* (evil spirits) have killed the woman.

Life is Fine
Liselotte Wolters (Uganda)

The death rate here is extremely high. The way Ugandans cope with relatives dying is admirable.

Patrick just comes back from his hometown where he has been for two weeks.

'How were things at home, Patrick?'

'Oh yeah, everything was fine. I found my uncle had died and on the way to the burial my aunt collapsed and died as well and my cousin had his leg amputated, but yeah, home was fine.'

That's life and when your time is up, your time is up.

What an amazing attitude the Ugandans have towards life. I've been in Uganda for more than a year now and still I'm not used to this attitude. I don't think I ever will be. But everyday I think how strong the people I meet here are.

The same attitude to life can frustrate me terribly when I try to look to the day, week, month or even year after today and they just live day by day. But well, this is life in Africa.

Rebuilding Rwanda
Mandy Unsöld (Rwanda)

Rwanda, the so-called 'land of a thousand hills', lies in the east of Africa in the Great Lake Region, about 8 million inhabitants and a surface area of some 26,000 km. With a density of more than 300 persons/km, it is the most populated state in the continent. The west side has the big Lake Kivu with border to Congo, in the north lies Uganda, in the south Burundi and in the east Tanzania.

In contrast to the green landscape with a tropical but soft 'spring' climate, it is not easy to live and work here: in 1994 perhaps the most horrible murder in African history took place here and about 1 million people were killed, most of them the minority Tutsi. The Rwandans themselves often say that they don't understand why this genocide could happen: different from other African countries, Rwanda had no 'classical' ethnic groups with different languages, territories and customs. A social order divided Hutu, Tutsi and Twa but intermarriages were possible. The Germans were the first who colonised Rwanda, but the ethnic separation was cemented by the Belgian colonial authority who introduced ethnic passports based on property. If a person had more then ten cows, they were a Tutsi; less than ten cows, a Hutu; without cows, a Twa.

As a consequence of the genocide of 1994, there are refugees who left in 1959 and have recently come back to Rwanda, and those who fled the country after the victory of the Rwandan Patriotic Front in July 1994, and have now returned. Daily, I am faced with displaced, handicapped and traumatised people, widows and street children. About 115,000 prisoners have not yet been sentenced, and President Kagame's new government wants reconciliation.

In Kigali, you do not see at first sight that grief and sorrow lie behind many laughing faces. The capital nowadays has a peaceful image: the building trade, renovation and commerce are growing. Rwanda has very few raw materials and export articles – just coffee, tea, and pyrethrum. Methane gas from Lake Kivu is not yet exploited.

The countryside is poor, so the Natural Resources Management Programme is concentrating on soil conservation and agro-forestry. We work in collaboration with the Ministry of Local Government in nine districts all over the country, with a staff of more than 100 people. I am a member of the co-ordination team with five experts from abroad, three local experts and the local co-ordinator. We support our partners in creating tree nurseries and building terraces to combat soil erosion on the steep hills, to increase small farming households' income.

We also work in the new agglomerations called *Imidugudu*. Thousands of people have been settled in these villages by the government. Such villages were previously untypical in Rwanda, as most farmers lived in isolated subsistence farms up the hills with their fields around them. This new political strategy must be seen as controversial and sometimes the farmers have been forced to live in these artificial villages. But land is scarce in Rwanda and the development organisations cannot ignore the new agglomerations. We are helping the villagers to build hedges around their homes with natural materials which can be cut and used for compost and animal food. It is important to strengthen these communities because, after the civil war, neighbours have found themselves thrown together randomly, as if by a throw of the dice.

A proverb in the Kinyarwanda language says, *Ahoguha umuntu ifi wamwigisha kwiroba*, which means, 'Don't give me fish but teach me how to fish.' Development efforts have to consider and encourage local know-how, and this is what we are trying to do.

The administration of such a big programme includes staff management, stock and car park control, budgeting, book-keeping, calculation, banking affairs, etc.

How about the private life of a development worker? In Kigali everybody seems to know everyone. You can go to the French-Rwandan Culture House to see old films. You can swim and do sports. You can go out to Chinese, Indian, Italian, German and, of course, Rwandan restaurants. In the capital life is safe now, but we are still not allowed to visit the Dian Fossey's famous gorillas and some other places in the north and west frequented by rebels.

Without music my life here may have been a bit boring. A young Rwandan-Congolese musician showed me how to play the drums. One of the famous Rwandan rhythms I have been learning is called *Kirimba*. During the performance dancers usually spread their arms and fingers up like the big horns of Rwandan cows. We like to mix it up a little and play the Rwandan drums and the Cameroonian balafons together. *Musique sans frontières.*

Two books I recommend are Philip Gourevitch's *We wish to inform you that tomorrow we will be killed with our families*, and André Sibomana's *Hope for Rwanda.*

A Mobile Clinic Day
Clare Fitzgibbon (Uganda)

It is just before 8:00am as we finish loading the Land Rover with supplies for one of our Mobile Clinic days. The skies are overcast and the surrounding hills dark.

A bicycle pulls up in the gateway of the hospice and the rider carefully manoeuvres it to allow his passenger to dismount. Mzee is easily recognisable by his limp and a heavily-bandaged cancerous foot, well elevated by a block of foam fastened in place with a strip of old tyre. He had been staying nearby with his son and is now returning to his village more than 75 km away in the direction we are going. Father and son part with an exchange of money and little more than a perfunctory nod.

By now Hassan is at the wheel and we are off, leaving the town of Mbarara behind us. The road to Ibanda has been recently tarmacked and stretches before us like a blue, grey ribbon, disappearing round bends only to reappear in the far distance against sloping hillsides.

The skies are clear and blue, the distant hills in splendour before us and the Psalm in my heart that comes to me on mornings like this: 'I will lift up mine eyes to the hills, from where cometh my help.'

We slow down at a small trading post where for some months now we have been meeting Feresta. She is one of our patients with cancer who walks 6 km from her home to the roadside. She is not there, but a boy of about sixteen, with a striking resemblance to her, approaches our vehicle. Can we give him her medicine? His mother is too sick to come. Martha, Hassan and I look at our watches. 'Let's go,' we say and make room for Feresta's son who will direct us home.

Feresta's home is of mud and wattle, with a grass roof and wooden-shuttered windows. It is worth the extra distance to see her radiant smile.

Leaving her home, we detour across country to check on a young woman with AIDS who has been on our programme for some months. Jay has a twelve-year-old son by her first husband who went missing in Rwanda, presumed dead. Her second partner died two years ago. On our last visit she had been pain free on our medication, but very weak, mainly as a result of her inability to eat because of the Kaposi's Sarcoma (tumours) in her mouth.

We approach with some apprehension, fearing sad news. A quiet lies over her home and the tall, straggling maize we pass through whispers a low lament. The two bent figures sitting in the compound shelling beans, do not call out in greeting but merely raise their heads and look mournfully towards us. Her mother and her aunt open their arms to Martha and me, and accept our cheek-to-cheek condolences.

Jay died two days ago. The flowers are still fresh on the mound of earth beneath the banana trees, where we are taken to pray a quiet farewell to yet another of our young friends.

Our next visit en route is to Francis, a young father of five children, who has cancer. He is a peasant farmer and has no money for treatment. Our organisation is treating his pain and supporting him and his family by listening, advising and encouraging.

As we park in our usual clearing off the dirt track, Fatima comes to greet us. She is the mother of a small child who died from cancer two months back and a distant neighbour to Francis. She has come to carry our case of medicines on the ten-minute walk, and to give us a sack of maize in return for our care of her child. A typical gesture from those who have no other means of payment for our service.

Francis expects us and is dressed, sitting in the one chair in their small living room where one corner is piled high with shelled and dried, multi-coloured beans. A wide smile breaks across his handsome face. This despite the frustration he must be feeling over his disabling condition, which no longer allows him access to his *shamba*. His wife, with three of their small children in tow, comes to greet us and exchange news.

It's hot now as we make our way back to the Land Rover for the last leg of our journey to the rural hospital.

Bottled water and sweet bananas replenish us, and we set off again. Hassan has put the radio on, playing low African music, allowing us the privacy of our own thoughts. I sigh deeply as I reflect on the richness of health services and resources back in the UK, compared to the poverty of health for most Ugandans. Will we ever begin to bridge the great divide between our worlds?

Back on the tarmac road, we soon reach Ibanda (our destination) where Mzee gets out with his month's supply of medicines, to continue his journey home. We drive to the hospital and park in the grounds in the shade of an acacia tree. Numbers of people sit waiting on wooden benches in the open-sided outpatient department. Several lift their heads and make eye contact with us. A woman quiets a fretting child and comes towards us.

Her child of four months, who has AIDS, was the youngest that day; the eldest told us she was a hundred. After consultations with each of them, carefully assessing, prescribing, dispensing and writing up records, we gather our files and bags and prepare for our return journey. Before departure, one of the staff brings us a very welcome refreshment of a bottle of soda each and freshly cooked *chapattis* (flat bread).

As our Land Rover heads home, I find myself remembering those we had hoped to see who had not reported. The reasons were likely to be: no money for transport, the patient had died or, in some few instances, made a temporary recovery.

There is always a sense of wholeness when members of a family return home at the end of a day. Something very close to that exists with Hospice Team in Mbarara. It is well after 6pm as we arrive back, yet other team members are there to welcome us on our safe return. Nothing is taken for granted. As the Land Rover is unloaded, stories are exchanged, support expressed, and appropriate humour shared until everyone leaves to make their various ways home. The sun will set, darkness will fall, doors and windows will be closed and sleep taken for the start of another day.

Fishing with the Men
Kath Ford (Philippines)

'Would you like to go fishing with us?' my host asked. I was a children's health volunteer on a small fishing island off the Philippine coast of Luzon, between the river and the South China Sea.

'It's a hard life here on the island,' the men kept telling me, 'hard to be a fisherman'. I wondered how hard it could be, when they seemed to have so many excuses not to go. Either there is a wind, or the waves are too high, or there is a typhoon on the way, a full moon . . . it seemed to me that very little fishing was actually done, so of course very little fish for sale or to eat.

When not fishing they sat drinking beer or Ginevra. The fact that they had no money did not affect this activity too much. The whole community lived on a system of *utang* (owe) and *bulod* (borrow) and many local stores went bankrupt because of it. They did not go short of *Palutan* (nibbles) either. The men would kill a goat or a dog or whatever was available, singe, chop and cook it. Although not officially sanctioned, dogs were bred in the rural communities for this purpose, or as birthday meats.

I had been there for about nine months and had been out in a dawn fishing expedition, in the small outriggers, for *pingpingan* (a small flat fish); but I had not had an all-night trip to sea for the larger fish, so I replied immediately to the captain's question, 'Yes please – when?'

We went the following night – the Capitan, his son Dante and his partner Lito. The women exclaiming at the ageing American going fishing with the men. I suddenly had reservations about the wisdom of such a venture. Filipinos in rural communities are for the most part very superstitious and I prayed that nothing disastrous would happen so that I would be blamed for bad luck.

The boat was a larger outrigger owned by the Co-op and powered by diesel. The river was very low and she had to be pushed out into deeper water and carefully manoeuvred to find a navigable channel to the sea. The sun was low in the sky and blazed a pathway across the swelling sea. We went up and down in the troughs of the waves and the Capitan kept asking if I felt faint. I assured him that I was fine.

It was a longer journey than I expected, with the sun an orange ball ready to sink into the sea. There were splashes to the right and left and two dolphins rose and curved back into the sea, racing us. I was very excited, it was a first for me, but very ordinary for the crew, although they were pleased to have provided me with such a spectacle.

They started to light the kerosene lamps – wicks in bottles, looking like an accident waiting to happen. These were attached to a small bamboo raft, which was fastened to the end of the fishing net. The sea rolled and swelled a steely grey in the twilight. We were heading towards an artificial reef when the engine faltered and stopped. Something had caught in the propeller and cracked it. I thought this would be the end of the trip and we would return, but after hanging over the side and feeling the propeller with his feet, the capitan decided to feed out the nets at this point. The tiny bamboo raft headed out to sea trailing the net. Dante and his father fed out the net whilst Lito used the oar to keep headway. Quite a methodical process, it soon trailed behind, with the tiny light getting further and further away.

After about fifteen minutes of this, the Capitan said 'bad,' and proceeded with his son to haul the net back on board. We turned round, travelled for an hour and stopped again, with Capitan grumbling about the propeller. They fed out the nets once again and the lights floated off into the night. It took over an hour and a half to set out the net, which was over a kilometre long. By this time it was eight o'clock, so everyone settled to sleep, after a snack of dried squid, cold rice and water (which I promptly threw up, much to my disgust and their amusement).

One stayed on watch for two hours and then changed over. I grew more and more queasy as I lay wrapped in a thin blanket trying to sleep. The night was pleasantly warm and the stars so bright that I wished I knew more about the constellations. The bamboo slats were comfortable and they had given me a pillow, but all I could think of was the rolling motion of the sea and my empty stomach. It seemed an interminable time of waiting, listening to the snores, the changing of the watch, feeling the sudden lurches of the boat and the slap of water against the side as she veered.

At last at 1am there was a flurry of activity. I was told to sit or lie on top of the boat – a precarious position I didn't relish. The bamboo slats I had lain on were rolled up and positions taken for hauling in the nets. Again one man maintained the position of the boat with the paddle whilst the others worked together. This went on for about one hour with nothing to show for it, eventually a small tuna – about 6 kilos, then a smaller fish, basloogan, about 12 inches long.

More hauling and suddenly a shout of excitement and what seemed to me an enormous fish rolled sideways on towards the boat. It was a swordfish – a prize catch because its price is high in the market place. I attempted to help pull it in, but was told firmly, *tugaw* (sit down) which I did – they knew their business best.

The catch was big, with a body of about two metres and a sword of one metre. He had to be untangled from the net and I was surprised to see them tear at the net, which would have to be repaired or replaced. The crew were jubilant – it was the largest catch they had personally made, and came close to that of the largest catch on the island; that of a 60 kilo tuna by a very skilled old fisherman, who consistently had good catches and whose record for the Co-op was high.

More pulling in, everyone wide awake now, but after discovering a large hole where a large tuna had probably escaped (the one that got away) – nothing more and the small raft drifted closer with the light showing the end of the line. The nets were stowed and we started back. The Capitan cut up the smallest fish into pieces. A piece was thrown over each side and on to the net, with a short prayer. The rest was cut into pieces, washed, sprinkled with salt and chilli vinegar – a delicious local dish called *kilawen*. We nibbled on this, presumably as a thank you to the gods for the catch.

The lights were out now and it was very dark except for a sliver of moon and the brightly winking stars. The engine was started, but because of the propeller, we had to go carefully. The Capitan sat with his feet entwined in the tiller, navigating by the stars as well as the lights on land – in this case the Bacnotan Cement Works.

The journey home was long and to me, frightening. No lights, just darkness and the rolling sea, which seemed to tip the boat alarmingly to one side. The wind increased and so did the wave movement. The lights of the land seemed no nearer. The engine stopped and I heard mutters of 'gasoline' and a search was made for a spare can. We started again (so did my heart). Eventually the sky lightened and the stars paled and the land seemed a little nearer. We arrived back in the river, which was very low, just after 6am.

Lito had gone on ahead and the Capitan and Dante had stayed, to truss the fish and bring it ashore. The word had already got out and we were greeted by wide smiles and dubbed 'lucky'.

It wasn't luck, of course, but hard work on the part of the fishermen. Theirs is a risky, at times uneventful and often unrewarding life. I now understand why they don't take risks, I wouldn't either, if there was the slightest wind or high waves.

And the swordfish? It weighted 55 kilos but only half of it was sold as not many people came to the market that day. The catch isn't everything. It might have been better to catch something smaller and more readily saleable, like squid or tuna or bas-loogan; or to catch the

The swordfish catch

swordfish closer to the weekend.

Set against the catch is the cost is the cost of seven hours travelling in diesel – kerosene, the damage to the propeller, engine and net.

So I now understand . . . . It *is* a hard life in a fishing community.

Meditating
Lou Olliff (Cambodia)

Sit quietly, now, and centre yourself. Sit quietly and focus on the light – ignore the aching chaos outside, the small child squatting in the dirt with sores covering his small dark skin, waiting for me to come out and give him money for watching my bike. Sit quietly and breathe deeply, now.

Cast the line and pull yourself back from the edge. Take each thought slowly and study it. Turn it over. How does it make you feel? Watch the small nun sitting in front of you, breathing so slow and heavy it is at any moment now that

you think she will stop and walk peacefully from this earth, despite all that aching chaos outside. Watch the half-light reflected on the warm linoleum tiles. Feel the tropical wind blow through the open wooden doors and lift the heat delicately from your skin. Drink in the ethereal calm of a place of worship. Seek the eyes of the giant Buddhas who smile like the Mona Lisa, all-knowing and a little smug.

Listen to the subdued chattering of insects in the soaring old ceilings. Sit quietly and repeat in your head: it's time to think, time to think, time

'Sit quietly now'

. . .

The stillness of the monks confounds me. The air moves their orange robes almost imperceptibly and I wonder how they can sit so stoically in this temple, in this city, in this country. How can they be so still when out on the streets of Phnom Penh humanity thrashes around in the sludge of the afternoon's rains, gnawing and crawling for a morsel of food or forgiveness? When in this country – Kampuchea – the guilt and shame of the past lingers just beneath the surface. When the whole country is reeling with the knowledge that their own kind wrote one of the darkest chapters in human history. When even through your half-closed eyes you can see limbs missing, faces swollen, mothers holding oh-so-quiet babies close to dry breasts. I COULD SHRIEK!

Instead I sit quietly and try to centre myself. I want to process my thoughts.

I want to sift through them to see what sense I can make of it all. I want to meditate on what I have seen because I am afraid I will no longer see it if I cannot make it make sense. I wish I could write the word 'injustice' and somehow, by writing it, I could make it just. But there is no sense in this. The only sense is in the calm of the temple and the stillness of the monks.

I walk out at nightfall wrapped in quiet. I draw it closely around me and sit on the steps for a few minutes. I feel like I'm sixteen again, afraid. The small boy is not waiting.

Famine
Eva and Bernard Batchelor (Cameroon)

Greetings from Cameroon, West Africa. Lat. 10W Long. 4N.

Our first round of travels is over. We have bounced and flown some 5,000 miles throughout the Cameroon in eight weeks. We have stayed in five locations and have not completely unpacked since we left the UK and we don't think we ever will.

Global warming has reached the far north, where it was unseasonably hot and the prospect of crop failure and famine looms. We visited a number of rural villages and were welcomed back to our established project villages. We were invited to the Paramount Chief's palace for lunch but were not sure what to expect. In the event we had a beautiful lunch cooked in the traditional way over an open fire outside. Pudding consisted of fresh milk and, although we immediately freaked out at the thought of liquid TB, it had been boiled. It was thick and creamy and tasted nothing like the white stuff that passes for milk in England. The chief then insisted that we drank tea. It was another of those events when the chief is laying back on his couch and we sat in the chairs of honour around the walls while one of his sons served us all, not a wife in sight even though we know he has many.

We visited the western zone of the Far North which overlooks Nigeria. This area is one of the tourist attractions, as it is a site of prehistoric volcanic activity with deep craters surrounded by columns of the remaining volcano cores. Over thousands of years the soft rock has eroded away leaving these stalagmite monsters scattered all over the landscape. It is the most beautiful and awe-inspiring sight. We plan to run one of our projects in a delightfully remote village in the heart of this area. While we were in this area we saw at very close quarters a troop of chimpanzees passing across the road.

It was a privilege for us to be invited into one of the compounds for lunch. The straw and mud huts are so well designed, cool and very comfortable. Once again, we were filled with fear and trepidation about what we were going to be given to eat since food is very scarce and is mostly variations on millet or maize, but we managed and live to tell the tale. It is very humbling to be fed by people who do not have enough to eat themselves and who are so poor.

One day we parked in the shade of a tree while our colleagues went off to inspect a bore hole. Having seen many bore holes, we decided to stay out of the sun in the shade. Sharing the shade of this tree was a young girl no more than eighteen, who was nursing a very young baby. As we watched we noticed how thin and very sick the baby was. The girl was sitting alone looking very sad as if she was waiting for the baby to die. To sit alongside such human tragedy and not be able to help or even communicate is a very disturbing experience.

So while we are enjoying some exciting experiences, we are constantly confronted with the abject tragedies of the developing world. It is these experiences that drive us forward to do the best we can with the limited resources that we have.

So Little Can Mean So Much
Christopher Osborn (Thailand)

Yesterday Sompop, the director, told me of a brothel raid that had occurred in Bangkok. The place was shut down and the girls were escorted to a safe island in a river near Bangkok where they are being held while their case is being considered. He opened his briefcase and twenty-nine forms with a picture attached to the top of each spilled out across his desk.

'They are frightened of the agents that sold them to the brothel owners, they are afraid their families will be killed, and they refuse to tell anyone where they are really from, because they have been told if they say they are not from Thailand, they will be put in prison and their families will be charged by the brothel owners for the debts they have racked up.'

After being smuggled into Thailand and sold into a brothel most girls are told they now owe the agents and brothel owners 50,000 baht or more in 'processing and transportation' fees. This is the equivalent of telling a fourteen-year old girl in the US that in order to see her parents again she has to come up with $500,000 – she can earn $1,000 per month if she has sex with people, and if she refuses, her parents will be killed. Frequently brothel owners will charge them for food, clothing and 'incidental charges' such as electricity so that their debt gets larger the longer they work.

A group in Bangkok asked if we could find a place to keep them safe. Sompop said to me, 'Where do you think we can put them?' If we can't think of anywhere, they will be driven up in a government truck and dumped on the bridge to Myanmar, where brothel agents will wait, pick them up and send them back to work in Malaysia, or further away.

Despite the guns, the threats, the violence and agents, there is no sense of foreboding. There is no fear in the air – like when you walk down the wrong street in NYC and realise you are now a target – there is none of that. It is a bright, sunny (and hot) day. Rain seems likely later today, last night I went to a rock concert with some friends . . . . I wish I had some cheese to eat for lunch; kids laugh and play, chase one another, play marbles. And yet, Sompop asked me yesterday, 'When you see these children, here, safe and doing exactly what they should be doing, making noise, laughing, trying to get away with not doing their homework; do you wonder where they will be in ten years?

What hope do they have? There is absolutely no money in their families, and they are not recognised as citizens of Thailand, so are not allowed by law to work or go to college. What hope is in their future? Where will they go after they leave here?'

This school has changed this region. Ten years ago, the threats, the violence, the rape and sales of girls to brothels went on just as it does today. But ten years ago there was no safe place anywhere for girls and families to run when they decided they wanted to end the terror. Ten years ago there were no kids playing marbles, or trying to avoid homework. Ten years ago this region was stricken with poverty and completely owned by the agents and Mafia who trolled villages to find girls they could buy, kidnap or coerce. Ten years have made a profound impact. For the first time, there is a glimmer of hope.

I don't have any answers for how to make this place better. I translate documents. I take photos. I laugh and teach children, work on the website. I feel agony for the villages two mountains away that are beyond our help. Perhaps that is enough. What is needed here is so stunningly small, so inconsequential, in the face of such terrifying problems and huge criminal organisations, it seems ludicrous. A shirt and a pair of pants. $10 worth of plastic pipes for a village of 200 people. A bunch of rowdy college boys to dig a drainage ditch for a few weeks. Paper, pens . . . I never realised what an astonishing difference the little tiny infrastructure bits that make up life in the US make – shoelaces, rulers, rubber bands, file folders, a screwdriver . . . .

So, for the next twenty-four hours, try to keep track of how many things you use that cost you less than $5 each. You'll be astonished at how many of these things we use without even considering their source. Imagine a world where you cannot for any price have access to *any* of them and where they make a world of difference to someone's life.

Evalina's Story
Colin Murphy (Angola)

Evalina is smiling. Nerves, or simple excitement – I don't know. She runs to fetch three chairs, carrying one herself, slung over her back, to where Beatriz is waiting in the shade. We sit under a tree at the edge of the *praza* – the small, local market selling coal, firewood, tomatoes and old shoes. I talk to Evalina in Portuguese, and Beatriz repeats, in Umbundu, what I've just said. Evalina hardly talks at all.

Evalina is seventeen. She doesn't have a husband, doesn't want one, or children. She grew up in Kunhinga, 40 km from here. She came to Kuito in '97, after her landmine accident, when she was three months in hospital. She fiddles furiously with a small twig as Beatriz asks her about her parents. When she raises her face slightly from her work, I see a tear hanging on the edge of her left eyelid. I don't know how long it's been hanging there, which question it was that brought it. Or maybe it's simply a tear of nerves, for the occasion. It's her first time talking with a *branco*, a *shindayle*, a white person.

Her mother died of *doença*, an illness – any illness – in 1996; her father was shot by UNITA, the *enemigo*, the Angolan rebels, in 1997. She has an older sister, but the sister treated Evalina so badly after she got out of hospital that she left home, and came to live in the kitchen of a friend of her mother's.

There is the noise of a plane circling overhead, a light breeze, people walking by, kids watching.

Evalina's livelihood is corn. She buys it at three kwanzas – twenty cents – a kilo, brings it to the mill, and sells the corn flour at four kwanzas a kilo. She sells maybe twenty kilos a day, so she earns just over a dollar a day.

A man comes up, on crutches, with one trouser leg flapping emptily. Another comes afterwards, an odd shoe betraying his prosthetic foot. He wears a flip-flop on his good foot, and a runner on the plastic one. The amputees I work with often wear footwear like this – the good shoe stays on the prosthetic foot, and hides it. The good foot goes barefoot, or sandalled. At night, they simply take off their leg, and so the shoe stays on it.

The men ask me, apologetically, if I will write their names down. I am sitting talking to a girl with one leg: I must have a reason; they want to be included. We can't include them; I have nothing to offer them; I won't write down their names because the project is specifically aimed towards women. They leave.

I ask Evalina what she owns. She has a pot, a plate, a cup and a threadbare blanket. She also has a pair of crutches and a prosthetic leg, which she is not wearing at the moment. It hurts, sometimes, the prosthesis.

She is wearing a light flowery skirt and a pink t-shirt. She owns another skirt and blouse. She has a bamboo mat to sleep on.

'Do you go to school?'

'Yes.'

'Don't you have a copybook?'

'No.'

I ask her what she most needs. She says, 'The first thing is a blanket and a basin.' She has to borrow a basin from her mother's friend – the same one to wash in, and then to bring her corn to the market.

Two women approach us, on crutches; their question is the same as the men – can they be included? We take their details, and they move on.

I ask Evalina about Christmas. She is Catholic, but doesn't go to church. She mentions an uncle in Kunhinga, 30 km away, who doesn't visit her, so she won't visit him. She won't do anything for Christmas, because she won't have any money. She owes fifty kwanzas to the nurse at the health post for medication she had to buy last week, when she was sick with malaria.

Beatriz asks her what other business she knows that would make greater profits than the corn.

Oil and sugar, she says. This means buying oil and sugar wholesale, and selling them on. The oil comes in tins, donated by World Food Programme; she will buy it, and then sell it in plastic wrap-fulls, enough for one meal in each wrap.

If she could make some more money, she would move out on her own, out of the her late mother's friend's kitchen. I have seen this kitchen. It is a small hut annex to a small adobe house, in which the owner cooks over an open fire. There is an open doorway, no windows and no chimney. Beatriz asks her would she not be afraid, would she not want a friend or a partner to live with? No, she says, she's used to being on her own.

Having the Nerve
Naim Ali (India)

I always thought real courage meant the willingness to pay the ultimate price. The line from *Point Break,* 'It isn't tragic dying doing what you love' (cheesy, but semi-true), seemed to be fun words to live by. How exhilarating to live at the summit of one's nerve and wit, when the margin for error is small and the ultimate consequence so great. Walking the edge of oblivion . . . the narrower the ledge, the more successful the navigation of it. But this past month, as I began my study of the *adivasi* (tribal) women of eastern Gujarat, I have been witnessing something different.

Maybe real courage *is* doing and being something totally different from what society expects and *living* with it. Maybe real courage is risking something that might force you to rethink your thoughts and suffer change, humiliation, doubt and failure and suffer the short term for a better long term. But I can also see real courage in the eyes of these tribal women.

The work itself is tedious – the need for interpreters, for example, slows things down considerably and I stumble along in this new experience. But it is all part of a learning process. My work for an NGO takes me out of the safe haven of the SADGURU offices and into my town of Dahod, aiming to interview the women that come into SAHAJ handicrafts to work. They enter barefoot, their faded saris are often full of holes and frayed, yet it is easy to imagine how colourful the cloth once was. Silver bangles on their ankles and wrists jingle when they walk or fold their hands. A large piece of nose jewellery in the design of a flower blinds me when the sun glints off of it. They are so shy in front of this Westerner, that they can only look down or away. I have to strain just to hear them say their name. The ants on the floor hear it before I do.

But their precarious lives are so incredible, so finely balanced, like the brown clay waterpot on their head. Children, food, water, farming, handicrafts, and life – their days start before the sun gets up and end long after it has gone to bed. They are indentured to a harsh life they did not choose. I feel so guilty stealing their time for my petty needs. Even the act of coming into the city and participating in this handicraft scheme is wrought with difficulty. Many cannot read or write and the thought of leaving their villages to learn something new must be nerve-racking, not to mention the harassment they get from their peers. But the drought forces them to search for new avenues to generate income for their families. And so in small groups they come, so scared, yet so brave. And it is in them I have redefined real courage, and maybe even found it . . . .

* * *

India smells like *chappals* (open-toed sandals) and cow manure. Mix in a little bit of *chai* (tea), some rotting fruit, wisps of a *beadie* (an Indian cigarette) and the stench of life always fighting for life . . . there, you have it. It does sometimes make me nauseous. Other times, it is close to being a carnival.

I used to walk home through a concrete jungle (downtown Calgary), now I dodge people and cows and goats, and scooters and auto-rickshaws, and horse buggies and buses and people spitting out of those buses and water buffalo . . . people pushing things far too large for far too little money and dirt-covered children and clouds of flies and raw cesspools of sewage, wild pigs . . . and garbage everywhere. As I walk through India's breath, I know it will stain my olfactory senses for the rest of my life, long after I come home and the dry-cleaning gets done.

A Tear-Soaked Day
Derek Thorne (Tanzania)

Wailing. I can hear wailing.

It was already light and warm. My sleepy eyes stared at the dusty stone floor of the room, and the interesting patterns of light created by my mosquito net. I liked sleeping with a net, even though there was hardly any call for it at the moment. No buzzing around my head at night. But the net was my personal cocoon, it made me feel cosy and safe, and if it were true that we had rats running around (it turned out to be true) then it would probably keep them away from me too. Unless they were very determined.

From somewhere, I can hear wailing.

I shared the room with Joshua, a twenty-two-year old Tanzanian. Curiously, we both went through a very similar procedure as we got up in the morning. We'd remove our nets from our mattresses, climb out from under them, and then just sit, staring into space. We'd do that for about five minutes, perhaps. I wondered what he thought about. Maybe he was like me, and thought about nothing. I needed the world to flood into my brain gradually before I could consider myself fully awake.

Faint, distant wailing.

. We didn't actually have beds, just thin foam mattresses. The village were meant to supply us with beds, plus more furniture, but somehow this was overlooked. I didn't mind. My back hurt for the first few nights, but I got used to it after that. And anyway, we were given the best house in the village to live in, by some distance.

Our house was sat by the road in the centre of the village. It was large, built from bricks and had an iron roof – all the mod cons, basically. The village tended to use it as their storage house, and so the front room was usually home to engines, buckets, water tanks, sacks of grain and more. There were two tractor tyres, which made good seats. One of our younger friends was able to squeeze inside the tyres, and one idea of ours was to roll him down the road, all the way out of the valley and into town. It might help him get to school, we thought. He laughed, but he didn't like the idea.

Almost subliminal wailing.

Right now, I'd like to be able to say that I reacted to those wailing sounds in a positive and inquiring manner. But I hardly even noticed them. I had been living in the rural Tanzanian village of Kilala Kidewa for around two weeks, and to me, practically everything I heard was strange and unexpected. Bizarre people, surreal activities . . . at least for me.

So I ignored the wailing.

The rest of our house was up as well. Catherine, the other Briton in our group of four, was often up first – she never seemed to sleep too well. I remember when I first met her, she told me that she didn't really sleep, period. She'd been working a lot of night shifts at a petrol station before travelling out to Tanzania, and this helped her to develop this ability to keep (somewhat) awake twenty-four hours a day.

And the other girl was Grace, Tanzanian, about twenty-one. Grace was quiet and friendly and, I would say, very beautiful too. During our first month in the village, we heard that she had become one of about forty finalists in the 'Face of Africa' competition, but I didn't hear much more than that, so I don't think she won.

It was a bright, warm, and therefore utterly normal morning. Being near the equator, the sun came up and went down with incessant regularity all year round. The village started moving around dawn (6:30am or so) but we generally stayed in bed until 8:00. Undoubtedly, we were very lazy – I've often thought that never again in my life will I average as much sleep as I did during my months in the village of Kilala Kidewa. Eleven hours a night. Surely babies don't sleep that much. Either Catherine regained the ability to sleep, or she was very bored. But the strangest thing was that I found it just as hard to get up in the morning as I normally do, and that through the day I would sometimes feel tired and worn out, even if I hadn't been doing much. It must have been the heat, although being at high altitude (maybe 2,000 metres), I suppose the heat wasn't so bad, maybe averaging 30°C throughout the day.

The morning, normal as it was, passed wholly uneventfully, until it became completely abnormal when Grace explained to me exactly what that wailing was.

* * *

I can hear wailing. There's nothing subtle about it now – it is extremely loud, disturbing, and close, being as it is in the very next room to me.

I am at a funeral.

The funeral was about three houses down the road from us. I'd walked with Joshua out of our front door, and before I knew it we were in another house, being led through the empty front room, with its bare stone floor and dried mud walls, to a small courtyard at the back. There were maybe half a dozen men sat outside there – only men. The women, I gathered, were in the next room, their number being possibly twenty. It was the women who were wailing.

How on earth can I describe it? Perhaps try to imagine twenty people being tortured, in some undisclosed fashion, and the sounds they produce as a result are so horribly ugly in themselves that they serve to torture that collective even more. We found ourselves in a vicious circle, a loop of positive feedback, as the wailing, screams, bawls and so on become ever more intense until they reach an upper limit, because those who were wailing literally can't wail any louder.

It was, in fact, completely ridiculous. For just one moment, I stared up at the sky and tried to remove myself from the situation, to listen to those sounds as they really were. Problematically, I found myself close to laughing. But I am at a funeral, I reminded myself. I cannot laugh. I get away with an incredible amount here, being a white visitor, but I think that might be pushing it.

So I tried to shut it all out as Joshua led me around the men. We said *pole* to each of them (the Swahili word for a sympathetic sorry) perhaps elaborating it with a *sana* (very). I had read in my Swahili book the day before that one can also say *rambirambi zako*, which means something like 'condolences with you', but Josh told me saying that would only make me sound cocky. As we said *pole*, we shook each man by the hand. Perhaps only one of them actually looked genuinely sad to me – the others looked either emotionless (numb, perhaps) or even cheerful.

After we had been around everyone, Joshua and I sat on a bench. Joshua started talking to someone in Swahili and I couldn't really follow the conversation, so I switched off for a moment.

And the wailing was back. It was truly unreal. I wasn't sure how long I could last, listening to that sound. In fact, I wasn't really sure what effect it was having on me. It was deafening – not in absolute terms, not like a pneumatic drill or the roar of a crowd, but it was extremely difficult to listen to anything else at the same time, to follow any other conversations.

How big was that room? I didn't know, and I didn't want to have a look – I was scared. The individuals in there seemed to be making their best efforts to avoid being even remotely in tune with anyone else. Some women would sing a rising note, some would sing a falling note, some would be screaming in anger, some would stubbornly pick two or three notes and hum them repetitively. It became even more surreal when, once in a while, a lady would emerge from the room, bawling her eyes out. Her face was more tear-soaked than anything I had seen, and she was doing some kind of dance and wandering aimlessly around the house before returning to the room again. I found it hard to take my eyes off her, but I noticed the other men there paid her very little attention.

Probably about twenty-five minutes after Josh and I came in, Grace and Catherine arrived. Since men and women evidently mourned separately, we had decided not to turn up together. Significantly, Catherine entered with nothing on her head. It was her original intention to cover her head in some way, preferably using a *kanga* (a large piece of traditional cloth), but Grace must have decided it wasn't worth the bother.

We didn't exchange any words, but I gave Catherine a raised eyebrow as she followed Grace into the room – that room. I remember thinking: that's going to be very hard.

Another twenty minutes passed (I hadn't done much – just looked around at the the red earthy ground and the bright blue sky) and Grace and Catherine had left again. Catherine had walked boldly out, possibly muttering 'that's enough of that' or something similar. Grace looked more uneasy about leaving.

Time passed slowly after that.

Joshua was being the social animal. He was brilliant – everyone loved to talk to him. As he was from 'the big city' (Dar es Salaam) he was new to the rural Tanzanian village. People asked him about where he lived, his family, and more, no doubt. But it was all in Swahili, and I couldn't really follow it.

It was getting towards noon when a man came around holding an exercise book containing a list of names and numbers. He was making a collection for the bereaved family. The prospect of giving money made me slightly uneasy, as I didn't know how much they would expect from me. I whispered to Josh, 'How much should I give?'

'One hundred is fine,' he said. One hundred Tanzanian shillings is about 10 pence. I fished the money out of my wallet. The man collecting it didn't appear to think of me any differently, and simply took my money and moved on.

It started raining, so we moved the bench inside. We were there for another hour, or maybe more. There was more talking. I was getting quite bored and very hungry. I had no idea how long we'd be staying – when we arrived, I thought it might be only half an hour. Now it had been three.

When Josh and I were momentarily left alone, I asked him how much longer we'd have to stay. 'Oh, until the end,' he replied. The answer seemed obvious to him, but I felt very downhearted. How much longer with that sickly wailing in the background, these conversations I can't follow, this empty stomach?

Not long after that, though, the body was carried out of its room. It was wrapped in white cloth from head to toe. I had learned that the body was of a young lady, in her twenties, who was originally a native of the village. She had recently been living in Ilula, the main town situated about fourteen miles away, where the bumpy sand road met the smooth tarmac. She had become ill and moved here to recover, which she never did. I had also learned that the funeral was an Islamic one, and so the division between males and females would remain strict throughout the burial.

The rain had almost stopped as we walked out alongside the body. There were many people out on the road – maybe one hundred and fifty. The women were at the back of the procession, the men at the front. Everyone started walking in the direction of our house, and beyond, and then off the road to the left. People split into different groups and followed different footpaths as we skirted around the clumps of houses on that side of the road, and emerged on the other side in a large field. I stayed as close to Joshua as I could.

We arrived at the grave, and I found myself in the large group of men, stood around the grave but away from the women. The pit was maybe three metres deep, and three men were stood in it to receive the body. Shortly after we arrived, Josh and I were dragged forward by someone we didn't recognise, who proceeded to point at the grave and explain it, like some kind of tourist guide. I couldn't decipher much of his Swahili, but I knew he was saying, 'can you see?' over and over again, and I just tried nodding a lot and saying, 'yes, yes'. He was actually trying to explain how the body is buried in a Muslim funeral – it is not placed at the bottom of the grave, but in a cavity that has been dug out of one side of the pit, like the beginnings of a horizontal tunnel. The body is placed in that cavity. It means that no earth is placed on top of the body, just to its side.

Next, people started filling the grave in. Some of the wailers were now very animated indeed, shouting what seemed like abuse down the grave. What were they angry at? I wondered. Were they berating the body, as if it was a broken-down car and they were the thin-tempered owner? Were they angry with God?

At this point someone I didn't recognise came up to me out of the crowd and started speaking, once again in Swahili. I couldn't make it out, but it was something to do with a camera, as he was gesturing the use of a camera to me. I must have looked quite confused, and I wondered where Joshua had got to – I needed help. Another man started talking to me as well, gesturing something about cameras. Joshua explained that they were trying to tell me that it was okay for me to take pictures of this if I wanted to – they didn't mind. What? Take pictures? There's no way in hell I'd want to do that, I thought. But perhaps they are common in many African funerals.

The pit was nearly full. I observed that only the men were moving the earth in, using *jembes* (hoes). However, most of the men there were getting involved, each man only moving earth in for thirty seconds or so. Some men were clearly more committed, and held onto their tool for a while. I thought they might be the family members of the deceased.

Then Josh went forward and took a jembe from someone. They handed it over gratefully, and he committed himself for half a minute, before another man came along. He retreated back towards me in the crowd.

'Do you think I should help out as well?' I asked him as he returned.

He paused. 'I don't know,' he replied.

But I was anxious to do the right thing, whatever that might be. 'I'm quite happy to do it if you think it's a good idea.'

He paused again. 'Uh . . . yes. Okay.'

And so, for the first and only time in my life so far, I had to assist in the burial of a fellow human being. I stepped forward from the crowd and went up to the nearest man with a jembe. I nudged him and tried out a phrase, *nikusaidie*? (May I help you?)

He looked at me but I did not look back. He handed me the jembe and I started digging. At that moment, I suddenly got a very clear sensation that I was being watched, intently, by everyone. In truth, my attempts at moving the earth were quite pitiful – my arms could hardly pick up any of the earth, and there wasn't much left to move anyway, such that to the onlooker I merely looked like I was gently and uselessly stroking the ground with the jembe.

I could hear a few titters of laughter. I tried my hardest to keep my head down and to carry on digging/ stroking/whatever. I wondered if they were aware that this experience was truly alien to me. It was certainly one of the longer ten-second spells of my life. A man put me out of my misery by tapping me on the shoulder and relieving me of the tool. I retreated into the crowd.

Joshua came close and murmured in my ear, 'Well done.' I had never felt so thoroughly out of place in my life.

I thought the digging would end when the pit was full, but in fact the men continued until all spare earth had been piled on top of the grave in a big mound. When this was done, they laboriously shaped the mound so it was perfectly smooth and elliptical in shape. They took great care over it. Then, when they had finally finished, the women closest to the grave (the most emotional ones), rushed forward. They flocked around the pile of earth and patted it intensely with their hands, packing the earth down and further smoothing it off. As they did this, some of the men continued to pour small amounts of earth onto the mound, which only aided in getting the women dirtier as they beat away with their hands. When the women were finally done, the mound was left alone, bearing only a large number of eerie handprints all over it.

The women went straight to a number of buckets of water and washed their hands in them. I had earlier been wondering what those buckets were for. Now I knew. Every detail taken care of.

Presently, the gathering quieted down. And then, finally, it was all over.

We walked back through the field and the houses. Big heavy clumps of earth clung to my leather boots. Joshua was a few paces ahead, engaged in conversation with the village chairman. A chairman is often a mere figurehead, but I got the impression ours was rather more involved in running the village. He seemed stern and formidable to me, and whenever we spoke I thought I could detect a faint trace of suspicion or cynicism in his voice. Perhaps he thought my presence here was superficial, that I had little knowledge of any relevance to the village itself. Or maybe I'm assuming too much about a man I never really knew.

Later on, the four of us were back in our house, cooking the evening meal – an operation that usually took at least two hours. It was a nice evening, dark at 7pm as usual but still warm and with no more rain. As I sat on one of the random sacks of grain in our main room I asked Joshua what the chairman had been telling him earlier on.

'Ah! Yes, I meant to tell you. Tomorrow, some people will go back to the grave and will search for ant holes.'

'Oh? What, like big ones?'

'No, just any ant holes, or ants hanging around the grave. If there are any, then they will know the death was caused by a witch.'

'A what?'

'Well, they will know that the death was not because of the will of God, and they will know there is a witch somewhere here. So, if there are ant holes, they will get a witch doctor to track down the witch.'

'How do they do that?'

'I'm not sure. I know one way – the witch doctor gets the family together, and they all sit around a basin of water. The doctor says something, and a face appears in the water. That's the witch. The witch doctor then asks the family if they want the witch killed. If they say yes, he gets a knife, and –' here, he gestured a cutting motion with his hands – 'he cuts the face. And the witch is dead.'

Catherine was also listening to this. 'But wouldn't the witch doctor just see his own face in the basin?' she contested. 'He's not going to kill himself, is he?' We all laughed.

I continued my questioning. 'So how likely is it that they'll find these holes, then?'

'Uh . . . I don't know. Not likely, I think,' Joshua replied.

Later, I went to bed. There was no wailing now, but it probably hadn't stopped. I was informed that the women continued mourning for at least forty days, and would not sleep on any kind of bedding for that time. They would huddle together on a thin carpet, or just lie on the bare stone floor. They would cover their hair, and would dress all in black. And once in a while, they might pay a visit to the grave and sit around it, crying, as the mound slowly sank back into the earth under its own weight, all the while being eroded by the wind.

Uttam's Fall
Clare Jephcott (Nepal)

One Saturday I left the teachers to do what they usually did on their day off – snooze in their beds, having washed their clothes and themselves in the ice-cold water at the local tap – and set off to explore the Buddhist temples up the hill.

Children had spotted me and started yelling 'American! American! American!' Two scruffy dogs barred the entrance but bravely I walked up the steep stone steps and patted one on the head. Judging by their temperament they were definitely Buddhist. Inside, peeling frescoes adorned the walls, drums hung from the ceiling; conchos lay at the ready. On the pillar hung many framed photos of people, some of whom looked young and healthy. The key-holder told me they had all died but looking at her I dared not ask how.

Late that evening Uttam (17), his friend from Choser near the Tibetan border and Elina (16) were up on the roof peeling leaves of the maize they had harvested that day. I was squatting over the toilet before climbing into bed when I heard Bina's twin sister Rina call Uttam to come down. Suddenly there was a resounding thud and his singing stopped. The frantic wailing of the three sisters broke the silence. In the courtyard I found them gathered round an unconscious Uttam, each desperately clinging onto and rubbing a limb.

In a state of shock I soon learned there wasn't a doctor, nurse or even health worker in the village or the next village or the village after that, though I recalled neat flowers outside the health post next door – there just to offer a false sense of

Clare with Uttam's sisters

security to the passing trekkers. I wished my first aid knowledge wasn't so scanty. The boy came round. What if he couldn't walk? He was the only potential breadwinner left in the family. The nearest hospital was a four-hour walk away. Their mother had died at age fifty-two after having had seven children, the father had died of appendicitis. The sisters instinctively helped him to move inside where they had made a bed on the floor. There was no point leaving him where he was until help arrived. Thankfully, he could move his limbs and only his shoulder seemed hurt.

Next morning, I found the living room crowded with anxious villagers. Luckily, Uttam had been calmed and was able to walk. The local traditional doctor rubbed a grey paste onto the affected area. Uttam got up and set off to walk slowly the ten miles or so to Jomson. But on arrival four hours later, he found there was nobody there skilled to work the X-ray machine. Luckily, Uttam's family had some savings and managed to scrape together the huge sum of 900 rupees to fly him to Kathmandu for treatment.

Some time later, he returned from Kathmandu wearing a sling with, luckily, nothing worse than a broken collarbone.

IT'S A STRUGGLE TRYING TO FIT IN

Wiki Ya Sita – Week Six
Stuart Marriott (Tanzania)

On the road – or rail – at last. There are four of us going to Kasulu – ourselves, Jim, a young agricultural advisor, and Geoff, who is expected to set up IT courses in a Folk Development College, whatever that is. As there are no scheduled flights to the region at the moment and as the roads peter out halfway across the country, the train is the only option. So, on Sunday afternoon the four of us piled all our goods for our two-year stay up country onto the bi-weekly train to Kigoma, which is right at the other end of the line and sits on the eastern shore of Lake Tanganyika. From Kigoma, it is another 90 km by road to our placement in Kasulu. Our agency had written a letter to our employers to meet us at Kigoma railway station and take us up to Kasulu by car.

All very efficient. The train journey is approximately 1,000 km and is scheduled to take 36 hours. We were booked in first class, which means two people (same sex only unless you are married) sharing a sleeping compartment. It's simple but perfectly satisfactory – two bunks, a fan and a little sink with running water.

There is always something about setting off on a long train journey – a wonderful sense of occasion, especially here. The platform is crowded with families saying their farewells and hawkers flogging stuff you might want on the journey – water and snacks – and all manner of things you wouldn't dream of buying. How many people are likely to buy a copy watch or plastic calculator as the train is pulling out? And pull out it did, right on time.

It seems that if you are a young dude, it's not done to jump on the train until it's got up a fair head of steam and is moving at jogging pace – years of practice boarding Dar (es Salaam) buses, I suppose. We made our stately progress through the suburbs and shanty towns of Dar and into the African night.

Central Tanzania is a vast plateau. The landscape varies somewhat between scrubby bush, desert, marshland and quite lush tropical countryside. What impresses most though is the vast emptiness of it all. There are only two towns of any size along the whole route. We stopped at lots of villages – after all, the train is their only lifeline – and quickly realised that the urban population which we experienced in Dar is mirrored in village after village. At every stop people clamour desperately to sell you things – food, water, pots, utensils and mats. The little kids run along shouting 'naomba chupa, naomba kopo', begging for your empty bottles and cans, which will no doubt be converted into something useful or saleable.

We trundled on and on and early on Monday afternoon stopped at a village called, I think, Itwa. And there we remained for six hours. At first I thought the engine had broken down but I learned later that this station is the passing point for the train heading for Dar from Kigoma. So it means that for one of the trains to reach its destination on time it's necessary for its opposite number to be equally efficient. But the delay doesn't bother anyone. No-one frets; no-one looks at their watch. It's just part of life and a chance to have a chat with the folk sitting around the station and a few handshakes with the passengers on the other train when it eventually arrived.

This delay meant that we first sighted Lake Tanganyika 43 hours after leaving Dar. Geoff was met by Irena, his contact, but there was no sign of anyone from Kasulu Development Programme to meet the rest of us.

So here we were, 1,000 km from Dar, 90 km from our placement like a trio of refugees with all our worldly goods piled up and no idea what we were supposed to do. Luckily Irena has been in Tanzania for a few years and wasn't entirely surprised that travel arrangements hadn't gone according to plan. She managed to telephone our project co-ordinator in Kasulu, who told her that they weren't expecting Jim until the following day (strange, as there is no train on that day) and Barbara and myself until the following week.

Irena, well used to dealing with such problems, bungled us and all our kit into the back of a UNDP Land Cruiser and took us back to her house for a much needed shower and then on to the Lake Tanganyika Beach Hotel for a bite to eat.

The plan was that Geoff and his luggage would be taken up to Kasulu but the rest of us would have to suffer a night in the hotel. A car would be sent down from Kasulu for us early the following morning. This gave us time for a late afternoon stroll around the town. Kigoma is a pleasant little place with a tree-lined main street running down to the lake and a few lanes branching off, including Stanley Avenue, named after THE Stanley, I presume. Stanley and Livingstone had their famous rendezvous at Ujiji just up the road so these names feature large in the local psyche.

Virtually every other vehicle in Kigoma is either a Land Cruiser or pick-up truck emblazoned with the name of an aid agency – UNHCR, UNDP, UNICEF, Caritas, Care. This place is very much 'Aidsville', which is not surprising as it is the control centre for the refugees fleeing the civil war in Congo across the lake. We hurried back to the hotel to see a different sunset from the one over the boring old Indian Ocean, which we had witnessed in Zanzibar last week. This time – cold beer in hand as usual – we watched it set dramatically over the lake and the mountains of Congo. So tranquil, so peaceful, so difficult to imagine the terrible civil strife being waged there.

The following morning we parked ourselves lakeside with our Swahili grammars to await the promised car. Late into the morning we received a message that the car hadn't set off from Kasulu until 11am so wasn't expected until three. At 5:30 we got another message from reception that the car had been sighted in town but nobody knew where it was now. Strange. By 6:30 there was still no sign and it was anyway far too late to risk the Kasulu road at night, so we abandoned our plans.

In the middle of the night there was a message at reception that a car would pick us up at nine the following morning. I was a bit sceptical about this and I was rather surprised when the familiar UNDP vehicle turned up at 9am to take us to Kasulu. The 90 km road lived up to its reputation – no tarmac, just dust, rocks, deep potholes and the surface bashed to pieces by the regular trucks taking refugees and supplies to the refugee camps in the area which house refugees from both the Congo and Burundi. First impressions of Kasulu were rather as expected – a long, dusty main street bordered by shack-like shops, reminiscent of a Wild West set. It wouldn't be surprising if tumble-weed were to blow across the street.

We were just a bit pleased when the car took us through the town and up a pleasantly green hill at the other side, the comparatively posh side of town, and delivered us to the house of Jean Mutamba, the Project Co-ordinator and our neighbour to be. He was rather taken aback to see us as he had sent a car down to Kigoma that morning to pick us up. This was the car referred to in the message we received at the hotel. It seems that the UNDP driver had delivered us to Kasulu out of pity for our plight, or, more likely, to boost his expense account. But we had arrived – four days after setting out.

We were shown our house. Because our arrival was unexpected, someone was still living there. It is rather beautiful, set on a hillside above the town. It is one of a semi-detached pair with two bedrooms, a study, a lounge and, at the back, an enclosed courtyard with kitchen and bathroom. To the front of the house a veranda overlooks a really beautiful garden full of flowering and fruit trees – frangipani, hibiscus, bougain-villaea, eucalyptus, banana, passion fruit, pomegranate, and papaya among others. Through the trees we can glimpse the town below and the hills of the Western Great Rift Valley beyond.

The most wonderful surprise is that, as well as having running water for about half the

Barbara at the door of the
District Education Advisor's Office

day, we have electricity generated by the nearby UN generator from seven in the evening until one in the afternoon. This is supplemented by a solar energy system, which caters for back-up lighting and small appliances.

We are temporarily (I hope) sharing our house with a Kenyan lady called Wanja. She works for the UN World Food Programme and has responsibility for ensuring a regular supply of food to the refugee camps, many of which are close to Kasulu. Our next-door neighbour is a Croatian woman called Jasna who works for UNICEF and is responsible for 'tracing', which means locating lost refugee children and reuniting them with their parents. As the success rate is very low, this must be harrowing work. Both ladies have been extremely helpful in all sorts of ways.

We have been encouraged to keep on the household staff, which isn't nearly as colonial as it sounds. It's standard procedure for a foreigner to have a day watchman/gardener and two night watchmen who work shifts. We share these with our neighbour in the compound and VSO, properly security-conscious, pays for them. We were easily persuaded to take over the 'housegirl' already working in the house. It's rather nice not to have to cook, wash up, clean, do the ironing and shopping, but very odd to me when she shows respect by dropping a curtsey every time she passes me. This afternoon, when she put the dinner on the table, she fell onto her knees and said, 'karibuni chakula, bwana', 'welcome to your meal, sir'. I didn't know how to respond.

Then there are the dogs, Tanga and Nyika (they were born by the lake), which we have inherited from our predecessors in the house. Neither of us are doggy people and we are a bit uncertain about looking after these big bouncy mongrels but we'll give it a trial period. There are some advantages – they are good for security, of course, and their presence forces us to take morning and evening walks. We have already discovered some lovely paths up and down the local hills.

Friday morning we went to the office for the first time. Our employment status is a bit complicated. Although we are VSO volunteers, VSO acts in a sense as a kind of agency rather than an employer. So who employs us? Both of us will be working as Education Advisors (with slightly different briefs) in the District Education Office. However, Kasulu District Office enjoys the support of a development fund called, not surprisingly, Kasulu District Development Project (KaDP) which is funded by the Austrian Government and administered by an NGO called the Austrian Development Corporation (ADC). When this was first explained to me I felt I was drowning in acronyms. Jean Mutamba is the Project Co-ordinator for KaDP and it was he who recommended that the District needed some professional support for education. So in summary it looks as though we have two chains of accountability – one through KaDP and the other through the District Office hierarchy. Could be interesting.

Protocol demanded that we begin by shaking a lot of hands – in the right order, of course. For example, you can't shake the District Education Officer's (DEO) hand until you have shaken the District Executive Director's (DED) hand. Our office is in the District Office complex and the place is very, very basic. If there is a telephone in the whole office complex I haven't found it yet. And certainly none of the schools have telephones. Kasulu District is a couple of hundred kilometres long and a hundred or so across, it has few roads – none of them tarmacked, no mains electricity and about ninety rural villages, each with its own primary school. There are five secondary schools scattered about the district too.

Communication is a nightmare. This was brought home to us when we met the Chief Inspector of Schools. He welcomed us with open arms, told us he was looking forward to running school-based seminars with us like he had done with our predecessor, Anne-Karin. But when we told him that, unlike her, we did not have our own transport, his face dropped. The poor old inspectorate team are supp-osed to inspect ninety rural schools without transport of their own. There are rumours that the KaDP might supply them with something next year but . . . .

So that is our introduction to Kasulu. The town's major 'industry' is aid for refugees, so just about every aid agency you can think of has an office here. The advantage of this is that there is something of a social life and access to a very limited range of western-style goods. You can even get cornflakes if you are prepared to pay a fortune. And, very important professionally, aid workers tend to be very well equipped – far more so than poor volunteers. Will they take pity on us?

A Newly-Built Home
Kathleen M. Moore (Ethiopia)

Just when the 'small rains' started and the dry, dusty path became a sea of sticky red glue that would suck the shoes right off your feet, my *saar-bet* was finally built. Saar-bet is the traditional Ethiopian house – round, grass-roofed, mud-walled, dirt-floored, windowless, home to humans and animals together. *Bet*, like the Hebrew *beth*, means house and *saar* is grass. Fortunately for us, the Guragi people are allegedly the best *saar-bet* builders in all of Ethiopia.

They begin with a tree, felled and stripped of its bark, as the centre post, two storeys high and six feet around. The body of the house is one round wall made of eucalyptus wood, the rough-hewn boards placed tightly together and open spaces filled in with thick red mud. Long poles are lashed to the tip of the centre post, slanting down to the top rim of the wall, making a giant pointed cap. These are held together with strips of thin wood and bark woven over and under, pole after pole, layer after layer, as tightly as if they were thin threads in a piece of cloth. Not a dot of light comes through the roof.

The intricate pattern is enhanced by the shadings of the wood from the almost white of newly-cut young trees to the deep ebony of an old board aged with smoke from years of cooking fires in a former *saar-bet*. When I lay on my bed at night staring up at my roof, my eyes reaching up and up higher than I could climb to the tip of the huge centre post, I felt like Michaelangelo looking at my own African Sistine Chapel.

New grass was thickly packed on top so very few drops of rain came in even though mine was a brand new *saar-bet* and I cooked so little in my fire circle that there was no soot to clog the air spaces among the grass. I felt awe when I went into a villager's home, aged with the breath of family members dead and present, with the smoke from the constant fire, with the pungent aromas of the cattle or sheep. The wood had become dark, the warmth never left, soft light came in through the open door during the day or spread from the fire circle at night when the door was closed against the hyenas and the cold.

While our new saar-bets were under construction, Phil and I convinced the builders to cut three windows in the round wall. We had bought screening in Addis Ababa and tacked it up on the outside of the square holes. Phil drew a picture of shutters and our Guragi carpenter made a pair for each window. We even had two tiny windows cut in our *shint-bets* (outhouses) and screened and shuttered them, too. This was a strange sight to the Guragis for whom windows only meant a hole to let in flies and cold night air.

I made curtains for the windows of my house from a *shama*, a shawl with a bright green and gold embroidered border. They hung unevenly from rods made of thin eucalyptus branches. In the morning, after getting dressed, I'd open the curtains, then the shutters and watch the sunlight make patterns on the table top, bounce off the centre post and beam over my bookshelf balanced on the Butagas tanks standing like soldiers awaiting their turn to do duty at the kitchen stove. Later in the evening, the setting sun would paint stripes across the boards on the upper wall and over the roof poles turning their dry, whiteness to a golden glow.

From my east window, I could see the small house where the boy students from Hosanna slept. They had to walk to Emdeber, sixty kilometres from their home, to go to high school for Hosanna had none. So we had a little house built for them to live in during the school months. They were always up before me, making coffee. I could see them squatting around the *jabana* (coffee pot), in one hand a glass of black coffee thick with sugar on the bottom and a chunk of bread in the other. I would call to one, '*Nay, anteh* (come here, child). Come in and get some jam for your bread.'

If I had ever thought of keeping my precious gifts of food from home all to myself, I would have learned a better lesson from Emdeber. The night I had moved into my *saar-bet* and was relaxing in my stuffed chair by the fire circle, a neighbour's daughter came to the door with a stand of bananas as big as she was. In Emdeber there was only *enset*, the 'false banana' tree, so named because it looked like a huge, lush banana tree but never produced fruit, although the Guragi nurtured this plant and made food from it. These bananas had been brought from Jimma, a town a long way off where the soil was rich and the rains plentiful and fruit grew all year in abundance.

They were expensive and this was an extravagant gift my neighbour gave me. He could have made a lot of money selling those bananas in the Friday market. My students and I picked bananas from the huge bunch, invited my landlord and his large family and soon other children began to show up. Everyone got a banana and still there were some left for me the next day. How could I not share my small gifts with them when they shared all they had with me?

The west window was my view of the countryside. My *saar-bet* was on a small knoll and from that side I could see over the high fence that surrounded my compound, my little space of house, garden and outhouse. I could see into a valley, green in the rainy season, red the rest of the year, dotted with *saar-bets* like giant toadstools, wisps of grey smoke coming out of the top of each one and disappearing into the cloudless sky. An occasional moving dot in the distance would be a bony steer or cow. The rust red stripe in the foreground was the river, emerging from the eucalyptus woods still a mile from the bubbling and steaming waterfall, the only place where the river resembled the image of African jungle I'd seen in movies.

From my third window I could see Emdeber's only road. It wound from school, through the little town, past my compound, Phil's, Jack's, and down to Abba's Mission. On Fridays, I could see women carrying enormous packs of pottery or baskets of live chickens on their backs to trade in the market. Their bodies were hues of colour from pale beige to ochre to deep brown. They fitted in with the place, blended with the trees and the earth, seemingly sprung from the ground, the soil just extending upward into a human form that moved and spoke. They were puzzled by my whiteness. I looked unbaked, undone, as if from another planet where the soil must have been white powder to produce this insubstantial, almost invisible creature with transparent skin and see-through blue eyes and hair that disappeared in the sunlight.

I saw little children running to school carrying scraps of paper and tiny stubs of pencils, their frayed tunics blowing out behind them revealing caramel coloured bare bottoms. I saw teenage girls in bright blue plastic shoes walking slowly and looking out of the corners of their eyes as they passed my house, giggling when the boys called out to them.

As I walked to school, I saw the littlest children, hardly more than infants, sitting on the ground in front of their saar-bet, dirt clutched in their little fists. Their black eyes stared at me but all I could see were the flies crawling in and out of the corners of their eyes, around their nostrils, into their mouths. They never brushed the flies away.

Other children, old enough to run around, but still too young for school, screamed at me, 'Ferengi, ferengi!' I chased them with my *dula*, my walking stick, but they scampered just far enough away that I couldn't reach them. I hated that word, *ferengi*, an incessant reminder that I was a foreigner, that I wasn't one of them, that I didn't belong here. I hated the word and the sound of the children's voices as they screamed it. Walking along the road every day, in the heat of the noon sun, when those children yelled 'Ferengi!' it was like a knife in my heart. This is how racism feels, I told myself – disdain based solely on the colour of your skin. It hurts your soul. Once when walking down a back street in Addis Ababa, a child not as high as his mother's knee, pointed to me and said, 'Aleecha, aleecha.' *Aleecha* is food made without the spicy berberay that turns everything bright red. Aleecha is pale, without colour. I so hated always being called 'ferengi' that 'aleecha' made me want to hug that little poet.

I could feel at home in my saar-bet after school with students sitting around singing or studying, the boys cooking or washing dishes, one of the students making coffee at the fire circle. The fire circle is just to the right of the centre post in every saar-bet. It is about three feet in diameter and, like the floor, is just the ground, refinished occasionally with an application of cow dung and water to keep down the dust. There is usually a smouldering piece of wood in it, easy to blow into a cooking fire with the addition of some kindling, collected every day by the littlest child. The supper hour is late in the evening.

After dark, as I walked down the road back to my house, I saw the gold-red flames through the open doorways, scattered over the hillsides like giant fireflies, too big to catch and put in Mason jars but as magical and entrancing as those flickering lights were on summer nights in my grandmother's back yard in Pittsburgh. They did not close their doors against the night too early. I could see silhouettes huddled close to the fire, making coffee or just sitting there feeding a stick of wood to the embers. It was a soft, earthy glow, red like the ground, red like the river.

This village had become home to me.

Champion Pineapple Eater of Somoto
Roderick Jones (Nicaragua)

I have achieved unprecedented fame down here. From now on, call me the Rocky Balboa of pineapple eating.

This week, Somoto celebrated its independence from the state of Nueva Segovia. The mayor's office has a bunch of low-budget events planned. Yesterday's 'Running of the Bulls' was cancelled, presumably due to a lack of bulls. But tonight's main event, the pineapple-eating contest, went ahead as planned.

My site-mate Lisa had mentioned that she, me and Rosalío, the health centre doctor who's now Lisa's *novio* (boyfriend), should enter the contest. I was like, 'Yeah, maybe, we'll see.' Tonight I went to visit someone in the hospital with my co-worker, Francis, and we decided to pass by the park, where a ton of people had gathered. As luck would have it, they were hanging the pineapples on strings, and Lisa and Rosalío were up and ready. I had to join the fray.

I sized up the competition. No-one there was as big as I was. Unfortunately, no-one's pineapple was as big as mine either. The other people had something like softballs hanging before them, while I had one the size of a watermelon. But I was not discouraged. For sure, I thought as I perused the crowd, I had to be the favourite.

I saw many familiar faces, since the main people an event like this one attracts are street kids (my street kids) and thugs from the baseball crowd (my thugs). The park was stuffed, the entire basketball court covered with spectators.

The mayor came up to me, looked me in the eye, and said, 'The record is eight minutes. I want you to break it.'

I took an early lead, but it was fleeting. Yes, I was eating more, but my pineapple was a monster. Hands tied behind my back, my strategy was this: duck down below the pineapple and stab up at it, lunging my whole body into the motion like a shark. This really got the crowd going, I'm telling you. When I'd rip myself off a big hunk, I could hear what sounded like a half-gasp, half-laugh. I'd turn around and chew wildly, letting the juice squirt over my cheeks and drip down onto the cheering kids below me.

I had to steady the pineapple with my lips or nose to ready it for the next lunge. I was at the edge of the platform, and next to me had appeared a manager on-the-spot, an old baseball team-mate of mine named Juan Gallina (John the Hen), who is well known around town for having been a guerrilla trainer early in the Sandinista years. He yelled out the strategy – it was he who told me to attack my prey from below. But he also called out, '*Al suave*, Rodrigo, *al suave*,' meaning, pace yourself and don't try to finish it off all in one bite.

Shreds of pineapple got into my hair, nose, eyes, and clothes. Through the juice I could see that victory was not to be mine on this night. But I had no doubt, judging from the crowd's noise, that all eyes were on me. So I took my cue from the great Johnny Rodz, the World Wrestling Federation stiff who was never allowed to win any matches, but always got thrown around pretty good and was a crowd favourite for that reason alone. I continued to attack. But now I didn't bother to steady the pineapple between stabs, and this seemed to make my pursuit of the hanging fruit all the more amusing.

In the end, Rosalío won. But when I looked over at him, I saw he had blood in his mouth and a big puddle at his feet. Could it be?. . . no . . . yes! He did! The man lost his lunch, tossed his *piña*, gave back his vitamin C. Even though Rosalío speaks no English, as we filed down from the platform, I whispered, 'I wanna rematch.'

The people charged up to me.

'Your pineapple was bigger than theirs!' they said.

'You should have been declared the winner!'

I scanned the crowd for Francis, my first and best friend.

'Francy!' I called out, blinking pulp out of my stinging, swollen eyes. 'Francy! Francy!'

Once I found her, we walked back to her house.

People kept coming up to me on the street with their analyses.

'At least you're really full,' one said.

'You're gonna have the squirts something wicked tomorrow, you'll see,' said another.

My response to all of them was the same. 'Wait until next year. I'm going to start practising. One hanging pineapple every night before bed. No, make it two. Mark my words. I, Rodrigo, will return to claim the crown that is rightfully mine – 'Champion Pineapple Eater of Somoto, Nicaragua.'

Seeing Differently
Liselotte Wolters (Uganda)

I'm in Kiwoko, a small village in a rural area of Uganda. I am manager of the hospital laboratory.

My fear of not knowing how to diagnose malaria was gone after a month. Some other tests still demand some study from my side because I am simply not used to doing all those tests manually instead of using apparatus for everything. But although I ask the lab staff to explain the different tests to me they still think that my being white makes me know everything.

I do not notice that everybody around me is black, but when I see another white person among Ugandans I think – wow, that person is white.

Recognising the different Ugandans gives some problems sometimes.

'How would you describe Sue?' (another white here) I ask Lornah, the secretary of the hospital. 'What colour is her hair?'

'Well . . . something like you, or maybe a bit more like hers,' she says pointing to another white. The difference between my hair and hers is that I'm blond and she's dark.

'What colour are my eyes?' I ask.

'Colour? What do you mean "colour of eyes?"' Lornah says.

'Well, I mean blue, green, brown . . . .'

Lornah just doesn't understand my question.

Patrick the principal tutor of the lab school was looking for me the first week I was here. He came to my house. Helen, an English student, opened the door, but Patrick didn't see if it was me or not (my hair is blond and straight, Helen has dark, short, curly hair, and glasses). When Helen walked away he recognised in the way of walking it wasn't me.

There are two female first year students in the lab, Rebecca and Annet. One of them has long braided hair, the other one short hair. My only problem is I don't know who is who. So I ask Patrick who of them is Rebecca and who is Annet.

'Easy', Patrick says, 'the brown one is Rebecca and the black one is Annet.'

'What? All of you are black here.'

Patrick just laughs. 'All black', he says, 'Don't you see that one of them is brown?'

'Well . . . no, not really. Is the brown girl the one with braids or is that the black girl?' I ask.

'Braids?' Patrick looks surprised at me.

I guess I know now why they don't see the difference between the different whites and why I had trouble differentiating the Ugandans. But after being here over a year now I perfectly see the difference in brown and black people.

Misbehaving
Gina Perfetto (Ethiopia)

On the way to the Berhanu restaurant, she walked with Alex as she had for the two weeks since she arrived. The children were still gathering, still yelling, 'Farenj!'

'Money, money.'

'Stomach zero.'

Alex ran a hand over his head that Sara began to see more and more as a bowling ball. They struggled over the erosion gullies filled with mud from the summer rains. 'Don't worry, in three months' time, they will forget you.' He burst into what she thought were expletives.

They passed the boys with their goats, the principal who she already learned had a serious reverence for his official stamps and ink pads, the naked children, the welders, the carriage drivers.

She broke free of his hand and skipped into the patio with its blue plastic awning.

'Miss Sara, you must not skip. You are a teacher and people will not take you seriously.'

He clapped loudly for the waiter and seemed angry when he did not come right away. He clapped louder. 'This is what we do to call the waiter,' he said proudly.

She pressed his hand down. 'I think he heard us. In America, that is rude.'

She began to compile a list of facts. People clap for waiters. It is okay to hit children you don't know. Women don't run or jump. Old people always get a seat, and anyone who is very young must run errands for you if you ask. When a beggar comes by, give only change, or say, 'May God give you.'

The waiter came. He was one of her students. 'How are you, Miss Sara?' he said.

Alex ordered roasted meat with rosemary and onions, a Coke and seltzer water. The flies were everywhere and she brushed them away when they landed on her face and arms. Alex meticulously smacked the dust from his shoes and pants legs. 'Goddamned dust. Really it's terrible,' he said.

There was too much to absorb in such a short time. He asked her last week if she wanted a servant to wash her clothes. Teachers must have a servant, he said. And he said it was his job to find one who was honest, because most servants would steal. She sat and listened in the main room while his wife Tsegereda swept the floors and offered her popcorn with her coffee.

She suddenly realised Alex was still talking and turned to him, 'I'm sorry?' The other tables were full with people eating and sucking marrow from bones. Each glass swarmed with lazy bees.

'I said that after today you should not eat outside your house. That does not look good. You are a teacher and should cook, or have a servant prepare the food. And you must not have beer in public. People will not think highly of you.'

The rules mounted. She nodded vaguely and saw her students walking up the road in their brown, issued uniforms. All except Rina, a pretty tenth grader. She had gotten her hands on a bicycle, and was riding past them and circling around again. Sara looked at her. Rina was standing up and peddling around while the students threw up their hands and tried to catch her. 'Where did Rina get that bike, Alex? Is it okay if she wears pants?'

'The bike, I don't know really. Rina is a cripple, it's very sad,' he sighed.

'She's not a cripple.'

The waiter brought out the large tray with the circular *injera* on it, and the meat placed on top in a pile in the centre. Injera served as the clean surface for the meat, and when pulled off was used as a spoon to grab the food and place it neatly in the mouth. When only a little was left, the last remaining piece would be used to mop up the oil and magically, everything would be gone. The waiter bowed to leave while another poured each glass half full with seltzer and then soda. They left and Sara hadn't forgotten what Alex said.

'How do you think she's a cripple? I've seen her walk, she's riding a *bike*.'

And he laughed. 'Don't you see, one leg is shorter than the other. She's a pretty girl but she will not get a husband. She has many friends – that boy, Addis? They are friends, and she wears pants and runs, it's okay. It's Rina, and it makes her happy.'

'Alex, I barely even noticed. God, I limp sometimes, and in America I could marry.'

'Yes, Miss Sara, but here it is different. It's the way things are.'

'I think it's the way things are only because many people say it is.'

He looked at her blankly, 'Yes, of course.'

She planned on eating here tomorrow, and having a beer with some of the other teachers from work. Almost four months, and she was tired of being afraid of doing something wrong. For the whole time in training, and the two weeks in Butajira, she asked as many times a day as the fingers on her hand, 'Is that wrong? Is this bad culture?' As a child, she remembered feeling the same way when she was yelled at for dancing in school when it was time for work.

She finished her soda before the bees landed. The bill came and Alex proudly pulled out the money from his back pocket. 'We do not tip here,' he said smiling.

'I'll remember that, Alex. I don't know what I'd do if you were not assigned to show me around and help me.'

'It's nothing, really,' he said. 'Now I will take you to market and show you the foods you need and the right price for everything. Then I will take you to the private bar where teachers may drink secretly.' He was beaming – even his head glowed.

It was always painful to her to disappoint the people who tried to make her believe in the world as they saw it: her mother and father who didn't understand why she'd want to come to a developing country, her grandfather who said social work was a sappy, thankless pursuit as he cracked open chicken bones and gnawed them to shreds. Alex was smiling so broadly she thought his face would crack.

But she called to Rina when she saw the girl peddling towards her. 'Oh Alex, I haven't been on a bike in years.' And Rina pulled up. Sara pointed to the bike, which was scratched up and dented. Rina was smart and immediately got off.

Alex said, 'Miss Sara, you will fall and your skirt will go up. This is highly improper for a woman teacher to ride the bicycle.'

She turned to Rina, 'Is it okay?' and Rina nodded, and covered her mouth when she smiled like all proper girls do. 'Alex, I think you are right about the children. They have already forgotten me. And if the children can forget, so can the adults. One minute, okay, and then we'll go to the market.'

He had a look that she had already seen several times before, the glazed eyes that focused on something else as he hauled up a thin smile. 'Of course,' he said evenly.

'One minute,' she said to Rina, and as she hopped on and rode away Rina was laughing and the children that Alex said would surely forget ran after the white teacher, screaming and singing, and calling her names.

Drinking Kava
Michael Eccleshall (Vanuatu)

I was a volunteer in the South Pacific, on an island in Vanuatu called Pentecost. This island is famous for its ritual known as *nangol* or land diving. It is this ritual which is the forerunner to bungee jumping (AJ Hackett saw it on Pentecost and turned the practice into the bungee jump). Unfortunately, it was the wrong time of year so I did not view the ritual, but I did meet people that had taken part.

Vanuatu is also famous for its intoxicating brew, kava. Kava is a very powerful drink. It comes from the root of the kava plant and there are over ten strains, some so strong they are used as powerful anaesthetics in western drugs. The average plant, when prepared properly, will produce a drink that relaxes and calms you after a few 'shells'.

In order to prepare kava, the plant is first selected from the garden. On Pentecost kava is grown as a cash crop and thus there is always plentiful supply. The roots of the plant are then separated and the top section discarded. Muddy sections of the roots are then 'peeled' using a bush knife, the remains are washed in a bucket and diced, leaving a pile of roots that look not dissimilar to a pile of chopped potatoes.

The next part of the preparation requires the greatest skill. A piece of sharp, phallic shaped coral is used to grind the pieces of kava to a pulp (the kava is held in one hand and the coral is ground against it, much like sharpening a large pencil). On occasions where there are large amounts of people waiting to drink, this process can be replicated by pounding a large amount of kava in a bucket with a large pole.

Once the 'mush' is obtained it is ready to be strained. It is placed on a thick wooden tray and a shell full of water is poured over the mush. The water mixes with the kava, which is then strained through coconut fibres (or a pair of tights) to give one shell full of fresh kava. This is drunk in one go (tasting like a cross between peppery water and dishwater).

After a few minutes the effects begin to be felt, and after a few more shells (one every fifteen minutes or more) you begin to feel relaxed and a real appreciation of the fact that you are sitting in a village consisting of mud and straw huts, accepting a strange brew from a chief with whom you share almost nothing – linguistically or culturally. However, it just seems like the most natural thing in the world. And is just one of the many extraordinary experiences that taking a GAP year can provide.

The Engagement
Helen Grant (Zambia)

Siza was a pastor in a rural village and often came to Lusaka for meetings with his church leaders.

'Good afternoon,' he said, smiling politely.

'Good afternoon.'

'How are you?'

'I'm fine. How are you?'

'Fine.'

This long preamble always went on before any conversation ever took place. I decided to be rude, for once, and speed up the chat.

'I'm just getting in the bath. What did you want?'

He flinched at my directness, noticing the towel. He was surprised that I should be having a bath in the middle of the afternoon. Bath times in Zambia were generally only expected to be early morning or late evening.

'I wondered if you found Lucy?'

Lucy, the maid, had recently stolen all the hard currency I had, leaving me with nothing. When I tried to find her, it quickly became apparent that she had given me a false address. The references I had checked before employing her turned out to be from strangers who had accepted money to vouch for her. At that moment in time, I felt the whole city was full of thieves and corruption.

'No. Unfortunately not. We spent hours walking around and I'm shattered.'

'Oh dear. Sorry for that.'

He was a friend and, as a man who had visited England twice, he understood Westerners' ways. I felt I could speak to him more freely than to most of my acquaintances.

'To tell you the truth,' I said, 'I'm absolutely fed up with Lusaka. Everyone just seems to want to get things from me and nobody seems to care about me as a person.'

He nodded, understanding. 'Well, you are a *muzungu* –'

I had no defence. The fact that I was white made it acceptable for everybody to use me as some sort of public benefactor or entertainer.

'Maybe you need a change of scene,' Siza suggested. Then his eyes lit up with an idea. 'Why don't you come to my parish next Saturday? It's a traditional Zambian village. You can see a different way of life from this fast-paced city rush.'

I actually felt like spending the next weekend lying in bed with a pillow over my head, but the constant stream of visitors would put paid to that idea. Perhaps a trip to the countryside was just what I needed.

'Okay,' I smiled, 'I'd love to.'

***

The bus throbbed with people, livestock, baggage and the energetic rhythms of the Congolese rhumba beat played at full blast on the distorting cassette deck. I was the only white person through the entire one-hour journey. As usual, everyone wanted to talk to me and touch me. Pinioned to a few inches of seat space, with seven passengers and all their possessions squashed onto three seats, I had no room for manoeuvre. Siza seemed to find it all rather amusing.

After a while, he said, 'this is our stop,' and hammered on the thin tin wall of the ramshackle minibus. It stopped in the middle of the potholed road. On either side lay the African bush. There were no roads visible, nor any signs. I clambered over protesting people and flung myself out into the hot afternoon sun.

'This way,' Siza said. I clutched my bottle of water for comfort, already feeling uncomfortably hot.

I was wearing a skirt because I had been told that people in rural areas would be shocked at the sight of a woman in trousers. The foliage was thick, so we couldn't see very far into the bush – the whole landscape consisting of spindly trees and thigh-high grass. Siza tacked his way along a narrow dusty footpath. I sweated and asked inane questions about living in the bush. Was there water? Electricity? Drainage?

'You'll see.'

A few rangy cows rustled in the grass nearby, tended by young boys.

The stresses of the city began to fall away. I drank carefully from the water bottle and ignored the aching in my legs as we continued walking. I was determined to enjoy the trip and to learn something from the villagers. We continued walking.

'It's not far now,' said Siza.

I glanced at my watch. It was three-fifteen already and I was hungry. We had been walking in the sun for over three hours. I contemplated eating a bag of crisps or some of the sweets which I had brought as gifts, but decided against it. I drank some more of the water, offering the bottle to Siza.

'I think you need it more than I do,' he said. 'Aah, here we are.'

We approached a clearing with a few round mud huts in it. Three small children came hurtling along the footpath towards us, oblivious to Siza, yelling, 'Muzungu! Muzungu!' at the sight of me. I despaired – this constant refrain followed me from my door to my bed every day. A small boy leapt at me and touched my arm with thrilled trepidation.

'Muli bwanji,' I greeted him, and he dissolved into peels of laughter. His friends joined in, throwing themselves one by one to the dusty ground, kicking up their legs in hysterical joy. Siza and I laughed with them, and more people came running out of the village.

First came two women, wiping their hands on the chitenges they layered over their skirts, as an apron and for modesty. They shook my hand, curtseyed, clapped their hands together and smiled. 'Muli bwanji.'

I copied their actions, head down, smiling, trying to look submissive, like them.

Siza said something to them and they hurried back to the huts.

As we neared the buildings, I could see a lot of activity going on in the circle between them. One woman was pounding maize in a wooden pot, throwing her entire bodyweight into lifting up and then hammering back down a pole as tall as herself. One of the women who had greeted me earlier was crouched on the ground, washing a huge pile of crockery with a stick, the flayed twigs working as a scourer. Another swept the dust around the huts with a twig broom, and a fourth put a kettle onto a fire and grinned at me.

'She is making you tea,' Siza explained.

I smiled at the woman and clapped my hands in a gesture of gratitude. I reached inside my bag for the gifts, but Siza stopped me, his hand over mine.

A young man bent double as he clambered out of his hut, blinking in the sunshine and wiping his eyes. He held out his hand to shake mine and spoke in English.

'Welcome to my home,' he said, smiling. 'And welcome to you, Pastor.' He shouted aggressively towards the young woman by the kettle.

Siza said, 'This is Moffat. He is the Chief's son.'

'Come, please –' Moffat gestured inside his hut.

I had to duck down to step inside the open doorway, because the roof thatch reached down to below my knees. Inside, the one-room building was so dark that I edged carefully forwards, unable to see anything.

'It is an honour that you are visiting us,' said Moffat.

I smiled and sat down, gratefully, on a short three-legged stool that he indicated.

As my eyes grew accustomed to the dimness, I saw a narrow bed in one corner, an incongruous glass-topped modern coffee table taking up most of the floor space, and four tiny stools. They sat down.

I knew that I couldn't speak first. My status was confused, however – as a muzungu I was held in high respect; as a woman I was considered lowly. I waited.

'I am the son of the Chief,' Moffat said. 'First we will have some food and drink and then I will guide you around my village.'

'We have brought you some gifts,' said Siza, nudging me.

I pulled out the sweets and drinks from my bag and Siza bellowed.

A young woman scrambled to the doorway in response. He pointed at the goods and she gathered them all up, never looking at our faces, but trying to conceal a smile. She took them outside.

'The latrine has burnt down,' said Moffat. 'Someone nearby was burning the fields and they unfortunately burnt their whole village down. The fire reached our latrine but we stopped it before it came any further.'

'I'm sorry,' I said.

'But you can sleep in the new house we are building for Gielgood. He is returning from Lusaka.'

'Oh really?' asked Siza. 'Why?'

'He is very sick. He has an illness.' The two men cast their eyes down to the compact-mud floor. Gielgood was evidently coming home to his village to die of AIDS, a common story around here.

Nobody spoke for a while. The peace of the village was very restful, the only noises from the maize pounding, the chickens and small children outside. From further off was the sound of cattle lowing, their bells ringing softly in the bush.

'Is Chief Mutabeza around?' asked Siza, finally.

'He is visiting in Machinga, but he will return today. He wishes to meet you.'

I felt slightly nervous at the thought of an audience with a Chief. As the conversation meandered slowly on, I grew more tired and thirsty by the minute. I finished the last of my water and Moffat shouted at the woman outside to hurry up with the tea.

It was over an hour later when she appeared in the hut's open doorway carrying a tin tray heaped with floral-transfer Taiwanese plastic cups. She bent over, placed the tea on the table and poured it for us, then backed out, crouched down virtually onto her knees, never looking us in the eyes, clapping her hands in respect as she retreated.

The tea tasted smoky and nutty, but it felt good to drink something.

'Where is that damn woman?' shouted Moffat, clapping his hands loudly. The same woman came running back to the doorway. 'Bring us food, woman!' he demanded, imperiously. She scuttled off.

'She is my first wife,' Moffat said. 'My father has three. I intend to have more.'

'You know, as a Christian, God only allows you to take one wife,' Siza reprimanded him.

'But I am also a Lozi,' replied Moffat, 'and in my tribe we take many wives.'

It interested me how Zambians lived with many different belief systems simultaneously – all Zambians belonged to a tribe and followed the conventions of that group. They all believed in witchcraft to one degree or another, many also believed in foreign religions – Christianity or Islam – and they believed in the Western ideal of science.

Moffat's wife brought us some food and we gladly tucked in.

'My father is very old,' said Moffat. 'Also, he has an illness, here,' he tapped his chest. 'The medicine man says it is witchcraft put on him by a woman in the next village – that's why he has gone for an insaka at Machinga today.'

'Has he seen a doctor?' I asked. 'I mean, in Lusaka?'

'Yes, of course,' replied Moffat, as if my idea was idiotic. 'He saw a Chinese doctor, who told him that he had heart disease and should cut down on rich foods!' he snorted disgustedly. 'These Chinese!'

I knew about the Chinese doctors, brought in to counter the local doctors' strike for better pay and conditions. The President had sacked them all and imported foreign doctors from Russia and China. The incentives he had offered these new doctors included large houses, cars, and huge salaries. The Zambian doctors, understandably, were furious, but powerless to do anything.

'The problem with these Chinese doctors is they don't speak English,' Moffat said. 'And they don't understand the African way of life. They told my father not to drink wine or eat foods like cream cakes. How can my father find foods like that?' He shook his head and considered the alternatives. 'It must be witchcraft.'

Siza and I both nodded. I wondered if it was witchcraft that had tempted Lucy to steal my money.

A young boy stuck his head through the door and yelled something excitedly, before racing away.

'Ah. My father is coming.' Moffat led the way out of the hut.

Siza held me back and whispered to me. 'Don't speak to the Chief unless to answer his questions. Make sure you sit lower than him and keep your head bowed, don't look into his eyes.'

I was grateful for the instructions, not wanting to appear rude.

A group of older men entered the village and all the villagers threw themselves down to the ground, hunched over, clapping their hands in respect. Siza and I did likewise. The men all wore ragged and torn, dusty clothes. I had no way of knowing which man was the Chief, until one sat on a stool in the centre of the village. The women brought a straw mat and laid it at his feet, beckoning for me to sit on that.

The Chief's stool, like all the others, was only about twelve inches high, so for me to keep lower than him I knelt on the mat and bent over, head down, clapping.

The Chief didn't speak for two hours. I crouched on the mat in front of him, silent, eyes down, immobile. I became desperate to straighten my legs. I wanted to urinate. But I stayed where I was, my whole body seizing up.

At six o'clock dusk fell, as always. The Chief stood up and walked away to his rondavel. I shook out my legs in great relief and limped to Siza. 'I need to go to the toilet,' I said. 'Where shall I go?'

'In the bush.'

I half-walked, half-ran out of the village and into the bush, squatting behind a tree in relief, agonising pins and needles in my legs.

The night was suddenly pitch black, the only light from a fire in the village where some of the women were preparing the evening meal. Preparing and cooking food seemed to take their entire day, as did pounding maize, sweeping the dust around the huts, washing clothes and crockery. The utter tedium of life in a place like this must be awful.

I returned to the rondavels.

'Now,' Moffat said. 'We will eat and then you will bathe before bed. My father says you are a very nice young woman.' He smiled and eyed me up and down. For a moment, I wondered if I was being considered as his possible second wife.

Dinner was exactly the same as lunch – *nshima*, the thick maize meal staple food, with cooked leaves. This meal, though, was served with warm Coke and Fanta straight from the bottle, which was considered the height of sophistication.

After dinner, one of the women brought me a basin of water which had been warmed over the fire. 'Zikomo,' I thanked her, and she looked me in the eyes and smiled. All afternoon I had been kept with Siza, Moffat and the Chief, at a distance from the women. In truth, though, I supposed I had more in common with the men, able to move freely and make my own decisions. The women's lives appeared to consist of drudgery and obedience.

She led me across the village to the 'bathroom', a fence made of straw which wound inwards like a snail's shell. She handed me the water, some soap, and a clean chitenge. I took off my shoes and entered the fence, walking around until I was in the middle. The fence came up to my chin. I stripped off completely and washed slowly, feeling relaxed and calm in the quiet night.

The moon was bright and reflected off the only white thing for miles – my skin. I looked luminescent, and wondered if my body showed clearly through the slats of the fence. I felt as if I was being watched, imagining that men from miles around might be standing in the bush right now, watching the show. I dried myself with the chitenge and left the bathroom carrying my clothes.

The same women re-appeared and, without speaking, led me to a hut. This was evidently Gielgood's new hut. Someone had placed my bag inside, on the thin straw mattress lying on the ground. I thanked her and got dressed in the dark. Then I sat in the hut and wondered what to do.

After a few minutes, Siza appeared in the doorway. 'Please come,' he said. 'The ladies would like to speak to you and they say I can translate.'

I followed him to the fire. Women were sitting around on stools, on hard-mud bricks or just on the ground. They whooped with delight when they saw me and started chatting.

Where was my husband? How many children did I have? Why was I travelling alone? Where was my car?

All the same questions I was asked every day in Lusaka. I answered them politely and Siza translated.

Does my skin hurt in the sun? What are these? One woman pointed gingerly at some moles on my arm. Why is my hair not curly?

The questions went on and on, but there was a good sense of camaraderie as I laughed with the women, despite not understanding.

Then Siza suddenly became serious. He said to me. 'This lady, Matilda, she says her son wants to marry you. He fell in love with you when you came here today. If you agree, you can stay here in the village.'

My heart sank and my pulse raced. I had heard how some tribesmen literally kidnapped women they wanted to be their wives. I didn't know Siza that well, how could I be sure that he would escort me safely back to Lusaka? What if Matilda was Moffat's mother?

Matilda laughed at the look of horror on my face. She spoke to Siza.

'She asks if you want to meet her son,' he said.

'No,' I replied, immediately. I feared that her son might come to my hut later and rape me. With the prevalence of HIV and AIDS in Zambia, rape was often a death sentence.

All the women laughed. Siza laughed too. Their white eyes and teeth glowed in the firelight. I shuddered, wanting to be polite, to go along with their accepted codes of behaviour, but terrified of being trapped in a place like this for the rest of my life, a slave to some local villager.

Helen meeting her fiancé

Amidst all the laughter, Matilda stepped up and went to a nearby hut.

'She will fetch him,' Siza explained.

Matilda emerged, carrying a sleepy four-year old boy in her arms.

'This is her son,' said Siza, laughing.

The boy rubbed his eyes and looked around at all the laughing women, saw me, and buried his head bashfully in his mother's breast.

'Do you accept the engagement?' Siza asked.

Relieved beyond all measure, I nodded seriously. 'I do,' I agreed.

* * *

Siza walked me back to the main road the next day, after his open-air sermon. The passengers on the bus back to Lusaka were very pleased to let a muzungu climb aboard and I put up with the usual interest with better grace than I had done the day before.

A Zambian fiancé could be a useful, I thought, to counter the constant questions about lacking a husband. And I would have left the country before he grew up.

I laughed aloud and a baby burst into tears. The rhumba tape played on. I was engaged.

Home Sweet
Michael Shann (China)

These two words I wrote with a wet finger
in the outer dirt of my door, braced myself,
turned the key, dropped a shoulder, pushed.
And pushed, marking on the floor a perfect
fan-shape in the dust. I looked up, blinked:
my new flat.

The walls are Celtic, striped, green and white;
the windows are tinted with coal dust.

The air is a dry cough
and the electricity is a nervous laugh.

The plumbing is a patient with poor circulation
and the gas-hob is the countdown to an explosion.

The lino is Lake Ontario or the Gobi Desert,
endless; the bedroom light is a floodlight, fluorescent.

The fridge is a noisy neighbour
and the sink an abandoned quarry.

The view is a scrap-yard,
honest, and the mirror is an iced pond, skated.
The water is burnt umber, from the tap,
a blizzard in a glass. The bath
is a mud bath, an ex-cattle trough,
and the armchairs are the sources of springs.

The view is a scrap-yard, honest . . .

The orange bedspread is a Pre-Raphaelite dress,
nylon, will have to go unless
perhaps it will do for a shower curtain.
A waterfall heard from the next field, that's the cistern.

The toilet has been condemned, then pardoned.
The phone is clear, the bed is bugged.

But the rooms are large and full of my dreams.
The balcony will be my garden, my time-piece,
the slow measure of my eight seasons in this town.
I sit down in the bare echo of the afternoon,
drink a toast of tea to my days here, then stand
at the window and trace on the glass, with
the same smudged finger, in eight-inch high letters,

the mirror image of the word **HOME**.

On the Periphery
Christian Brackin (Thailand)

Chris and I definitely facilitate each other's laziness with the Thai language. We spend more time every day with English, letting the Thai lessons fade into background noise. I've recently discovered that I do understand much of a conversation in Thai, though just as often discover that I'm completely baffled. This is really not such a surprising phenomenon, considering that people from this province speak both Central Thai and Northern Thai, two completely different languages. This fact was another blow to my original zeal in learning Thai, though now it is only a pitiful, yet persistent excuse.

Admittedly, I've gone through a depression of sorts. I've spent days on end wallowing in the idea that I could leave for a full week, and as long as I didn't take Chris, no-one would miss me. I've dreamed up plans to go back to Chaing Mai to learn from the Thai teacher we met there and come back months later vastly more valuable. While I was there I could get a certificate in Thai Massage and would be an undeniable asset to the vocational training project. Truth be told, I finally got to the bottom of my mood and realised that I was just trying to justify escaping to something, anything where I felt even vaguely proficient.

Language really does comes quite naturally to me, though not the intellectual variety. My true talent with communication is in understanding non-verbal language. This is one of the vagaries that can make or break someone in the Therapeutic Massage field. Being at the organisation every day has taught me more valuable lessons about the universal human language than I could have learned in Shiatsu school. And acutely discovering that I was standing on the inside of a glass box for two months formulating this realisation this is one of the reasons I have never taken my dreams of leaving seriously.

Many of the children who come here are from the tribal villages that lie on borders and in the no-man's-land without a nationality. Many of them come to the DEPDC with no knowledge of Thai language, Central or Northern, but find themselves surrounded by fluent Thai speakers. There may be a few other children or even teachers who speak their language, but when it comes down to it, they are *farangs* (foreigners), just like me. They are separated from home, albeit willingly, and facing great mental and emotional changes at a very young age. When I was three, I would have thrown a fuss in the kitchen, too, if I was suddenly surrounded by people who spoke, acted and smelled completely unfamiliar. Finding this innate human kindredness has given me more spirit to stay and learn, just like many of them come to understand in their first months here.

If I look at the children from my heart, I see budding young people who just want to become. Some of them will be great social innovators, anxious to learn anything and everything new that comes to the campus. Chris is teaching one young man how to use computer graphics programs, and I've been asked to help a group of girls learn conversational English. These kids have sucked up every morsel of knowledge they could get from the time they arrived, and I am another source on their continued hunt for self-actualisation.

Other kids just want to be kids, to play ball and marbles, to have friends and community. I see them every day, and they greet me as they would any elder, overlooking any barriers, seen or unseen, with traditional Thai customs. They have learned from their early days at the DEPDC that farangs on the campus represent continued flow of funding, as all of the granting agencies are from outside of Thailand. Some past volunteers have worked very hard to help get agricultural programmes in place so the vocational training extends beyond the sewing and weaving schools.

Some other of the kids are very special people, and the most interesting to me. There is one boy in particular who does not hang out with any particular crowd, who stands aside and fields stray footballs while the other boys are playing, and often watches from a distance with his hands behind his back. It is the attitude of someone who hasn't found the right place to put his peg. It's as if all the other children have round or square shapes, or maybe a right triangle that fits perfectly into the running of everyday life, and he's here looking for the octagon he was born with, thinking, 'I'll know it when I see it.'

He's probably the most knowledgeable person there is on the social interactions of the playground, but who's going to ask him for that information? After watching him in wonder for the last few months, it is only recently have I realised that this child has been bequeathed with the gift of patience, though he probably wouldn't use those exact words. In some ancient eastern proverb I have read that the most rare blossoms bloom late in the season. If this proverb were translated into Thai, would he recognise himself?

A Singular Face
Holly Twiname (China)

Sometimes, just when I think that I might be able to forget that I'm a foreigner here, something will happen to remind me that that won't ever be possible. The other day, I was cycling home and this girl gave a great big shout of shock/surprise/disbelief as she saw me whizz by (okay, maybe not whizz, more like a gentle whoosh – cycling here is never exactly fast). I was approaching a junction and slowing down anyway, so she came running after me and could hardly find the words to express herself. She said she'd seen my picture in a magazine (although to my knowledge I have never been in any magazine) and she loves English and wanted to make friends with me. Every other word she said was 'oh' (as in, oh my goodness, I can't believe this is happening). I never knew what it was to feel like a celebrity, but now I do, and it is absurd. (Hearing whispers of 'foreigner, foreigner' wherever you go, however, is not funny.)

A friend is coming to visit from the States tomorrow. I wonder what effect it's going to have on the locals, having discovered the foreign population has doubled overnight.

Hospital
Bronwyn Hudson (Vanuatu)

On Tuesday night I had another little incident/accident. Those who know me well know that I have a little habit of sleepwalking. It's not really a dangerous habit, just enough of a habit to give my family and friends some amusement from time to time. Well, I was chasing this little boy who was holding two pot plants (as you do) and my feet got all caught up in my sheet as I was getting out of bed, but I didn't realise this (because I was asleep) so I proceeded to fall out of bed with my feet still caught in the sheets, therefore my knee was left to take the full brunt of the cement tiled floor. So then I had a swollen knee and a swollen face.

I was housebound for a week, which is just torture in a place like this. I have now run out of my supply of reading material. I was once again well looked after; on one day I had three different people bring me lunch. Human kindness is a magic cure.

It was a really confronting experience going to the local hospital. I had to wait for about two hours to see the doctor (keeping the locals amused with the state of my face) and while I was waiting I was doing a bit of people watching, contemplating the state of the health system in Vanuatu. I felt a real sadness at knowing that people die from curable illness here. The hospital runs out of food and medicine on a regular basis and this is the central hospital in the capital. I couldn't let myself think about what it is like on the other islands, my fragile emotional state would not have coped.

It was interesting to observe the system that was in place in the clinic. In Australia you make an appointment, go to the doctor, they get out your file, you sit and read an out-of-date mag for a while and then get to see the doc. Even if you don't have an appointment it runs on a first-in basis with all the little white cards lined up on order of who came when. In Vila, people come into the clinic and sit on long wooden benches and wait to see the doctor. The nurse comes out and takes the patient in to see the doctor, only there is no system for determining who sees the doctor when. Unfortunately for the women and children, the men see themselves as much more important and worthy of the doctor's time, therefore they just go with the nurse regardless of how long the women have been there.

The women didn't seem to mind and sat waiting patiently until the men had been attended to, because they also see themselves as being inferior. I can deal with the women having to wait at the hospital on some deep cultural level, except the men just keep on coming, so the women just keep on waiting. One woman was there before me (7am) and was still waiting when I left (10am). It was all I could do not to get pen and paper from my bag and set up a system but I'm a woman – so what would I know? It's hard to get over the mentality of wanting to 'fix' things. I settled for having a chat to the Australian doctor about it.

The inequality of the sexes is mega-hard to deal with for an egalitarian like me, especially when the traditional or customary role of males is used to justify everything from workplace discrimination to domestic violence. Men see it as a right to beat their women if they are in a bad mood and the women see it as their role to be the punch bag. It is uncommon for me to go a week without seeing a woman with a black eye. There are many advocates here for gender equality and women's rights but the process of change in such a fundamental customary way of thinking is slow. After all, we can't even manage equality in Australia.

Hey Dolly!
Annette Hearns (Angola)

Life as a white expatriate in Malanje is like living in a goldfish bowl. Everyone knows who you are and what you are doing, so quite quickly you learn to adjust.

The Concern Worldwide office here is next door to the house. One Saturday I was returning from the office to the house, when a neighbour called out 'Hello'.

I crossed the road to chat. He is the guy who, every weekend, takes the huge yellow truck parked outside apart then puts it back together again, with a hammer. This little bit of maintenance is carried out every Saturday, then to be sure again on Sunday mornings. Of course the bit I like most is the fact that he starts at 6am each time.

This is beside the point. As I spoke to the man he interrupted his hammering to ask where I was from, did I like it here, and did my father mind my being here.

Seated in the shade of the raised bonnet was his little girl playing with her dolly. The child was about three years old and was staring at me open-mouthed. Her dolly was a typical white doll with long blond hair and blue eyes. She and I resembled each other in these features. The child refused to talk to me, so I continued my chat with her dad. Then I felt a tug on my sleeve, and there she stood, huge tears in her eyes and her lip wobbling. Dolly was fiercely clutched to her chest.

I bent down to her, and she said, 'Are you my dolly's mummy?'

The dad laughed, and told me she was afraid I had come to reclaim my child.

Minor Irritations
Margaret Goverde (Namibia)

It was quite a relief to see my husband again. The year had not been easy with all the new and hard work, and some little problems like a mugging, and a hurt foot, and a blocked toilet, and the neighbour's houseboy who appeared to have been pilfering things from our house for some time, and some Oshakati dogs that came after me and bit me, though not badly. That's what they are trained to do, to defend their master's property, and they hate cyclists especially, it appears. There aren't too many cyclists here: there are quite a few thorns lying around, and the sandy roads can get quite soft. The tarred roads are for the cars – they feel that you as a cyclist have no right to be there.

So the first half year was eventful, and then to be among complete strangers and miss your own home was not always easy. Of course we had been on email and after some time we also managed to chat online, and I got letters from friends and relatives, but still you miss the 'warmth of the nest', as we call it in Dutch.

Still, I am not sorry I did this – all those friends and relatives I had known for so long will still be there after I return, and in the meantime I have lived in a different society and made new friends and had an interesting job. It was interesting to get to know the ideas about the world from the students' essays, and to visit them in their homesteads in the country and to introduce them to lots of 'western' things like computers and all sorts of ideas that came up in the texts we studied, from the Roman Empire (and the British Empire of course) to the millennium bug.

We have visited three students who live in 'homesteads' – a collection of huts (of wooden sticks or stones made of dried clay) within a fence made of wooden sticks or of the stalks of palm-leaves (there are not so many trees around nowadays). Usually there is also one smallish brick house in the homestead where the parents sleep and goods are stored. The *mahangu* (millet) is stored in big baskets with a lid.

The last family we visited was a 'nuclear' family: parents and eight children, of which our student Magdaletis is the eldest. Like most people in the country they are subsistence farmers: they eat what the mahangu field and the vegetable patch and the cattle yield. Everybody is now waiting for the rains to come so that they can start sowing. It is a bare and sandy country, except for an occasional fruit tree or palm tree. If you are a subsistence farmer, finding money for clothes and medicines and the children's school fees is a problem.

In this case Magdaletis's mother goes to nearby Oshakati (12 km) in a taxi six days out of seven to buy a goat in the market, slaughter it and sell it in a stall. On Sundays she officiates in the church with some other people (mainly women) because a properly ordained priest is only available once a month.

On the Sunday we visited them, we went along to this service from 9:30 till 12. Church services usually last a long time, with lots of singing, mostly hymns that sound rather European but there was also a young people's choir who now and then sang some African songs which sounded beautiful. Half the church was filled with schoolchildren. It will be difficult to give all the children of this country a good future. At the end of the service we were asked to stand up and introduce ourselves, and we were thanked for the work we did, which was nice.

Usually you are seen as rich whites in the first place, people unashamedly ask for things once in a while, even people with a proper job. Can I have that necklace? Will you buy me a cool drink? Why don't you give that cardigan to me? The other day I was buying a sort of pie at our tuck shop and the garden boy turned up on one side and asked if I would buy him one, so I gave him half of my pie. Then the cleaner turned up at the other side asking for my pie, but I said I would have nothing left myself. Sometimes you get tired of it.

Who is the Lucky One?
Karen Andrae (India)

9:50pm – ten more minutes and my boyfriend will call. Though it is much too early, I leave my tiny little room and jump down the stairs to sit in the lobby and wait. I don't want to miss the call that I have been looking forward to over the past two weeks. In the hall, a few women are sitting around the table, reading or chatting, always with an eye on the only phonebox in the hostel serving about sixty women. You can't make calls – just receive them. So, if you want to talk to someone after the 9pm curfew you have to arrange a time to be called. Apparently, I am not the only one waiting and my heart sinks. I hope the other girls won't talk forever, I hope he will get through . . . .

I am employed as a Physiotherapy Trainer by the Spastics Society of Tamil Nadu and live in the Working Women's Hostel of the YWCA in Chennai (formerly Madras) in southern India. Initially, I was a little disappointed about the room of approximately eight square metres and the 'bathroom' at the other end of the corridor that I share with fourteen other women (would I be able to cover the distance in time if I had an acute onset of diarrhoea?) but got used to it quickly. The women on my floor are very nice and go out of their way to make me – the only white western woman in the house – feel welcome. But I do get lonely sometimes and long to hear my boyfriend's voice. While I am now taking my seat among the other waiting women they smile and nod. We chat a little, always keeping an eye on the phone.

9:57pm – Rashmi hangs up, finally. With a rather happy smile she returns to her room and the phone rings again. Lakshmi and Jeeva jump up. Lakshmi is quicker and answers – the call is for her. The other girls, including myself, disappointedly turn back to books and conversation. Every few moments I look at my watch and at Lakshmi. God, why does she have to talk for so long? Doesn't she realise that all of us are waiting for important calls?

10:00pm – Lakshmi is still on the phone and doesn't appear to have any intentions of hanging up any time soon, despite my repeated coughing and sighing. Outside, an old watchman slowly shuffles to our big front door. He meticulously locks the door from outside and even fastens a chain around the handle as if to make doubly sure. Then he shuffles away again. It is the first time I witness this daily routine. The Women's Hostel has a curfew starting at 9pm, and we may consider ourselves lucky as most other hostels expect the women to be at home at 7pm. After 9pm you need a special permit to leave the compound or to be let in by the guards at the front gate. No permit – no way in or out. They take their job as guards very seriously. So it is, 'No ma'am, you can't leave. It is too late to go out. Please go back to your room.'

Arriving at the physiotherapy clinic even in
torrential rain

And then there is the 10 o'clock lock up of our front door, which is only reopened early in the morning. We precious women have to be protected against intruders, bad people on the streets and ourselves, because we would surely 'go astray' if we were allowed to come and go as we pleased. So the hostel, it appears, has a responsibility towards our families and us.

Until now I didn't think too much about it. I was tired enough after the long daily trips to the seven communities I was visiting with my colleagues. I thought I was going to address the problem of my lack of freedom later when I had adjusted a little. But sitting here, watching the old man locking the only door to our building suddenly makes me cringe. What would happen if there was an emergency – a fire, for example? Would we all have to wait for this old guard to make his way over here and unlock the doors in time to save sixty desperate women from catastrophe? I suddenly feel quite vulnerable. God forbid that something happens. Locked doors and one phone from which you can't make outside call: that's not what I call reassuring, really. Eventually, I need to find another place to stay. As much as I like my floor mates, I am not prepared to reduce my social life to this hostel and ask for permission to go out. I am thirty years old and, come to think of it, I can't even remember the last time when I was told to be back at home at 9pm . . . .

Thank God, Lakshmi finally seems to be done with her call. What time is it? 10:08pm. Lakshmi puts down the receiver and the phone rings again immediately. She answers and turns to us. Three pairs of expectant eyes are upon her. Who's the lucky one this time?

'Karen, for you'.

She smiles at me, I jump from my chair and give her a big grin in return. But even while I make my way over to the phone I am conscious of the two remaining women waiting for their turn and I know I can't talk too long. Maybe I should arrange a later time for him to call. What a shame, I have so much tell him but some of it will have to wait.

'Hello love . . . .'

North-South
Jimmy Hendry (Namibia)

I had the problem the other day of one of my pupils stealing my compass. I know it was him as I saw him. Once the bell had gone, everyone made their way out. After the break he approached me to inform me that his pencil case had been stolen.

'Funny that, my compass is also missing,' I said. I told him, 'When my compass appears so might your missing pencil case.'

After ten minutes he had somehow found my compass and his pencil case appeared again an hour or so later, from somewhere.

What a surprise.

In Need of Attention
Tiina-Maria Levamo (Zambia)

At the dawn of the new millennium I felt physically miserable. I had severe pains in my stomach. The Canadian doctor in the Zambian capital of Lusaka was of the opinion that absolutely nothing was wrong with me.

The Zambian ultrasound scan, that coughing ancient machine from the '70s, showed that I was lonely. The young male nurse suggested that I should get a Zambian boyfriend and heal myself by going out on a date with him.

While he was scanning my stomach my eyes were following the movements of the crowds of cockroaches in the ceiling of the examination room. For a few seconds, I saw my life passing like a film on the screen.

The diagnosis of the specialist Indian doctor was that I was desperately homesick. The lady was in the mood for small talk, so I listened.

Finally she asked: 'Do you drink beer?'

I had to admit that I was not consuming beer much.

'That is exactly it,' she said, 'you should. You should drink much more beer, my dear.' She beamed with delight, shimmering in her golden sari.

That was the final conclusion and the Canadian doctor agreed. This case, the Finnish development worker, was to be sent back for diagnosis to her motherland. I needed to talk to a doctor of 'my own origin', to describe my symptoms in my own tribal language to someone from the same tribe. I could have not agreed more.

But I had not yet met Dr Rodwell Vongo, the traditional healer, who lived in Lusaka. That day, when I was about to loose my nerve in persuading the insurance company to pay for my trip to Finland, I met him.

He paid attention to me. He spent endless hours listening to my problems. He gave me some herb tea and suddenly I felt comfortable. The life in my body, let alone the pain in my stomach, was not that bad after all.

Later, back in Finland, when I was lying on an operating table in a hospital in

Helsinki, I somehow tended to agree that maybe I should have drunk more beer. I was able to count to eight and then I was gone, fully asleep and in the hands of the Finnish surgeon.

When I woke up the nurse was talking with her colleague on the phone, unhappy about her salary. Moreover, she was complaining how boring it was to work at the anaesthesia department. I asked for some water, but she was not interested in her patients. The doctor entered the room and said something which did not make any sense to me. I tried to interrupt her by saying that I was about to vomit.

In the evening, that same day, they asked me to pack my belongings and take a taxi home since there was not enough room in the hospital to keep me occupying one whole bed. I licked my wounds in an apartment in a block of flats in Helsinki. Even the neighbours did not care less what I had been going through.

Suddenly I missed Zambia and talking to Dr Vongo.

* * *

Back in Zambia, it was the rainy season. By a stroke of good luck, I slipped in some water and had a slight accident which damaged my little finger. I was so happy – I had finally a reason to go and see Dr Vongo again. I was longing to sit on his old leather sofa and tell him the story of my accident.

This article was first published in *Vihreä Lanka* newspaper.

Drawing a Line
Kinney Thiele (Sierra Leone)

Yes I've tasted guinea pig,
 monkey
and rat.

Yes I've nibbled baby birds,
bush beef
and cat.

We've stewed up lizards,
fricasseed a snake,
peeled and crumbled old dried fish
and chewed cassava cake.

I still hate okra.

YOU LEARN TO UNDERSTAND THE

LOCAL CULTURE: GOOD *AND* BAD

An Acceptable Alien
Jean Hales (Guyana)

We were going to Malali, a small village up the Demerara river, only accessible by boat. I was a wee bit apprehensive when the engine kept cutting out due to water in the carburettor, and we had to keep finding a landing spot to pull over so that the driver Malcolm, who we had only met once before on a boozy night when we had arranged the outing, could fix it. It was only then that I realised there were no oars in the boat, and no life jackets. No matter, he seemed to know what he was doing. We were chugging along nicely when suddenly figures appeared on the river bank. A group of about thirty men were waving and signalling for us to pull over. I thought that they wanted us to carry a message or a parcel upstream.

As we stepped off the boat we were surrounded by the crowd saying 'Welcome, welcome, we couldn't let you go by without saying hello, we hardly ever see any Europeans.' One was carrying a teapot. 'How nice,' I thought, 'they've made us a cup of tea.' It turned out to be the local brew. The men were stumbling over themselves to shake our hands and introduce themselves. 'Let me touch your hair, how do you get it so red? How come your eyes are so blue?'

I felt like a cross between an alien from outer space and Princess Diana. That's what is so fascinating about Guyana, it is a land of so many contrasts. It has technology: computers, the internet, email, cybercafés – I was once in an Amerindian village in the depths of the rainforest and they had a computer working from a generator – and of course all the latest sound system equipment; and yet there are people leading a way of life that has not changed for centuries.

Soyelsuren
Karen Harmatuk (Mongolia)

Soyelsuren escorted me across the barren steppe from my Russian-style apartment block to our school, a big brick building with a sports hall added onto one side, and a roof painted baby blue. The weather was warm. In Outer Mongolia at the end of August, the steppe and rolling mountains in the distance were still green and dotted with edelweiss.

It was my first day in Nisekh and I was moving into a Soviet-style apartment building and being introduced to the school where I would teach voluntarily for two years. Soyelsuren, or Soyela for short, was joined at my hip, escorting me to all the places I needed to be, which, that day, were many. In the early days of my arrival in Mongolia, Soyela was not only my counterpart in setting up an English programme, but also the personal guide I needed to cope with Mongolian life.

First thing that morning, we briefly met with Bayanjargal, the school director. Then, we were hurried into a crowded room where Soyela and I shared a chair during a staff meeting with eighty teachers. Next, we went up for my first look at my future classroom. It was an old listening centre whose desks remained bolted to the floor as wires ran through them. The walls were baby blue with orange trim. Within a few minutes, we were told to attend another meeting, this time with the language and history department. Just as it got underway, Soyela excused ourselves (which she was politely good at), so we could catch a lift to the market in Ulaanbaatar, about a half-hour from our community of Nisekh. Only we had no money to go to market with. Business and travel seemed to be two things that never ran smoothly in Mongolia. Having Soyela as my anchor made it easier to cope with the uncertainty. In fact, spontaneity became fun as I could laugh with Soyela about it, or chat during the waiting periods that break up frenzies of events. This first day with Soyela was a taste of what was to come.

Getting the money needed for market that day, for example. We went to Soyela's father's who broke the key to his safe, who took us to someone who could mend it who, unfortunately, said this would take many hours. So we went to the volunteer agency's office. That day was a glimpse of the whirlwind lifestyle that is often commonplace in a volunteer's life. It could be draining or entertaining, depending upon how the volunteer looked at it.

In contrast to the day's pace, the evening was mellower. When everyone checking on my housing needs, nailing bars on my windows, and redoing my locks had departed, Soyela asked if she could stay until her two and a half-year-old woke up.

'Of course,' I answered.

When Kholan awoke, Soyela breast-fed her and we had tea. We started chatting by discussing professions, and then the changes that occurred since the Russians packed up and left Mongolia in the early 1990s. While cradling Kholan, Soyela shared her life history with me. She was born 30 km outside Ulaangom, the provincial capital of Uvs. Her mother had five children, Soyela and her brother Enkhbold were the only two still alive. At eighteen, Soyela came to Ulaanbaatar to study. Soyela's mother died and her father moved to the city. Then Soyela married and moved into a flat in Nisekh, by the airport, where she had her first baby, Amiinaa.

Meanwhile, Soyela's husband worked along Mongolia's border with Russia. On the job, he was chasing a Russian thief when his car crashed, resulting in his death. Amiinaa was one year old. Because Soyela had a flat and a teaching job, she coped. Later, she married a man she had known from her days in secondary school in the countryside. He didn't drink vodka then.

'Now, he drinks too much,' she confided.

She assured me that when he wasn't drinking, he was a kind, smart, responsible man. When he drank, he could lash out. Her friends had varying opinions about drinking and violence, some supporting the prospect of divorcing violent husbands, others suggesting that children need to be with a mother and father, thought violent outbursts tolerable. It was hard for me to listen without sharing my opinion. I wished to remain the observer of Mongolian culture, trying to affect it as little as possible by my Canadian perspective. (My mere presence, however, meant that I was already having an impact on the community, so I struggled with my own hypocrisy.) Growing up in urban Toronto, where the media publicises support programs for violence against women, made it hard for me to restrain myself. Not to mention the human instinct to protect those you feel close to.

'If you're ever scared, you can come here with your children,' I told her.

Soyela took me to her brother's *ger*, or *yurt*, the traditional felt tent many Mongolians live in today as they did many years ago, although not all gers fit the romantic nomadic stereotype. In Nisekh, many were hooked up to electricity, and boasted stereos, fridges, and television sets.

She brought me a silvery-grey *del* (traditional Mongolian dress), the colour of a rain cloud.

'You should wear this del to school,' she kindly suggested. 'I will get you another del to wear in the street.' Later, she showed me how to belt it. (One must tie fabric around the waist in a certain way so that it doesn't come undone, and make sure it's folded in the front and back at the waist. Over my two years, teachers would constantly readjust my clothing while chatting with me, as I never seemed to do it quite right. In fact, it seemed people habitually touched each other in this way, as a socially acceptable gesture of affection. Sometimes I felt like every Mongolian woman was my mother.)

Daily routines and errands were important threads of our relationship. Contemplating life issues together was another.

Soyela talked to lawyers about divorcing her husband. To make her divorce clean, friends advised Soyela to give her youngest daughter to her husband. Kholan was his daughter, whereas Amiinaa was the daughter of her first husband. This way, her current husband would have no reason to visit her. Hence, in theory, he would leave her alone. I listened, trying to withhold judgement, but I couldn't help feeling shocked. Giving up your baby daughter to make your life easier? They made movies about this sort of thing in North America.

In Mongolia, children didn't belong to one set of parents as blatantly as they did in present-day Canada. Instead, the extended family and the community as a whole cared for little ones. In my experience of Mongolia, there was a stronger sense of community responsibility, which carried over into family and professional life. I felt my home culture could learn from this.

On a personal level, not only Soyela, but also the community of Nisekh took responsibility for me. When I was sick, neighbours brought me berries. At other times, they brought me meat when they killed an animal, yoghurt when they'd been to the countryside, and an iron or a big pot when they saw I needed one. Parents even sent their teenage girls over to spend time with me and the director got me a TV so I wouldn't be lonely. Everyone in the community shared in caring for me, something I'd never experienced in Canada. In all fairness, I had grown up in downtown Toronto, followed by six years of life in urban Montreal. Perhaps what I viewed as a difference in Mongolian versus Canadian culture was more the contrast between big city versus country life. Soyela was my gateway to the whole community.

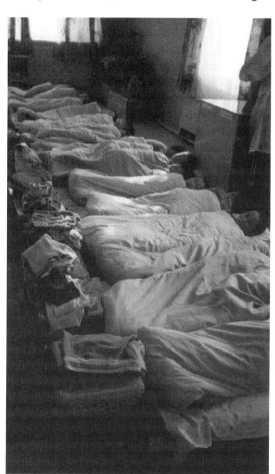

Rest time at school

In the workplace that Soyela and I shared, my value of community responsibility grew even more. Russians had a strong influence in Mongolia from the early 1900s until 1990. Among other institutions, they set up kindergartens and schools. Soyelsuren had studied abroad in Russia as part of her training to become a Russian-language teacher. The year before my arrival, she had been retrained, as had many others had, to become an English teacher. Schools were organised in such a way that groups and subgroups were assigned tasks to complete. The onus was rarely on the

On horseback

individual. It followed that teaching tasks were not my sole responsibility in Mongolia; everyone was a vital resource to me. I had felt alone in Canadian classrooms, fending for myself, sheepishly asking for help from busy colleagues.

Through teaching and living with Soyela, I was learning of the real-life values of all cultures. When you're in the fog of your own culture, you can't look at it, examine it, question it in the same way as you can from afar. When you live day in, day out, in the thick haze of a valley bottom, you aren't even aware that the clarity of a mountain peak exists. Through my friendship with Soyela, and my immersion into the community of Nisekh, I came to experience this clarity. In practical terms, I had more professional support in Mongolia than I had ever had in Canada. Soyelsuren, as my counterpart, was the main pillar.

So it followed that I noticed my own tendencies more profoundly from this new vantage point. For example, I was self-centred. When Soyela couldn't come to work, or plan the curriculum with me, or visit the methodology centre to collect resources for teaching, I got frustrated. Her absences made it hard for me to accomplish professional goals. Work never seemed to be a priority for her. How was I supposed to make a valuable contribution to education in Mongolia without the support of my local counterpart?

Self-reflection, followed by self-transformation came out of my friendship with Soyela. Soyela had legitimate reasons for missing work. Her best friend's mother died, her brother was tied up and gagged while working security on the night shift, her father's health was poor, her daughters needed medicine, she needed to visit the hospital . . . . Health, friends and family came before work. Through Soyela, I grew more compassionate. I began to understand Mongolian culture. How absurd it was that professional life in Canada often came at the expense of personal well-being. Seventy-hour workweeks, divorces, disconnected families and fast food became traits I remembered of Canada.

Unexplained Forces
Kenneth Carano (Suriname)

I was always agnostic. We agnostics are curious cynics by nature. A part of it is searching, overanalysing, and yearning for a feeling that always seems illogical. At least that is what it always was for me. I needed it spelled out to me. Faith had never been enough. For me seeing was believing.

My experience as a Peace Corps volunteer in the rain forest of Suriname, made me re-evaluate that position. I lived with a tribe of Maroons who were descendants of runaway African slaves still living in Suriname's interior. The jungle had always provided them a safe haven from the perceived western corruption and allowed them to continue their traditional practices like their ancestors in Africa.

It was like living inside the pages of National Geographic. The village was an enclave of thatched-roof houses. The community was run by a captain and what he said was absolute until death. Women walked around half-naked. Mothers and children washed clothes and dishes on rocks at the river. Villagers carried buckets on their head. Men fished for large piranha and hunted wild animals to provide meat for their multiple wives and children. Naked children ran around with their bloated bellies and pencil-thin limbs exposing the lack of nutrition prevalent here. At night the mesmerising sounds of old African-style drums and the traditional dance of the *awasa* could be heard as I lay in bed. But it was the *obeahman*, Tisade, and the many charms of this culture's ethereal ways that captivated me.

Obeah, a form of African witchcraft mixed in with Christian terminology and symbols. So feared is it that most places in the West Indies have outlawed it under penalty of death.

Obeahmen ply their trade of sorcery and divination with curses and poisonous herbs. They are known for their revenge hexes designed to murder the offending victim and considered to be 'four-eyed', a reference to their ability to contact the spirit world.

Tisade told me it was called 'catching winti'. It was a part of their obeah beliefs. It was when the spirit of one's ancestor entered another's body and took control of it. Of course I was sceptical. I came across this phenomenon within the first week of settling into my new living arrangement in the jungle. I was lying in my hammock reading a book in the shade.

A village man, wearing only a loincloth around his waist called a *kamisa* and some cloth tied around his neck to resemble a cape, marched past me with his arms swinging cartoonishly back and forth and his legs taking exaggerated high steps. He was spouting gibberish as he passed by on his way to the obeahman's house. A few minutes later he was running past me in the opposite direction. Tisade, the hobbit-looking obeahman, gave chase as his eyes were glazed over and bulging out and he was swinging a machete. I supposed even the obeahman thought the man was demented.

Scenes like that played themselves out on a weekly basis in the village. One in particular caught my attention. It was early afternoon, usually a very quiet part of the day. The sun was beating down. A couple of men were building a small table out of thin tree limbs in front of my neighbour's house. Once the table was in order they made a three-sided fence out of tree limbs to surround the table. The fence was decorated with thin green palm fronds draped over it. A bowl of leaves and water, covered by madras fabric, was placed on top of the table. The area around the fence was sprinkled with water and a white powder. They were preparing obeah.

A few minutes later a young man, dressed only in a kamisa, entered the area and began chanting. Tisade joined in and the young man began shaking a moracca. My neighbour, an elderly women, was then brought inside the fence. The men directed their chanting towards her and soon her normal subdued manner changed to one of ecstasy. She began dancing around while leaning forward, right arm behind her back, bursting out in occasional laughter and chanting with a distant and crazed look in her eyes. She had caught *winti*.

One morning in early January, as the village was still going through new year's ceremonies, I came across another strange scene. While walking around the village, I saw eight people sitting on wooden stools outside a house while two men were standing one behind the other balancing an eight-foot long plank on their heads. A third man stood nearby appearing to ask the plank questions. The two men, balancing the plank, would move back and forth as if the plank was directing their movements. It was like watching a human ouija board. Tisade told me they did this every year to ask the spirits when they can begin the planting season, the best places to plant, what they should plant, where the best hunting is and other questions they deemed necessary to their survival.

These events were all thought-provoking, but the straw that broke the camel's back was the death of a villager, a sixty-seven-year-old man named Pansa, and the circumstances surrounding his death that made me revise my philosophy. Specifically, it was the casket. Everything else I could manage to explain away. Maybe someone had been mentally unstable. Maybe the plants had been hallucinogenic. Maybe the will of their unconscious mind had made someone inadvertently influence the planks they had balanced. For the casket I could not find a logical explanation.

Just after 1am I was awakened by the sound of gunshots and eerie wailing sounds in the darkness outside. I put some clothes on. The gunshots had ceased, but the sound of women crying hysterically continued. I opened the door, crept down the steps of my house, and walked in the darkness toward the sound of the people wailing.

Five houses down people were gathered and sitting down outside a house. Pansa had just been discovered dead in his sleep. The gunshots were fired in the air to announce a death to the village. Everyone would sit around the house until dawn out of respect to the newly deceased. A couple of hours into our vigil a fine mist began to fall. At the same time, I could hear a couple of voices inside the house begin chanting. Then I heard a woman yell, 'Come help me! Come help me!'

Within seconds a young man wearing only a yellow kamisa ran outside of the house. The rain started coming down heavier. At first, I could not tell who it was because of the pouring rain. But then I caught a glimpse. It was Joe, an apprentice to Tisade, and his eyes were glazed. There were at least fifty of us sitting outside the house. We all stood and watched him. Someone placed a mortar in front of the young man. Another person brought over some leaves. Joe began pounding the leaves into the mortar with his fists and elbows while continuing in his tongues-like chatter and dancing around in his winti stupor.

After a few minutes, he stopped pounding and started marching around, while still squatting, chanting and flexing his muscles as if he was trying to break a chain. Then an older woman stripped off her shirt, jumped on top of the mortar and began dancing on the leaves, half-naked and wailing. As this went on, Pansa's widow was escorted out of the house and she started washing her body with the leaves.

By daybreak what had begun as a death mourning had, as was characteristic when someone died here, turned into a virtual revelry of grand proportions. After the widow had been washed with leaves the festivities moved to the area next to the dwelling where the body would lie until burial, the dead house. Drums played for the next few hours, villagers danced ecstatically, and more tribesmen caught winti. Some of the spirit filled people were swinging machetes in the air as they danced. A few others had white powder rubbed over their lean, chiselled bodies, hopped around like frogs and leaped into short, thin trees in front of a nearby shrine. Some villagers danced on one leg in a circle outlined with palm leaves, while many others let themselves be taken away by the soothing rhythms of the drums as they danced the traditional awasa. The gaiety would continue nearly unhindered for the next two days. The party was only put on hold for us to build the casket and dig the hole at the sacred burial ground hidden in the bush.

On the third day it was time to bury Pansa. The burial ceremony was to begin at the dead house and the casket would be carried to the burial site hidden in the bush about a kilometre and a half away. At noon all the villagers gathered around the dead house. The casket, carrying the deceased, was placed on top of a wooden base that sat on the dirt floor in the middle of the dead house. The box was decorated with many pieces of bright madras fabric. One person beat on a drum and another person held a tree limb up about ten feet away from the coffin. Six people lifted the wooden base that supported the coffin and began to carry it. In the next fifteen minutes, a bizarre scene ensued.

The people carrying the heavy load would walk backward and forward, zig-zagging around, and nearly running over onlookers. Every couple of minutes the men would come to a halt and a couple of them would drop out as new villagers would help carry it. Eventually, I was pushed out of the crowd into the way of the casket and told to relieve one of the weary pall bearers. As I helped carry the casket I realised it seemed to have a mind of its own. The pall bearers had not been the ones directing it in circles. The casket was controlling the movements.

I could feel a force from the casket running down my spine and dictating the movements of my legs. The casket was the puppet-master and I was the puppet – never had I been so out of control. This went on for a few minutes. My mind was in daze. It felt like a dream. An imaginary giant mural of psychedelic colours spun in front of me. I was light-headed and dizzy, like a feather. If anyone was to blow on me I felt sure I would be carried away.

Just as I was at the peak of my euphoria, Tisade came running out of the dead house. He circled the casket, eyes bulging, jumping up and down, tossing white powder on the casket and yelling, 'Enough, enough, enough. It is time for you to leave.' The casket began to drag us out of the village and took us to its final resting place as the obeahman continued to circle around, tossing white powder and shouting out orders to the box all the while. The remainder of the ceremony was rather anti-climactic. A few words were spoken as they lowered the coffin into the hole, and I stood in the background still shaking and trying to rationalise a logical explanation for this experience.

The following morning Tisade came over to my house. He said, 'Never write about what you have participated in or death will accompany you.'

'As you wish,' I replied and meant it. . . .

Freckles
Stephanie Lemieux (South Africa)

I sat with the small South African girl, discussing birthday parties, favourite books, and whether or not frogs believed in God. I had been teaching pre-school at the Sithabile children's shelter for two months, and was amazed at how quickly the children had entrenched themselves in my life; I loved them, fully and fiercely.

And so, on this bright and breezy January day, I dug my bare toes in the warm sand, shielded my eyes from a sun that would only get hotter, and savoured the comfortable companionship of young Jabu (not her real name).

Jabu, a precocious six-year-old child with bright eyes and an engaging smile, tugged absently at my sleeve as she chattered. Suddenly she stopped, staring intently at my arm.

'What's wrong?' I asked, a little bit concerned.

'What's that?' she replied, touching my freckles with hesitant fingers, as though the small brown spots may be fragile or dangerous.

'Freckles,' I said, laughing. 'They come when I spend lots of time in the sun.'

She contemplated that quietly for a moment, before lifting her eyes and asking me in a voice filled with wonder, 'So you mean you're the same colour as me underneath?'

I looked down at her, and I burst into laughter, thinking, 'Aw, how cute.' After a moment I realised that she wasn't laughing. Jabu, quiet and intent, was waiting for a serious answer to a serious question.

I looked at this little girl who was born in a country that, until shortly before her birth, stated by law that she was inferior to her white countrymen. I remembered taking her younger sister to a hospital, where white nurses glanced at the small child in my arms, and then stared coldly at me before walking away without a word and ignoring us for hours. I re-lived the moment when I realised, with a sort of sick horror, that both white and black South Africans were glaring at me and my black friend as we walked down the street together. And I suddenly wondered just how serious her question was.

Jabu held my gaze, cocked her head, waited. I considered her question again, this time thinking not of those people who had made my heart ache, but of those who had made my heart swell with respect and admiration. I thought of the South Africans of every hue that I'd met, people who were co-operating and working together to build the new South Africa. I remembered these people – the Zulu women who had fought apartheid in the 1970s and been exiled; the Afrikaans woman who married her black lover despite her family's protests; the English-speaking white teacher who opened a free school in the slums of Soweto; the Indian family who showed up at the Child Care Centre with a truck full of food.

They were all good people, people who respected and took care of each other. The new South Africa belonged to these people; they were giving birth to it, and the process was slow and painful, but also shining and beautiful.

I looked down at the little girl who was gazing up at me with trust and love in her eyes, and suddenly I knew, deep in my heart, that the world was a good place and that she would one day make it even better.

Slowly, I nodded and then wrapped my arms around my young friend. 'Yes, Jabu, underneath I'm the same colour as you.'

A Connection in the Amazon Basin
Miranda Thomson (Ecuador)

When I spotted Pascual's mother on her way to the river, I rapidly tried to remember the word for hello in Achuar. I was used to the women not replying, not even looking at me in response. So as I shyly mumbled 'wina jai', I was most surprised to see her turn towards me. She grabbed my hands, held them to her and smiled, a gloriously open, toothless smile. It was over in a flash so I hope that in my surprise I smiled back.

It was at that moment that I realised how special teaching English as a volunteer at Kapawi was. All the tremendous difficulties in dealing with this strange culture, being scared of the isolation and disease and being so wet and dirty all the time felt worth it.

Kapawi is the name of both an eco-lodge and an Achuar community that lie in Amazonian Ecuador. The lodge was started in 1993 as a joint venture between the FINAE, the Achuar federation and a tour operator to build a hotel for eco-tourism on land neighbouring the Kapawi community.

The goal of the lodge was to provide, through eco-tourism, a monthly means of support and jobs for the Achuar. In ten years, the lodge and all the installations will belong entirely to the Achuar and will be managed by them. I was brought in to teach the new generation of Achuar students in the Kapawi community school. It is these students who in ten years' time will be part of the team managing the lodge and who will find English useful to communicate with the tourists there.

Unknown in origin, the Achuar now occupy huge extensions of Ecuador and Peru's rainforest. The name Achuar comes from the Jivaro word *achu* meaning '*morete*' – a sort of palm that occurs in flooded areas and *shuar*, meaning people. Thus these people living in flat and flooded regions are known as *achushuar*, 'people of morete', or in brief Achuar.

The Achuar territory is 4,700 square kilometres of some of the last major trakless and roadless rainforests of the Amazon basin. It is truly a wild place, one of the last frontiers between man and nature in the world. From Kapawi to the nearest town is a two-week canoe trip. You can also take a tiny plane and watch uninterrupted tree tops for over an hour before landing on a dirt strip in the middle of an Achuar community.

I came to Kapawi as a volunteer English teacher but was at times nurse,

A view of Miranda's workplace

environmental educator, barmaid and guide. It was a role that gave me almost constant contact with the Achuar people. Trying to communicate with people from such an alien culture who have such different experiences in life is extremely hard and takes constant adaptation on both sides. I had an amazing opportunity since I was the first volunteer to work in the Kapawi community though others before me had worked in the lodge.

The Achuar were not contacted by outsiders until the early 1970s and even now live very traditional lives. Each member of the community has a distinct role according to their sex. Women work in the *chacra*, or garden, collecting the manioc to make the *nijiamanch* or manioc beer, a staple in the Achuar diet. They also do all the cooking and look after the children. The men help with community work, fish and hunt, often still with blowpipes. Men are also the leaders and the *shamans* of the communities.

For all its traditional roots, life in Kapawi community has been changing. A Salesian mission has been there for the last five years, a quartet of warm, lively Mexican nuns led by Sister Conchita whose home-made tortillas were wonderful. They had started the high school where I was teaching and recruited the other teachers. Among them was Luis, a happy, smiling dreamer from Quito who became my best friend there. They had introduced music, football and hygiene, though the first two were the more popular imports.

On my first day at the lodge, I was taken to the community to meet Sister Conchita and Luis. I think they were astonished to see such a rare creature as me – tall, blonde and blue-eyed.

I quickly realised that teaching was going to be a real challenge. Luis was the designated English teacher in the high school, even though he spoke no English.

Moreover, there were no books, music or radio in English and obviously no television or films. Sister Conchita and Luis told me that I was to teach two classes: Básico, whose students ranged between ages 12 and 18 years old, and Sexto who were the most advanced students where the oldest was 25. I was to start teaching the following week.

After a weekend of complete culture shock and a forty-minute walk through the rainforest to get to the school, I was met by Luis at the classroom door and given an enthusiastic introduction to the Sexto class. I was terrified. The classroom was a tin-roofed hut built recently by the government. It had a small blackboard at one end and a row of desks with eight expectant students.

I had planned to teach a greeting dialogue and so began slowly, 'Hello, how are you? My name is Miranda, I am from Britain, I have one brother and one sister.' The class was soon flowing, and I had one of the students in no time telling me 'My name is Marco, I am from Wayusensa and I have nineteen brothers and sisters.'

Several of my students (Antonio, Pascual, the two Mattiuses and Chowe) were among the most able students in the territory. Antonio was probably the best. He was extremely confident, always answering first and explaining to the rest of the class. To be a good speaker is a much admired ability in the Achuar culture so I am sure Antonio is destined to be a local leader.

Unlike Sexto students, Básico were still struggling with Spanish and, since they already spoke Quichua and Achuar, English was their fourth language. I wondered if they actually needed it. It was difficult to keep their attention so I ended up inventing games which usually meant repeating 'My name is . . , his name is . . .' endlessly. It was the only way to get everyone involved, especially the girls, who were so shy. Still it was always a struggle to get them to repeat the same material every class. I often wished that I had more ideas for games to play with them in English.

As well as teaching my students I also had time with them as they walked me back to the lodge after classes. This was when I had first met Pascual's mother. He and I had stopped off at his house for him to change and I was waiting in the visitor's part of the house when she offered me some of the ever present nijia-manch. We then surreptitiously watched each other from opposite ends of the house. It was these moments of intimate cultural exchange which I began to treasure.

Achuar houses are divided into two halves – the *tankamash*, the male area of the house used for greeting visitors, where women are not allowed except in serving nijiamanch to visitors, and the *ekent*, the women's part of the house.

Achuar women are not allowed to work in the lodge nor are they allowed much interaction with strange men. Women from the outside with their equal working roles are, therefore, treated with deep suspicion. For my first week in this very remote spot, where I was one of only two women employees at the lodge, none of the Achuar spoke to me. It was only after this trial period that things became more comfortable.

The patriarchal culture of the Achuar was not the only issue. In the middle of the rainforest there is every sort of bug, parasite, spider, snake and disease that you've thought of. In my first week, I was covered by microscopic, extremely itchy mites. They especially liked underwear. At Kapawi you just take it one day at a time.

There were also countless cases of malaria including a friend whom I had to nurse. We were once called to a house to help with a boy

Miranda's farewell

of six who was having a seizure from malaria, we were told. Unfortunately by the time we arrived the boy had died in his mother's arms. As I stood outside the house, one of the Achuar men I was with went in picked the boy up from his mother and laid him on the floor, covering his face. All this time all the family present was silent, no-one, not even the mother, cried.

So was the isolation, the disease and other difficult jungle realities worth it for me, as a volunteer, in the end? Were my efforts useful to the Kapawi community? I was absolutely exhausted by the time I left, both physically and mentally, though not sick. I was also only there for two months, not enough time to teach much of a complex language.

As I left Kapawi on my last day, taking a photo of the students, I thought how much I had learned from them. It had been an exchange of knowledge. They had learned from me as well – who I am, how I am different from them.

It is their generation that will have to fight for their freedom to continue in the world, fight the oil companies trying to enter their land, the loggers and colonists. The only weapon in their fight is education. If through learning English and understanding outside cultures they were taught to value what they have but to understand what the outside world can give them, it gives them choice. They can choose how they want to live and not have it thrust upon them. If Antonio, Pascual and the rest can be educated to understand the outside world they will be better equipped to fight for their land and their people. If in any small way I helped them to do that, my effort was worth the many challenges of Kapawi.

Coping with Winter
Holly Twiname (China)

The temperature has finally dropped here in Zhoukou . . . and I'm getting into the Chinese way of dealing with the harsh weather conditions, like layering my clothes. The trick is to wear five layers or more underneath your jumper and trousers. Everyone looks that little bit more chunky these days, especially children. They get padded out with layer upon layer of clothing.

The layering is quite necessary here, not because it's much colder than, say, England – it's just that there is generally little heating anywhere, so there is no refuge from the cold, apart from during the day when you can secure a place in the sun. Inside is always colder than outside. Insulation in the houses is very poor so even though I am lucky to have a free-standing heater, most of the heat just escapes.

In class I have taken to doing activities which require students to move around a bit because otherwise they would need defrosting by the end of the lesson. I'm usually okay as I'm standing up and walking around anyway. Some classes have taken to nailing cardboard to the bottom of their desks, to stop their legs from feeling cold (they have to spend most of the day in the classroom – 8am to 9pm – apart from ten-minute breaks between each lesson, lunch between 12 and 2:30, and dinner 4:30 to 7pm).

The day before yesterday a friend of mine (a teacher from the English department) invited me to eat at her house and told me just how important it is to eat *jao zi* (small dumplings) that day. Apparently, if you don't your ears will fall off. Not wanting to go against tradition, I ate and ate and ate (I wasn't taking any chances).

Getting Closer
Christian Brackin (Thailand)

Of these friends, I've become the closest with a Canadian woman. She has been here a few months longer than we have, and is looking at a much longer stretch of time here. She's also had her share of pre-Thailand life stories that we hear bits of from time to time, and though she is younger than me by a few years, I still consider her an older sister. Maybe it's because we talk openly about the constipation I had the first few months, or maybe it's that she offers her emotional reactions to the situation around her before I ask for them (I would have asked anyway, but she has a way of leaving space for me to offer my own perspective as well).

Whatever wonderful, non-verbal bond our emotional bodies are doing, it's the healthiest feeling I've ever had around a person I've only known for three months. On one visit she made to Mae Sai we were complaining about one of the Thai habits that continually trips us up, the tendency that people have to discount the competency of any *farang*, especially one who doesn't speak Thai, and she burst out: *'Ah ha!* You're jaded! You're jaded! I was jaded after three months, too!'

Something in that statement made me realise the timelessness of the experience. I thought of all the farangs who have come to Thailand, all the generations of Thai children who have been taught to identify them on sight with the loud cry 'Farang! Farang!' and how in this way we foreigners will always see the Thailand that is provided for tourists.

One Thai woman was speaking to me about an island that has become a designated spiritual retreat location. My first reaction was to mention that it is good for the Thai economy, foreigners in any country will pay exorbitant fees to have access to monasteries and temples where they can feel the ancient connection between the human and the divine, and to have so much foreign money coming in with such a small need from the local people is a great source of income.

Then I realised the error of my statement. There is a very strong understanding of respect for the religion here, though many tourists don't catch on before they violate at least one of the customs that honour Thailand's many holy places. In my own country the indigenous people keep their silence about holy rituals, preferring to be misunderstood rather than violated. In Thailand, there is an air of tolerance from both sides. The foreigners will condescend to remove their shoes, and even bow to the buddha before snapping photos inside the temple, and the locals will teach their children to look out for the big lumbering farangs.

It made me realise how difficult it is to really understand the inside of a culture. At least I can take the trouble to find out more about Thailand, though. And, hopefully, the Thais I get to know will see a different type of farang from the tourists.

Raisa
Sophie Forbes (Uzbekistan)

She emerged into the scatter of children as I passed down the dusty road and began to speak to me. She said hello in Russian and I responded with, 'Assalom Allaykum'. Her name was Raisa and she lived four houses down from me, behind a tan metal door. Her dark hair was streaked with grey, though I saw the reddish tinge of unflattering dye. She patted the wiry mesh, in a hasty remaking of her forward appearance. Smiling silently, her teeth showed yellow, stained from the unrecorded years of tea drinking. She switched quickly to the native language, discarding the instituted sounds of an empire nine years dead.

Making sentences easy enough for me to understand, she asked, 'How are you? How is America?'

And I answered, 'Good, good.'

'Come in for a cup of tea?'

'Oh not today, I must go home.'

Her eyes drowned in the failing light and their shadows left me feeling silly with my refusal. I turned away, soon listening to the many, 'HelloHello-HelloHellos' of the street children.

'Tell me about the old woman who lives down the street,' I asked Delia.

The answer mingled with the smoke of the pot that cooked over the gas flame. She never wanted to respond to my curious questions, and so she never did. I was researching the ancient Silk Road and its affect on the cuisine of Uzbekistan. I arrived young in years, with no husband or children, facts that were as alien to her as my cookbooks and measuring spoons. She frowned at my culinary certificate and wondered why my mother had not taught me to cook as hers had.

The next day, as I carried a bag of strawberries up to my front door, I heard Raisa's raspy voice echo in stilted Uzbek. 'Hello. How are you? How much were the strawberries?'

I began to imagine her life, as I drank up my strawberries in the yoghurt they sweetened. I had only seen what the gate's door reflected. But who was this woman? 'Tell me about the old woman who lives down the street,' I asked Delia again, as she taught me how to make the local rice dish. I listened to the swirling disregard that stirred out of her mouth, as I cut the onions and carrots for the *pilov*. Delia liked to teach me how to make the dishes she learned as a young girl. We often sat in the small kitchen forming a friendship as we exchanged cooking techniques.

The next time I saw Raisa, she beckoned me to a standstill. She did not ask me in for a cup of black tea with cherries. Her upturned palm bent and disappeared out of sight, into the pocket of her red, washed-out house dress. The vines of the flowers curved gracefully around her body, twisting and mimicking the movements of her arm. I had noticed before the dull sheen of her clothes. They were old and bought with lost roubles. Finally, her hand emerged with a small cardboard box.

At first I thought it was a gift. People were always revealing possessions to me. She told me her daughter had sent it to her from Israel – something for her diabetes. Yet it was useless in its foreign lettered alphabet that she could not read. 'Come for tea,' I said. 'Come later and I will read.'

There was still light when a slight knock sounded hollow on our door. I suppose Delia and the others expected a different, more familiar face. Their surprise reached high into their laugh lines, creating false welcomes. Greetings were passed, waterlogged with unsaid thoughts. The unsettling silence hung expressionless on everyone's mouth. I wondered what the past had wrought. I led Raisa to the courtyard table and asked her for the box. I stood with my back straight, trying to fend off the awkwardness of the situation. I hoped that Delia would greet Raisa with some famous Uzbek hospitality: a pot of black tea, round bread, and jam. None appeared.

I opened the little box and pulled out the directions. Then I lifted out various pieces. I set them out like an after-dinner dessert. I found a small triangular razor blade, meant to prick the finger red, an eye-drop tube to collect it up with, and a slide upon which to place it. Then there was the machine that analysed the blood. The paper read: this machine measures how close or far from diabetic shock one is at the time of carrying out the test. I wondered if it would tell a helpful fortune, for not much insulin landed in the snug white pockets of the local clinic's doctors.

I attempted to explain the technology. Raisa's eyebrows met and fought the confusion that sampled her mouth. Soon Delia's husband and son jumped upon the words I released. They understood my wide-spaced, mispronounced Uzbek. They related my thoughts in forceful Russian. I quieted their deep voices and harsh swift motions with a few questions.

'Do you understand?'

'No. Where do I put the blood?'

'Here.' I pricked my index finger and placed the blood on the shiny clear top of a slide.

'Okay.'

'Can you get blood from your finger?'

'Like this?' As she pushed up her shirt sleeve her cuff reached above her wrist bone. Old scars revealed nightmares of a world gone bad. Numbers that marked a time in history that few smile upon.

I began to suspect the mistake I had stepped in to. I looked over my shoulder and saw the ugly disgust that contorted their faces. Raisa was of the 'other' group, the one Uzbeks had been occupying for seventy years. In fact, it was in this very house that the 'others' once lived. Indelible Stars of David decorated the corners of rooms now belonging to this Muslim family, a place affordable only with the disintegration of a way of life that no-one ever dreamed would end.

Suddenly a bubble of her blood popped out of her skin. I gave her the slide with my own blood. Raisa's and mine commingled there as if mixed by an unfathomable ancient history.

I heard grumblings against her just after the courtyard door had closed. A current of dislike circled us as we sat around the pilov dish. I imagined Delia's hate lodging in the minds of her young children, as their ears imbibed the hiss against Raisa and her otherness. Her small face bent in harmful anger, the type that slowly strangles hearts of the innocent.

'Never would an Uzbek do something like that,' sprayed Delia.

'It is because she is Jewish,' responded her husband, Hakimjon. He patted his hand into the rice and ate.

I wondered about this family I had lived with for over a year. What would they say of me, their 'adopted' American daughter, when they learn that I, too, am Jewish?

Libasse
Susan Rosenfeld (Senegal)

Four years before coming to Senegal, I met a group of Senegalese students in Italy. We became fast friends and it was through them that I became interested in Senegal. I was very eager to see them on 'their own turf' and to meet their families.

A recently-arrived Peace Corps trainee, I'd been in Senegal no more than ten days when I figured out how to leave a message for one friend to tell him I was there, eager to see him. I didn't know where he lived, but he worked in the Presidential Palace. Finding the palace, huge, white, imposing, and elegant, was simple enough, but once there, then what? Two stern-looking palace guards, bearing rifles and staring straight ahead stood at the gates. Despite the heat, they wore heavy, cumbersome uniforms, bright red with gold buttons, and ornate headdresses. I approached one and asked where I might leave a message for an employee. He motioned to the gate house.

The gatekeeper wore a similar uniform, but his was blue. He didn't carry any arms that I could see. He told me that the person I wanted to see was travelling, but I could leave a message, which I did.

Later that day, back at the lycée that was our home during training, a visitor pulled up on a mobylette and asked for 'Susie'. Nobody called me Susie any longer, but as there was no-one else there named Susie, Sue, Susan, Suzanne, or Susannah, people rightly assumed that he was looking for me. He also worked at the palace, shared a mailbox with my friend, and was his next-door neighbour. He was bringing a message from Isse, my friend's wife. I was invited to her house for lunch on Sunday. I gladly accepted the invitation and eagerly awaited the day, excited and nervous. I was excited because I was finally going to meet a family about which I had heard so much for so long. And I was going to have a chance to spend an afternoon with a Senegalese family. I felt I already knew this family. The oldest child was Libasse, a boy of ten. Then came Mantou, a girl of eight, and finally there was Seydi, the baby, only two.

I was nervous because I had never yet spent any time away from the comfortable protective 'womb' of our training programme at the lycée. I wanted to do everything correctly à la sénégalaise, but how much did I really know? What if I made some terrible, gauche, insensitive, cross-cultural mistake? To compound my worries, my friend, the father of these kids, wasn't even going to be there to tell me what to do, to introduce me to the family, and to smooth things over if I made a mistake.

I found the place with no problem and was able to recognise Isse, Libasse, and Mantou from photos I had seen. The baby had to be Seydi. But there was another child, of about five, whose presence I couldn't explain.

'Is he a neighbour?' I asked.

'No; he's ours too,' replied Isse.

'What?' I never heard about him. 'Who is he? All these years I only heard about three children.'

'Yes; I know,' said Isse. 'My husband always forgets this one. That's because Djiby was born right after he went to Italy, so they didn't meet until almost a year later.'

It surprised me that anyone could 'forget' a child, but there he was.

We sat around making small talk and looking at photos until it was time for lunch. Isse asked me, 'Do you want to *lekk loxo* (eat with your hand) or do you want a spoon?'

Determined to show how assimilated I was, I hastily answered, 'Oh no; no spoon. I always eat rice with my hand.' That seemed to please, and somewhat surprise, everyone. And while it is true that I always ate rice with my hand, it was also true that I was not very skilled at it. You see, I am left-handed. In West Africa, as in many other parts of the world where people use their hands to eat, only the right hand is used. There is a very logical, hygienic reason for this. The left hand is used to take care of bodily functions and therefore is considered dirty. To put one's left hand into the common *ceeb* (rice) bowl would contaminate it for everyone else.

Therefore a special burden is placed upon southpaws in a right-handed society. Not only must we learn to eat in a new way, moving our fingers in such a way as to make a ball of rice, but we must do this with a hand that is clumsy, that lacks agility. To this day I haven't mastered the task. A lot depends on the rice, too. Sometimes, if the rice is sticky enough, it makes a ball easily. Even a child – or a lefty – has no problem. Other times, if the rice is dry, although a Senegalese adult has no problem, it is impossible for me, about as easy as making a ball out of handful of dry sand.

Isse's rice was neither sticky nor dry. Intermediate difficulty, I would say. Yet even 'intermediate' proved too difficult for me. Of course I was under close scrutiny. The kids, thrilled at meeting 'Susie', about whom they'd heard so much, never took their eyes off me.

I fumbled around, making a mess, dropping grains of rice on the mat and on my clothes, and had oil running down my arm. Isse again offered me a spoon and again I refused, partially out of stubbornness to 'do as the Romans do when in Rome', and partially out of a sense that if I gave up and resorted to a spoon, I'd never learn. This comedy continued several minutes longer; my dropping rice every which way, and the kids staring at me silently.

Finally, unable to contain himself any longer, Libasse, the oldest, blurted out, 'Susie, how old are you?'

'Me? I'm twenty-eight. Why?'

'Twenty-eight! You're twenty-eight and you don't know how to eat rice?'

Isse and I explained that this was a new way for me to eat, and besides, I did everything backwards. Why, I even wrote with my left hand!

Libasse understood, but remained sceptical and unconvinced.

Later in the afternoon we took a walk down to the sea. I had brought along my Instamatic camera and was snapping pictures all over the place. Only problem was, I was never in any of them.

Finally I decided that Libasse should take a picture of Isse and me. Isse said he'd never done it before and I said that it didn't matter; it was really easy.

'Libasse,' I called, 'Come here and take a picture of your mother and me.'

'Susie, I can't. I don't know how.'

'Libasse,' I asked, seizing the occasion, 'how old are you?'

'Me? I'm ten. Why?'

'Ten? You're ten and you don't know how to use a camera?'

After a second of confusion, a light dawned on Libasse's face.

He smiled slowly and then he winked at me and said, 'I understand.'

From that moment on, Libasse has been my special friend and guardian angel, always looking out for me and preventing me from making cultural gaffs.

One such instance occurred several months later. It was Tabaski, the most important holiday of the Muslim calendar, commemorating the day God told Ibrahim to spare his son Issaka and kill a sheep instead. I was spending the day at Libasse's house and I brought along an American girl who was just about his age. Although they didn't have much language in common, they were managing to communicate just fine.

The house was jammed with relatives, including Libasse's uncles and grandmother. A sheep had been slaughtered and all the women were in the kitchen and in the courtyard behind the house, preparing the meal. Before the main course was ready, the women cooked up a huge plate of liver, heart, and french fries to munch on. Mantou passed the plate around.

I was talking to an aunt and absent-mindedly reached for some meat with my left hand. Quick as a flash, Libasse was at my side. Although he'd been talking animatedly with his new American friend, he obviously had been keeping an eye on me all the while.

'Susie,' he whispered, 'I know it's difficult for you but my grandmother is here. She won't understand. You've got to remember to use your right hand.'

A Pleasant Afternoon Stroll
Helen Grant (Zambia)

'You men there – what are you doing?' our guide called out imperiously.

Two men clutched their plastic bags and answered, 'Picking caterpillars.'

'Let me see.'

Our leader thrashed through the knee-high grass to the men and turned one of their hands over. In his palm were three furry caterpillars, the same sort that were used in local recipes.

'Look at this,' said our leader. 'These people take these caterpillars off the trees and eat them.'

He said this in the tone of one giving a military lecture to a particularly slow-witted class. 'Carry on,' he said to the men. They went back to their work, startled by the intrusion from a crowd of twenty or so white foreigners trudging around common land in Zambia on a baking Saturday morning.

Our leader swished the grass with his stick. 'This way,' he bellowed. 'Follow me.'

The other members of our hiking party followed him, unenthusiastically. He was a singularly irritating and condescending man who seemed to be living in the last vestiges of British colonialism.

'Urgh – caterpillars,' shuddered a Scottish woman behind me. 'They don't really eat them, do they?'

'I think so,' her friend said.

'They do,' I turned around to speak to them. 'They're a bit gritty-tasting. I had some last week.'

The first woman's hand fluttered to her mouth. She didn't say anything, but seemed to think it strange for a foreigner to eat 'local' food. My suspicions were confirmed when I heard her say to her friend, 'Well, it's all right for the Zambians, I suppose, but, really. . . .'

Our leader had got lost and turned back on himself. We trailed listlessly behind him in his erratic, zigzag wake. The sun was boiling and I wished I had never come.

Everyone on this trip was white. We constituted the Zambia Hiking Club – a grand name for a few bored expatriates who had no idea where they were going. I had hitched a lift with a diplomat friend, and she was talking to a Danish development worker who had just arrived in the country.

'Everyone says the standard of living's very good here,' said the Dane, 'and, of course, the weather's beautiful.' Her naturally pale skin was pink and burnt already.

'Oh yes,' agreed her friend. 'I'll have been here twenty-nine years next May, and I'd never have had such a good lifestyle back in Britain.'

I marched ahead, furiously. The standard of living in Zambia was lousy. Over two-thirds of the population struggled to survive on less than a dollar a day. The average life expectancy had fallen to thirty-seven years – people's health ravaged by AIDS. Any walk or drive around Lusaka inevitably passed three or four 'high-density compounds' (shanty-towns), where people lived desperately hard lives, crammed into makeshift shelters without water, sanitation or electricity. They often had no money for food and had to make do with one meal a day.

'It's all right for you expats,' I snorted, under my breath, hacking at the grass furiously. We trudged down a slope to a river.

'Ah,' said the leader, in surprise. 'That stream shouldn't be here.' He consulted his badly-sketched map. 'Well, never mind, let's press on.'

He strode manfully into the murky stream. He wore an unflattering combination of khaki safari-style jacket, shorts cropped at the top of his thighs, thick woollen socks pulled up to his knees, and dark leather sandals.

He was already halfway across the river when an over-made-up Chinese lady refused to go in the water. An American joined in. 'We could get all kinds of diseases from that,' he commented. 'No way am I getting in there.'

Our leader turned to survey us. We must have been an uninspiring sight.

'I see.' He turned around and waded back out of the river. 'Well, our route is precisely over there. We would be there in a matter of moments, but if you're not prepared to ford the stream, then I suppose we'll have to walk the long way round.' He looked up at the sun, as if gauging the correct direction. I thought he had no idea at all where we were.

'Where exactly are we going?' I demanded, wiping the sweat off my face.

'I've got vehicles stationed over there,' he pointed vaguely to the west, 'to collect us at the end of our walk. It's all jolly well organised. Let's press on then.'

He walked up the hill and I spoke to Louise. 'He hasn't got a clue. Let's just turn back.'

'We can't go back,' she said, reasonably. 'We're totally lost. Unfortunately, we'll just have to stick with him until the end.' She smiled, finding the whole expedition extremely funny. I had lost my sense of humour about half an hour earlier.

I had only joined the walk out of boredom. Work was going well, my flat was fine – my only problem was leisure time. I had very few friends, no TV, there was no cinema, no sports centre within a reasonable distance and no other diversions. Shopping was basic and even the supermarket often had aisles and aisles of empty shelves. As a volunteer, I didn't have any money to spend anyway. The local currency (in which we were paid) kept devaluing, and my 'living wage', which had seemed adequate at first, only just covered the cost of food by the end of the first year.

I had read my limited supply of books repeatedly, listened to my talking book tapes over and over again, written copious letters home. Nowadays I spent hours sitting on the steps outside my flat, striking up conversations with passing neighbours, vegetable sellers, the gardener and security guards. I went to bed early.

I asked my colleagues and neighbours what they did on evenings and weekends. They thought the question strange. They were always busy. They farmed, did piecework, sold things on crumbling street corners, did one project after another in a desperate bid to make money. They looked after their immediate family, their extended family, cousins from neighbouring countries. They went to church. They had no such concept as 'free time' – all their time was fully accounted for by the demands of their minds, bodies, families and souls. I, meanwhile, only had work. I was bored.

Expatriate workers and diplomats, on the other hand, cruised around in expensive air-conditioned vehicles between their exclusive, cool offices and well-staffed and guarded homes. They bought food at a supermarket selling imported foods, or in their embassy shops. They went to an expensive gym just outside town, attended dinner parties, watched videos and satellite TV, drove to holiday resorts in neighbouring Zimbabwe and Malawi at the weekends. I pondered what they could achieve if some of the money spent on their luxuries was given to the NGO I worked for.

Louise and I became firm friends. She was sensitive to the discrepancies between rich foreigners and poor Zambians, and introduced me to some of the dwindling middle class of local people. Through her, I stopped feeling the need to prove myself being as poor as the 'ordinary' people around me. They all believed I had loads of houses, cars and consumer goods back in the UK, anyway, and couldn't understand why I kept up the 'pretence' of earning the same as a local counterpart. They were all convinced that I was paid the same as them **plus** a decent wage into some other imaginary bank account I wasn't telling them about.

Louise invited me to delicious dinners at her house, and sometimes let me watch her TV. I introduced her to people at grass-roots level, took her to local cultural events and dance classes in town.

'Ah.' Our guide looked flummoxed again.

'Has he lived here long?' asked the newly-arrived Danish woman.

'It must be nearly forty years,' replied her companion.

'Has he ever walked across this field before?' I asked, irritably.

We had stopped in front of a clump of reeds. They were over ten foot high and formed a barrier in front of us. The only option was to double-back on ourselves again.

'At least we might end up back at the beginning,' Louise said, optimistically.

We had already been walking for almost two hours without seeing much. The walk had been advertised as a 'pleasant afternoon stroll offering scenic views across Lusaka' and its duration given as one and a half hours. I wanted to make my dance class that afternoon, to work on a complex Zambian dance I had been learning for the last few weeks. Time was ticking on.

'Never fear,' said our leader, hacking away at the reeds. 'You see – it's perfectly simple to make a path through these plants.'

We followed him into the jungly-reed bed.

'Isn't this the sort of place where biting ants live?' asked the American man, hanging back cautiously.

'AAAAHHH!' The answer rang out from all twenty of us. I felt a piercing pain stabbing into my jeans. Another one in my sock. Another in my pants. I leapt up and down, trying to shake the ants off. The pain of each bite was immense – like a sharp needle slicing through my skin.

I ran as fast as I could out of the reeds and back into the field, pursued by the rest of the hikers. The American man was backing off, his eyes widening in amazement as everyone – young, old, male and female – shamelessly started ripping their clothes off. I pulled at my trainers, yanking the laces so hard that I broke one, so desperate to get them off, fling off my socks and brush the ants off my tender ankles.

'I can't get them off!' yelled Louise, ripping her shorts down beside me. I was in too much pain to help her, tugging at the big ants burrowing into my skin. Their large, razor-like jaws were clamped on too firmly to remove. I pulled at the black shiny bodies with all my strength, only managing to pull their heads and bodies off, leaving the jaws intact inside me. 'Urgh!' I felt sick.

'Help!' Louise called. I looked up and saw her neck being savaged by five or six of the insects, and tugged ferociously to get them off.

'Keep still,' I said, hopping up and down in pain.

'I can't!'

Nobody could. The dance of the biting ants went on for ten minutes or so. Then we rebelled, sick of the hike.

'Let's go straight back to the cars,' the Chinese woman demanded. 'My feet hurt.' I wasn't surprised, as she was wearing stiletto heels, but the top of her feet looked raw with deep red bites from the ants.

'There's no point, my dear,' our leader said. 'My vehicles at the end are nearer to us now.'

Nobody had much confidence in his orientation skills, but we were all hot, severely bitten and exhausted. We followed him as he led us straight into a barbed wire fence.

'It's just a smallholding,' he said. 'They won't mind if we walk through here.'

He pulled the wire down with his stick and gallantly helped us leap over it. 'A few obstacles makes it all the more exciting, I say.'

We trespassed across a field, being challenged by the owner who was tending his tomatoes. He spoke in Nyanja, but our leader replied in English. 'We want to get to Salisbury Farm,' he said.

The farmer continued to berate us for walking all over his crops, but our leader was unconcerned. 'Salisbury Farm,' he repeated. 'Where is it?'

The angry farmer finished his tirade and then pointed diagonally across where we had just come from. He tried to push our leader outside his fence, demonstrating that we should walk around the cultivated land and not trample all over it.

'Never mind about that,' our leader said. 'Come along, everyone, it's just across here. I recognise this place now.'

Louise smiled apologetically at the farmer. I touched my chest in a local sign of respect. Most of the other walkers were oblivious, marching directly through the crops.

I spoke briefly in Nyanja, greeting the farmer and apologising for our intrusion. I said that our guide had got us all lost. The farmer was surprised that I could speak his language, and calmed down, smiling and wishing us well on our journey. He thought we were going somewhere to do something, not understanding why we would choose to walk nowhere just for the sake of walking. It did seem pointless, when he put it like that.

'What did he say?' asked the woman who had lived in Lusaka for twenty-nine years. It surprised me that I could speak more of the local language than she could. I told her. She agreed that our walk had been disastrous.

'Now we know why people dance when they meet biting ants,' Louise said. She had overheard someone talking about dancing for the ants previously and hadn't understood the reference.

After almost four hours' walking, we finally reached the farm where our leader had parked his cars. I had missed my dance lesson and was tired and dehydrated. We drove back to the starting point and returned home.

'Hello, Helen, how are you?' asked my ten-year old neighbour, sitting on the steps.

'Fine. How are you?'

'Fine. Where have you been?'

'For a pleasant afternoon stroll,' I said bitterly.

'You've got a caterpillar in your hair,' she noted.

I stuck my hand into my bird's-nest hair and threw it onto the floor. 'Yuck.'

'Where did you go for a walk?' she asked.

'Nowhere. See you later.' I went into my flat, had a cool shower and picked ant pincers out of my skin.

YOU CHEAT – YOU GET MORE
THAN YOU GIVE!

Miraculous Medicine Man
Aynsley Moore (Vietnam)

'. . . Good morning. It's Monday June the 6th. You are tuned to South East Asia Today on the BBC World Service. I'm Jeremy Harmer. Here are today's headlines. . . .'

It was hot. I lay in bed, motionless, listening to the radio, staring at the world through the haze of a mosquito net. Bright light pierced the room's darkness. It shone like lasers through cracks and gaps in old wooden shutters where friendly little geckos slept, safe in the knowledge that their bellies were full with flies and that they were hidden from the predatory world outside.

The humming, buzzing, whistling world of invisible insects outside was in full voice. Passing mopeds, trucks and buses on the road fifty metres away from where I lay occasionally interrupted their monotonous chorus. They roared and tooted through clouds of cyclists, pedestrians and farmers with animals proceeding to work or school.

Out of bed, I opened the shutters. Geckos, startled at suddenly being cast in light as their safe world swung and vibrated, darted for cover. Some momentarily dropped on the window ledge, got their bearings, and scurried off.

I squinted as the bright light blinded me. The tiled floor beneath my naked feet felt cool and damp.

Everything seemed normal for late spring in rural northern Vietnam, except me. I felt weak and ill. I could do little more than consume liquids and basic foods. I visited the throne hourly. It was not pretty. I had had diarrhoea all weekend and today, Monday, I had to teach.

All I could manage for breakfast was a pint of sugary tea and some dry toast.

I left my room and went to class. Both places were in the same building. I lived downstairs and worked upstairs. The building was called 'The Guesthouse'. It was reserved for foreign visitors and important Vietnamese visitors but I was usually the only guest staying there and after being there for nearly two years I was hardly a guest.

I unlocked the classroom door, then opened it with a sonorous squeak and entered. I pushed back the shutters and closed the windows. I turned the air conditioning and the fans on. I dusted and watered the plants. This was my routine before classes. It was the most comfortable environment I had ever taught in.

The classroom was in the corner of the building, on the first floor. Two walls, one facing east and the other south, had windows running from one side to the other. There was lots of natural light, no need for fluorescent strips, and the views were fabulous.

Facing south, directly below my vantage point, were some beautifully tended gardens full of bushes and plants and trees and flowers. Further in the distance, acting as a buffer between The Guest House and the university's administrative building, was a façade of lush trees. Above this façade, attached to a roof, flew the red and gold flag of the Peoples' Socialist Republic of Vietnam. In the distance, only visible on clear days, were jagged limestone mountains rolling off as far as the eye could see. Their shapes and colours changed depending upon light and cloud and distance. They looked like a sea of writhing dragons and they rarely failed to amaze me – sometimes, out walking, I would stop and stare at them for so long that the light would change.

Facing east, forty metres from the classroom, was a road known locally as the Cuban Road. It was built with the help of Cuban money and fifty Cuban labourers during the American War. Some locals had fond memories of their interactions with the sympathetic Cubans and could still remember Spanish words such as *hola*, *amigo* and *buenos días*. Creatures with all kinds of shapes, sizes, colours and noises used it. It could be the basis of a story alone. Across the Cuban Road, was a huge flood plain. When it was flooded, locals fished there. When it was drier, locals farmed there. There would usually be something happening on the field or on the road to catch eye and interest.

My gaze was broken by the usual gaggle of laughter and high spirits echoing around the building as my class trickled in, smiling and chatting. Mrs Minh was, as usual, the last person to arrive. Panting and gasping from cycling and running, beaming the world's biggest smile, she apologised for being late.

My learners in this class were all senior lecturers or members of staff in the university, The Forestry University of Vietnam: Dr Chieu, Dr Hue, Dr Quynh, Dr Lam, Mr Thai, Mrs Phuong, Mrs Minh and Mr Nam. They were the warmest, friendliest, most intelligent group of people I had ever had the pleasure to know.

For a warmer, I wrote 'diarrhoea' on the board. I asked them to look it up in their dictionaries and then tell their partners what they did when they had it. It wasn't long before they wanted to know whether I had it. Then, in true Vietnamese style, they all wanted to help me. All of their theories came out. Some suggested cancelling the class so that I could rest. Others suggested riding me down to Xuan Mai town, immediately, to buy medicine. Mr Nam suggested something else.

'Come with me,' he said.

'Where to?' I asked.

'To the forest.'

'Why? What for?'

'Something, yes, I know something you can eat to help you now.'

'How long will it take?'

'Emm . . .' he pondered, '. . . ten minutes.'

Although I was ill, I felt adventurous and trusted him implicitly so I agreed to go during the break.

Mr Nam and I left the class. We walked outside and into the edges of the university's four hundred hectare experimental forest. Treading very carefully through the long grass, avoiding any sleeping snakes, I followed his every step. He was concentrating hard, inspecting everything around. What seemed to me like a nondescript screen of green foliage was to him a mass of definable plants and trees with different medicinal properties.

After a couple of minutes searching he exclaimed, excitedly 'arr, yes, here.' Then he began carefully selecting leaves from a vine. He picked exactly twenty-one and told me, 'eat seven now, seven before and seven after dinner.'

Sensing my disbelief, he began munching leaves himself. 'Look, no problem.' he said, cramming them into his mouth, chewing like a cow and smiling like a Cheshire cat. I followed suit, eating my seven and pocketing the rest. They tasted surprisingly good.

After class I felt hungry, so I ate the rest of the leaves. Then I went out for more before sunset, after which I knew that it would be impossible to enter the forest and pick more.

For dinner I cooked some pasta, which I'd bought from the western supermarket in Hanoi. I added a knob of butter and sprinkled a large helping of torn leaves in too. Then I gobbled and washed it down with some mineral water. It was delicious.

Very soon, however, I became sleepy. I hardly had enough energy to brush my teeth, get the mosquito net out of its wall-mounted box, let it cascade down, tuck it under the mattress, and crawl into my safe cocoon.

I fell into an extremely deep and powerful sleep, full of delicious dreams. The leaves were taking effect. Nothing could have woken me during the night.

In the morning, fourteen hours after going to sleep, I awoke.

' . . . Good morning. It's Tuesday June the 7th. You are tuned to South East Asia Today on the BBC World Service. I'm Jeremy Harmer. Here are today's headlines. . . .'

I felt like a new man. I felt fresh. My body seemed strong. My bad belly had been restored. I'd regained my health overnight.

I lay in bed, staring through the haze of the mosquito net. Bright light shone like lasers through the cracks and gaps in the old wooden shutters.

The humming, buzzing, whistling world of invisible insects outside was in full voice once again. Vehicles occasionally roared and tooted by along the Cuban Road.

Out of bed, I opened the shutters. Geckos darted for cover. One dropped on my hand. It felt like rubber. Then it leaped off and scurried away.

I squinted as bright light blinded me. The floor beneath my feet was cool and damp.

What a great day.

My work at the Forestry University of Vietnam and the people I met there helped me learn about the many benefits of Mother Nature. For example, a large percentage of western medicine comes from trees and plants in tropical forests. There are many more still to be discovered. This is one reason why the university, in conjunction with Vietnam's forward thinking Communist government and some international organisations, is responsible for reforesting five million hectares of bare hills and mountains in Vietnam. According to local sources, this land was once covered by lush, primary, forest. This forest helped prevent soil erosion and flooding, and it provided food for locals. Much of this land was stripped by American military attacks, which used Agent Orange. Then, after the defeat of the American invasion, the US instigated a trade embargo, which caused massive poverty. This forced locals to destroy the forest further, using it for firewood and building materials.

Night
Olwyn Ballentine (Angola)

Let me tell you about Huambo at night.

I only realised last night, as we drove through the pitch-black streets of the centre of town, that I rarely venture into downtown at night. Then I thought about it a bit more, and realised that I often do, but usually I'm chatting to whoever is in the car, and not really concentrating on my surroundings. Also, usually there are patches of town power, the odd streetlight, windows lit up, which changes the atmosphere. Last night however, was devoid even of moonlight, there was no general electricity, and it was if the town had gone back decades.

It's funny how darkness can both make you feel closed in, because the world appears to end at the boundaries of the headlights of the car, but also give you the sensation of being very, very small in a very big world, as you are aware of the enormity beyond the reality you can see. As we lurched from pothole to crater on the main street, running just parallel to the now defunct rail track, we caught in the momentary beam of the headlights kids playing on the streets, women carrying their bundles home on their heads, the odd *maluko* (mad person) dancing with abandon.

From above, you could see the light of candles flickering through the windows of high-rise blocks; the darkness hides the bullet holes, shell craters and crumbling walls. Under the first floor balconies sat groups of women and children, selling bread or roasted corn by their fires on the pavement. The convoy that just came in a few days ago – all one hundred or so trucks – are parked in the open area beside the old hotel that they always use. The more enterprising have rigged up some sort of electric lighting system, which peers out into the darkness from the confines of the cab. Underneath some of the trucks a game of cards is played by candlelight with a few friends and a bottle of whisky or a few cans of beer to while away the hours. Other trailers shelter families, with a bit of cloth hanging down to provide a makeshift wall.

At night, you cannot escape the realisation that here are people living real lives, and in spite of all that has been thrown at them, and all they have had to struggle and improvise, they will continue to live real lives. And above this living city, with thousands of people and their amazing stories, the stars shine, the milky way languishes in the sky, and I feel alive.

Of Rapids and Piranhas
Kenneth Carano (Suriname)

The morning stillness, unbroken since last night's drums ended, is interrupted by the crowing of a cock. He seems to be near my head. That initial outburst spurs a chain reaction as, one by one, roosters begin crowing in a clockwise motion around the village until inevitably it is right next to my head again. They are our alarm clock and alert us to roll out of our hammocks. It is barely past 5am. Erik, a fellow Peace Corps volunteer in Suriname, South America, assures me there is an ideal fishing spot about an hour down river where we can camp and catch large piranhas.

Walking the beaten dirt path to the river, we encounter some Ndjuka women carrying large buckets on their heads filled with clothes. These women are from one of the tribes of the Maroon people that are descendants of runaway African slaves and inhabit Suriname's interior rain forest. They hold onto many of their traditional customs and beliefs. You could easily believe you have been transferred back in time to old Africa. We exchange the appropriate morning greetings as they pass.

After packing the fishing gear in our dugout canoe, Erik and I paddle down river, through the dense fog. Erik's dog, Scrappy, stands at the bow of the boat. The vast green forest decorates the side of the river. Large branches dangle over the water's edge. As the sun begins to heat up, the fog starts rising above the jungle. Occasionally, we pass small, thatched roof, open-air canopies, built by local Maroons, along the side of the river. Small birds and butterflies glide atop the surface of the water. I search for the majestic six to eight foot long giant river otters that call the Lawa river home. The ride takes us along the winding river through some small rapids that churn where the current folds under and onto itself.

After paddling for an hour we come upon additional rapids. We navigate through and suddenly, without warning, approach a three-foot waterfall surrounded by rocks. There is nothing to do but go over it. In a moment of exhilaration we are over the chute and free falling. Our boat lands upright below. About a hundred metres away is the small island, covered in bush, which will be our fishing site. Rapids are to the left and the right, but there is about a four hundred-metre perimeter of calm water to fish in.

Just before noon my fishing rod, that has been sitting on a rock and leaning against a limb, is dragged into the water. The ensuing tug of war begins as I do battle with a piranha. He is fighting so fiercely I am certain the pole is going to break in two. Eventually, I win the battle and pull in a ten-pound piranha.

In the late afternoon, Erik takes our fish and prepares a meal over a wood fire as I go to a nearby sandbar for some more fishing. After dinner, another battle follows. Again, my rod looks as if it is going to snap like a twig. The battle rages on for what feels like fifteen minutes, but is probably thirty seconds. Finally, out of the water, I pull a twenty-pound freshwater stingray – allegedly more dangerous than their salt-water cousins, leaving you immobile for an extended period of time. So much for bathing tonight. The nearest doctor is at least a day away.

Not only was the fishing bountiful today, the scenic beauty is mesmerising. A full moon rises from behind the mountains in front of us and a swarm of stars light up the sky. It is a romantic scene that cries out for my wife to be with me. Unfortunately, I am stuck with the big burly, bald-headed guy. Don't get me wrong; Erik is a great guy, a real man's man, but not the one to have beside me with a portrait of this magnitude playing itself out in the heavens above.

Sleep comes early in the blackness of the jungle night. My body feels as light as a feather as I sleep in my hammock with a mosquito net wrapped around me like a cocoon. The night is tranquil with a slight breeze. The infrequent ghostly screams of the red howler monkeys engulfing the jungle airways are the only sounds.

The following morning, we break camp and head home. Within minutes, we are forced out of the boat due to the low water of the rapids. The boat will have to be pulled across. Approaching the three-foot waterfall, Scrappy attempts to swim through the rapids and over the falls. The stirring water pushes her down river about fifty metres before she struggles to get back to the nearby rocks. Seeing that she will not be able to swim through the rapids, I decide to carry her as I swim through them.

I have underestimated the fury of these rushing waters. I also forgot about my glasses. Approaching the waterfall, with Scrappy in my arms, the powerful force of the water knocks me back and has me stumbling and slipping on pebbles and rocks below me. Then, as the water is level with my chin, the strength of the rapids swipes my glasses off my face and carries them down river into parts unknown. Unable to see anything, except a blur, I swim back to the rocks on the side. Now it is every dog and man for himself. I stumble my way through the remainder of the rapids, sporadically slipping and scraping myself on the submerged rocks, until I reach the boat on the other side where Erik and Scrappy sit safely awaiting my arrival.

Two hours later we arrive safely back in the village. I have found an extra pair of contacts to regain my eyesight. Now I am relaxing in a hammock nursing my wounds and relishing another day of life as a Peace Corps volunteer.

Six Months in Male'
Jeff Bendeich (Maldives)

A month after returning from the Republic of Maldives and I have been through the barrage of questions everyone throws at you about what it was like. You answer the questions as best as you can but it is hard to put into words what it is really like. How do you package up six months of your life where you lived in a developing country working as a volunteer?

One memorable experience was when the staff from the ministry I worked for were at the home for mentally ill, disabled and elderly to celebrate its twenty-fifth anniversary. The official ceremony was over and we had distributed all the gifts to residents that we had brought down, and we went off on a quick walk around the facility. We reached the area where the elderly lived and there was a particular elderly man there who really made me think. He was probably here because he had no family to look after him and, as such, it fell to the government. They were doing their best; he had a roof over his head and a bed, but very little else.

It struck me how lonely he appeared to be, and how much he appreciated the small gift of chocolate and a few pieces of fruit that we gave him. To me he did not appear to have any apparent physical problem, he was eating the orange we had given him when we arrived, and it had obviously been carefully peeled. He even went to the effort of tidying his bed up, placing the knife and the remainder of his gift carefully under his pillow with a few other small things that were there, on his immaculately-made bed. He was one of the first people we said hello to as we walked in, and as we continued through I looked around and then back to him.

I realised how little the people living here had; a bed in a dormitory, a small table next to it, and a small area in a shared cupboard. This particular building was light and airy, the dormitory was clean and tidy, but this man looked so sad and lonely. I wished I could do more, even just a little more, to make this man's life even a little bit brighter. Unfortunately, we were only there for a few hours in total, and the group moved off to go through the other areas before leaving. It was depressing to think how lonely and sad this elderly man appeared, and how even a small thing like having someone to come in to say hello had appeared to lift him. To have someone from the community go in and spend time with him and the other elderly people, just visiting and talking to them, looked like it would brighten their lives just that little bit – definitely for this man. It seemed such a small thing to do, but it could make such a difference to a person's life.

I was also lucky enough to travel to some of the outer atolls while I was working with the Ministry. This gave me the opportunity to not only see more of the country and to get to know the people I worked with better, but also to meet and catch up with other volunteers. It is odd, you may only have met these people a couple of times, or in some cases it might be the first time you have met them, but it was so easy to talk and share things about each other's lives.

I remember one night, sitting in a 'jolly' under the stars of Hithadhoo, talking to a Canadian girl I had met for the first time about five hours before. I do not even remember exactly what we were talking about, but it was to do with our lives, the motivations that led us to where we were and what the future held. The conversation flowed so easily and seemed so natural at the time, but looking back afterwards, I realised how rare it would be for me to be having that conversation at home. This was not the only time this happened, I felt as if there was this bond between people you have only just met, solely because you were both volunteers working in a foreign country. Friendships were formed that are hard to describe, for some reason it seems different to back home, somehow more natural and more open.

The closer it came to me leaving Male', the more mixed emotions I felt rising within me. I knew my assignment was coming to an end, and I was looking forward to coming home to family and friends, but I didn't want to leave. It was hard to believe that six months passed so quickly. It seems like only yesterday that we stepped off the plane from Australia to start our volunteer assignment, and I wanted to spend more time in Male'. A couple more months would have been nice, but I had to leave. When I was there, I used to think about being back in Australia, but now I'm home, it's almost the opposite. I'm glad to be home, but I would still like to be in Male'.

Things have changed now, I have returned to the world I left six months ago, and everything seems to be the same. Friends and family are the same, just a little older, the town I live in is the same, my old workplace has gone through some change, but after a week back, it looks pretty much the same, though maybe I've changed. I've lived a different life for six months, met new people from around the world, and had the opportunity to experience new things and help other people in the process. Yes, it is me that has changed. My outlook has broadened; I have learnt things about myself and met some great friends along the way. It's a journey that I feel privileged to have been able to undertake and something that I will carry with me always through life. I have grown during my six months in Male' and no matter what happens in the future, I know I will always remember Male'.

A Big Impact
Ellen Boyle (Papua New Guinea)

Timing is what it is all about. Hot on reading this book's call for contributors, I toddled off to our struggling local VSO group. A new member arrived. I was struck by her youthfulness and listened as Margaret talked about her posting as a statistician in the Caribbean. The voice in my head wondered 'What do we share? How on earth would she understand my PNG days?' Yet for almost a quarter of century I have, to my continual amazement, found a bond with VSO volunteers, present and past. It hasn't got to do with countries, jobs, sex, age – so what is it? It's something to do with the 'ubiquitous' encounter that enables us to have a unique experience that's both individual and universal.

So, back to the writing challenge. Could I convey some of my most treasured but private thoughts and feelings of my volunteer experiences? I'm aware of an almost irrational preciousness about them; will people really understand, will I accurately represent – will I get beyond 'it was different'? Take Papua New Guinea (PNG), for example. So many images and memories flood my mind, yet some of the most painful are the most vivid. There were times when I could feel the sculpture of my personal growth like the young student nurses you see on wards in the UK who have to deal with very sober, adult, grown-up things. Dick's death was one such sculpture, forever carved in my being. An outrage to have happened, yet a privilege to have known both his life and his death.

When I met him, he was the leader of a band of 'Paras'. No, not the advanced division of the Air Force, but a 'quadriplegic', the result of a rugby accident. A formidable man who had had a very successful career in the army and headed a big extended family. Like at least ten others based in the hospital, his new 'life' had been narrowed to living in a rehab ward (with virtually no rehab) for years on end. My job, as director of 'Homes for the Disabled' was to support those people to leave the ward and reintegrate into the community. A simple enough phrase but a mammoth shift in both behaviour and attitude. People had lost physical capacity and over time had become de-skilled in most daily living activities, dependent on the relatives for everything, from finance to the next meal. The community saw disability in terms of *inability*.

Dick liked the idea of getting back out there and had the guts and the character not only to move but was a key figure in working with me to help the others move. He was very much the most important figure in his extended family and became the spokesperson of this new venture into the community. On a personal level, Dick managed the frustrations of his impairment very well, but he always had a watchful eye on likely health problems, especially infections and bed sores. He'd been in hospital two or three times whilst now living in the community, but was always supported by his wife Jane and his *wantoks* (extended family).

The people I was working with faced that challenge. Each had individual needs. With Dick, I played a back-up role so, on one of my back-up visits to the hospital, I saw Dick was not at all himself, not even his normal unwell self. I instinctively knew that something was up. The staff were 'unavailable' and when I finally succeeded in talking to someone I was given the run-around and, despite my best efforts at assertiveness, felt I was more or less ignored.

My feeling of unease was growing and as each minute passed I understood that these tactics, conscious or unconscious, had to do with Dick being a quadriplegic; an unspoken belief of a life worth less expectations, a life worth less. The medical condition was obliterating the person. As Dick weakened in front of me I felt we had to kick-start some action.

A frantic passing of time ensued as I tried to mobilise what contacts I had in the hospital, but Dick became critically ill within those couple of hours and died. I came back into the ward to the hysterical sound of his wife and family members wailing, all of them sprawled over Dick's dead body. I was filled with anger, helplessness and a sense of failure. I couldn't begin to know how to comfort them and I had just lost someone who I'd come to value and love.

Then the reality, the rawness of death took over. These same people, in their self-important way, in their cheap, dirty uniforms, who'd dragged their feet to answer my questions, were now pressing me to move the body. Yes me. No officials deal with the body, so I helped his wife and brother move Dick's body, still warm, onto the trolley they so promptly delivered. At that moment I hated them and the whole sordid hospital, but I seethed inside at the bigger picture of injustice. I found myself pushing the trolley; winding our way to the mortuary and trying to keep hold of Dick's big body on the bumpy paths. People went about their business, unperturbed by death, literally passing them by. Life seemed to be cheap and death commonplace.

It was as if I'd done this many times, even when I stepped inside the small frozen room. I was surrounded by corpses and, in a shared moment of silence, we realised there wasn't enough space for Dick. I held onto Jane whilst Dick's brother had to move some bodies, wrapped in shrouds, to make room for Dick. I will never forget him lifting a small figure, so small it had to be a child, so gently and placing it with dignity on the shelf above. After what seemed a long time, he too had his place, and we sat outside in a little pocket of calm, discussing the plan for his funeral.

It is customary to wail emotionally in PNG. I had heard it so many times but this was different. There I was in my buttoned-up British way, swallowing back tears. My throat and head were so painfully full of grief I thought I might burst. Jane was looking at me, saw my pain, and pleaded with her big brown eyes to stay and grieve with her. Against all my instincts I did. I let it go and howled in a way I wouldn't have thought possible. What a release. That dam of restraint (of sadness and anger) had burst and washed over me. It was such an emotional marker. It still lives with me to this day and touches something deep whenever I recall it. We are so often defined by our culture, but this culture and context into which I had strayed, had given me Dick in my life, also gave me permission to really cry for him without any loss of face.

The next day we returned to the morgue. I was again confronted by the absence of services. Dick's naked body lay upon a cold slab. The family would prepare the body for burial. They treated Dick as if he was still alive among them. They cleansed, manicured, embalmed and then dressed Dick in his best clothes. They did this in such a loving, sensitive manner that it quickly obliterated the cold, austere surroundings and I became aware that I was a participant in something special, something to behold.

He was to be taken back to his village high up in the Highlands. It was a long journey in a hired public service vehicle that gathered more and more followers as we progressed up the famous highlands highway. As we neared his village, the road ran out, the vehicle became redundant, and his friends and family orchestrated the ascent of the mountain. An enormous procession formed, each one eager to take their turn carrying his coffin part of the six-mile climb.

I was privileged to attend that colourful and dignified ceremony which embraced many animist rituals and some Seventh Day Adventist prayers. A wonderful combination illustrating the rich diversity of his life. It was a long climb up the mountain, but he was back in his boyhood place where he would once have been physically strong; full of health and promise and talent. As a mark of friendship, I was given the hunting arrows he used as a young boy as a memento. They were on my sitting room wall for a long time.

Some people didn't notice them, some people did, some asked or commented, 'Are the arrows from PNG?' I say yeah, and tend to leave it at that. It's too long and too special a story, about Dick and about me.

All you Sexy Ladies, Get Ready to Wine
Jean Hales (Guyana)

At the rear of the truck, speakers as big as a house, mounted by DJ Number One giving the hype, 'Come on all you sexy ladies get ready to wine.' At the front, an anxious DJ Number Two at the controls tries to maintain and regulate the sound, which he can hardly hear because the speakers are thumping the sound away from him. Desperately he attempts to communicate with DJ Number One, while struggling to keep his balance on the swaying vehicle and being jostled by the beer-swilling, rum-guzzling revellers, blissfully unaware of his difficulties; their main objective being to happily obey Number One's instructions to wine. For the uninitiated, 'wining' is the generic dance of the Caribbean. The nearest thing to having sex with your clothes on, on the dance floor – 'wine' from 'wind', which is what you do with your hips.

Bodies adorn the sides of the truck, swaying, shouting and waving to the lesser mortals on the street. Extroverts position themselves on the roof of the cab, heads thrown back, hands in the air and legs spread in the usual wining posture, they wiggle their hips with abandon at the world below. And in between them snake the electric cables, a safety officer's nightmare. Somehow they manage to keep upright as the vehicle sways and crawls through the crowd. But every so often it lurches to a halt throwing its occupants into each other's arms, threatening to spew them out onto the crowd below.

This was the defining moment which exemplifies my experience as a volunteer in Guyana. Life for me in the UK and, I suspect for many others, if they have the energy to drag themselves away from the sixth home decorating programme this week, long enough to think about it, was about being a spectator: going to the movies, the theatre, reading gossip columns, newspapers, books, getting stressed out at work then looking forward to settling down in front of the telly to get a fix from the latest soap.

Getting hooked on programmes such as *Big Brother* or *Survival* – programmes about other people taking risks or exposing their inner selves, so that we can take part in the endless discussions and analyses that follow – as though they mattered. Not so in Guyana. No longer did I carry around the phrase 'Life is Elsewhere'.

Some Guyanese friends had invited us onto their truck in the carnival parade for the Republic Day celebrations, *Mashramani*. No longer was I a spectator on life, I was a participant, a player. I was part of the carnival.

Never before have I felt so accepted, made to feel so welcome, appreciated and valued. Although Guyana is an ex-British colony and has adopted many British customs, habits and traditions – cups of tea, porridge for breakfast, dominoes, chess, *White Christmas* reggae style – thank goodness the Guyanese have not adopted that famous 'British Reserve'.

We could learn a lot from them about their attitude to foreigners. People would stop me in the street and ask what I was doing there, and when I told them, they would say 'Thank you' and 'Welcome'. Granted, in the UK it would hardly be correct to stop a non-white person in the street and ask them the same question. But the point is that Guyanese people, when they know you are a foreigner, they are genuinely hospitable and friendly and want to make you feel welcome in their country. In my home-town in England it would take a foreigner years to become accepted in the way that I was in my Guayanese temporary home-town of Linden. I was once asked why I did not accept lifts from strangers, and had to explain the dangers of doing so in England.

In Search of Tortugas
Tessa Blakemore (Mexico)

'Straight to the bottom of the property ladder.' Such was the gloomy prediction of family and friends on hearing of our plans to go travelling for six months. Indeed, it was to the bottom of this very same ladder that my husband David and I felt ourselves sliding as, just a few months later, we relinquished our well-paid jobs, sold the car and set off into the sunset clutching our 'round the world' tickets and leaving the dinner-party circuit far behind.

Our trip began with three weeks on the beach in Mexico. Sounds like bliss? Soaking up the sun, sipping sangria and doing the salsa until sunrise? Well, not exactly. We had forsaken the wild nightlife for night wildlife: we were looking for turtles.

Boca de Tomates is located on Mexico's Pacific coastline, just south of Puerto Vallarta on the magnificent Bahía de Banderas, one the largest bays in the world. Here, like many other regions of Mexico, illicit killing of turtles and egg-raiding is rife. Skin and shell are used to make clothing and adornments, the flesh is sold for food, and the eggs are considered to be a powerful aphrodisiac. Only one in every 1,000 eggs produces a turtle which matures to adulthood. For three weeks last July we joined forces with an international group of volunteers and local environmental organisation, *Nuestra Tierra* (Our Earth) in an attempt to curb the depletion and eventual extinction of this endangered species.

As dusk began to fall on our first evening, the group listened expectantly as the striking, self-assured director of *Nuestra Tierra* explained the rules of the camp by the low light of a gas lamp. 'Always empty your boots before putting them on.' Scorpions were not uncommon in this area and would kill in minutes.

'Be prepared for tropical storms.'
Hurricane-force winds frequently
rampaged across the bay, and, as we
were later to discover, destroyed
everything in their path. Looking
around us apprehensively, we began
to wonder if this had been such a
good idea.

Nestled amongst a group of palm
trees and encroaching on the jungly
vegetation of a river estuary, our

A leatherback turtle

home for three weeks was a rustic camp on the beach. A far cry from Leonardo
DiCaprio's Thai paradise or Brooke Shield's idyllic *Blue Lagoon*, our abode
consisted of little more than a canopy of palm fronds, supported precariously
by slanting wooden posts. A makeshift kitchen comprised a rusting two-ring
hob, a gas canister, and a plastic vat for collecting rainwater. A visit to the
toilet meant a trip into the undergrowth armed with a shovel and bathed in
mosquito repellent. As for sleeping arrangements, we were faced with the
choice of sweating out the night in a shared tent or communing with nature on
a camp bed on the sand. Neither option provided adequate protection from the
enormous crabs with whom we shared our home and which could be felt
crawling under the canvas of the tent and heard snapping their grotesque pincers
against the food containers at night. David, who had opted for a camp-bed
outside, awoke one night to find that one such intrepid creature had attached
itself to his big toe which when wriggled sent the impostor catapulting off
around the mosquito net, finally coming to rest on his pillow.

Fortunately, though, sleep deprivation came with the job. The hours of 10pm
to 7am were spent patrolling the beach in search of nests, tracks and, if we were
lucky, the majestic 'tortugas' themselves. During shifts of three hours, our eyes
soon became accustomed to the dark, and, assisted by the light of the moon, we
quickly learnt to identify the indentations in the sand which would lead to our
nest. Once located we would carefully remove the golf ball-like eggs (between
80 and 120 at a time) and carry them back to our protected corral for reburial.
After forty days of incubation the baby turtles would emerge from their shells,
push their way up through the sand and clamber frenetically down to their new
home – the Pacific Ocean.

One memorable night we discovered six nests, collected over 500 eggs and
encountered three turtles. Watching a mother heaving her way up the beach,
dextrously digging her hole and then laying her eggs with tears of exertion
rolling gently down her face was a truly magical sight. Perhaps more moving still
was witnessing her make her weary journey back down the beach, and waiting
until she became engulfed in waves, never to see the offspring to which she had
just given birth.

Other nights, though, were less productive. Patrolling for hours up and down
the long stretch between our camp at Boca de Tomates and the blinding lights

of Puerto Vallarta's glitzy American hotels we would see nothing. Only the eerie barking of some wild dogs, the distant chatter of some late-night tourists or the nightly patrols of the Mexican marines who surveyed the beach would occasionally disturb the peace. Once or twice we arrived too late: a pair of shadowy figures furtively rushed away from some turtle tracks clutching their pillaged booty. Being offered *huevos de tortuga* at a nearby restaurant was a harsh reminder that we hadn't saved them all.

Needless to say, turtle eggs didn't feature highly on our own dinnertime menu. For all of us, the Mexican staples of tortilla, guacamole, salsa and frijoles (refried beans) soon became our daily diet, all washed down with the obligatory glass of tequila. Our main difficulty came in deciding not *what* to eat, but *when*. As the Spaniards finished lunch, the English stomachs started rumbling for dinner, and by the time they were preparing for their evening meal, we Brits were ready for bed.

Despite cultural differences, we all got along well, communicating in a bizarre form of 'Spanglish' and spending time together on our cherished days off. One unforgettable afternoon we hired a speedboat and, James Bond-style, sped around the stunningly beautiful islands of Yelapa, Playa de las Animas and Quimixto, marvelling at the film-set scenery, drenched in the tropical sun.

Unfortunately, though, the weather wasn't always quite as kind. July is Mexico's hottest and most humid period of the year, bringing with it some ferocious rains and hurricane-force winds. During the last night at Boca de Tomates a violent tropical storm raged across the coast, stampeding through the camp and devastating our home. We watched in awe as the already-slanting structure swayed precariously around us, as chunks of the roof flew off into the sky and as a nearby palm tree was struck by lightning. It was the Mexican marines who finally came to our rescue, whisking us off to safety in their military truck. Hurtling through the streets in the failing light, our adrenaline pumping, our comfortable Brighton flat and the once ubiquitous chatter of house prices and internet millionaires seemed a world away.

Developmental Dilemmas
Kath Ford (Philippines)

Before becoming a volunteer, we had vigorous training to prepare us for change in our designated countries. We were all aware that we would have much adjusting to do, and would suffer much 'culture shock'. Nevertheless, we had skills to share and a lot of enthusiasm, so we set out hoping that these would carry us through. We were sure that the many problems we encountered would be a challenge and we would be able to effect some change in the poor communities where we were to work, we were after all, development workers. . . .

Unfortunately, it's not as easy as that. Enthusiasm and skills are fine, but there are many developmental dilemmas. How far do you go in adjustment to lifestyle, before you see the important issues to the community, not judged by western standards? Sometimes you can raise issues, which they do not see as a problem and so are in danger of creating discontent where there was none before. It's no bad thing to raise awareness of 'better standards', but good to stick to what it is possible to achieve. Do I in fact cause envy of western culture just by being there?

It is fine to introduce a commercial aspect to local skills – weaving, woodwork, etc. so they can gain financially – but what do they lose in an effort to be saleable? They are in danger of rejecting the traditional for the more popular 'modern' version, changing colour and style to suit the customer.

The big issue in the Philippines was 'gender' and the empowerment of women was part of my job description, but this cannot be done without the co-operation of both men and women. Given that women spend all day on those tasks needed for survival in a basic community – bringing water, collecting wood for fires, cooking, washing etc. – as well as working in the fields and market, they are in danger of being more multi-burdened if the chores are not shared.

As a health worker, I was initially convinced that I knew more than they, about health education for prevention – but did I? There were traditional healers, *sinang* doctors, spiritualists, local herbs – all of which I needed to know more about, to know what was truly needed.

From personal experience and ten days of agony from a trapped nerve, I can vouch for the fact that some traditional healers (*hilots*) were very good and some not so good. The first healer was prayerful, the second drunk, and the third practical and excellent. I had in my possession a book of Cordillera medicinal herbs, as well as my own herb books from home. There were many people around who were skilled in the properties of the local plants, but there were also those who used them indiscriminately, causing more harm than good; especially if an early diagnosis was necessary to save life. Sometimes western medicines were seen as miracle cures, and also used incorrectly. Money spent on these was often was more than the families could afford.

Where do you start then on a community health programme? It may seem obvious, but you need to learn about the community first . . . find out what they think the health priorities are. They won't necessarily have the same ones as you. For instance, they may see diarrhoea as a problem, leading to death in young children. They don't see that the underlying poverty and malnutrition cause low resistance to any disease that occurs in the very young and very old.

How then do you teach nutrition to people who have no food? How do you set up an accident prevention programme for children whose everyday life is a matter of survival, who climb trees and pick fruit for food, who cook food over an open fire, who play and bathe and fish in the river, who are out in boats without life-jackets at an early age? People who walk barefoot over rough terrain littered with broken glass and garbage, who live in houses on stilts with bamboo steps – not a safety gate in sight! People who use their father's *bunengs* for everything, because it is the only knife around and kept very sharp, who will scavenge around the neighbours garbage cans to retrieve anything edible e.g. egg white out of eggshells, bread etc. – if the dogs, hens and ducks haven't got there first, and where bleach

Sharing skills

bottles are left lying around the pump area where the laundry is done?

How do you motivate people who complain that life is hard, but seem to resist change even though it makes life easier? Why is it that there is so little planning ahead – they are satisfied if today is provided for – something will turn up tomorrow – they have a very philosophical approach to life? If there is a surfeit on one day they share it with others until there is nothing left.

Perhaps they have lived so long without the means to keep food cool, that they deem it better to eat it all while it is good, rather than it should waste in the heat. Although there are fridges now, this attitude still prevails. The sharing is also part of the survival pattern and part of a barter system. *Bulod* (borrow) and *utang* (owe) are a way of life there and not everything is paid back in money – it calls for a very complicated system of accounting, for which most of the women had their little notebooks with a separate page for each debt.

Despite the lack of money, there was never a lack of hospitality. If visitors arrived in between meals, Coke and Sky flakes were bought (utang), but if a meal were about to be served, then the hosts would stand back and allow the visitors to eat first. If the visitors were regarded as important, the meal was delayed whilst something special was cooked – a dog or a goat – tuna, if available, as this was a fishing island. The hosts could be paying for this for months hence, but when I asked about this, I was told, 'We would be embarrassed if we could not provide for guests.' Not so different from the UK perhaps – maybe we don't go to such extravagant lengths to prove that we can afford to feed visitors, but I know many a host in England who has disguised their meal, so that guests would not know they were eating their portion.

Though it was very frustrating at times, depressing at others, there were many rewarding moments too. I went to the Philippines prepared to share skills and work on better standards. Like most volunteers, I'm not sure who got the best of the deal.

Namaste
Laura Kyle (Nepal)

Plenty of successful graduates suddenly balk at the prospect of entering a cold salary-fuelled world at the end of their cosy period amidst the security of academia and quite simply, I was one of them.

Having raised £3,000 by completing a solo five-day, 250-mile bike ride from Manchester to Farnham, I travelled to Nepal with Student Partnerships Worldwide. Our programme was designed for young westerners to team up with young Nepalis and, together, promote environmental awareness throughout Nepal's remote rural areas.

Two months of intensive training in and around Kathmandu had ended. Thirty young English and Nepali volunteers were about to face the biggest challenge of their lives. Armed with enough skills to make bricks out of cow dung, buildings out of mud and stone, plus the odd nature collage, we were sent off into the unknown.

On board a public bus imported from the subcontinent (one of the ones that was too damaged even for the Indians), five volunteers began to get to know each other. I had been placed with Rita and Sujit who were Nepali and Adam and Mia who were on their GAP years. None of us had particularly bonded during training and the choice of group had come as a bit of a surprise. Seven hours east of the capital, in Dolakha, the road ended. We piled out and began the two-hour trek towards our village, Kshamawoti, with two very small and worryingly old porters, loaded down by five backpacks, striding far ahead of us.

It was a truly beautiful area – a series of spacious terraced valleys with jungle-topped ridges enclosed by the towering Tibetan mountains. When we first arrived, the land was golden with wheat. Within a couple of weeks, the wheat had been harvested, corn planted and the whole area was covered by a lush green blanket. The smell of grasses, the river and good clean air immediately filled our nostrils and began to chip away at the city's pollution etched in our lungs. A cuckoo echoed its call across the valley and I knew I was going to love my three months there.

Seventy-five percent of the village was Thangmi – one of many minority ethnic groups of Nepal. They had their own separate language, culture and traditional religion and I found them to be a fascinating people. Sadly, however, they were considered of low caste and alongside a shocking history of exploitation from the not so scrupulous higher castes, they have been left with little land, income or status. Many Thangmi people expressed feelings of shame and inadequacy towards their position and were working hard at becoming assimilated into one large Nepalese identity. Most of the children spoke Nepali as their first language and English as their second.

All five of us had to get right back to basics in all parts of our lives. We rose with the sun at 6am and the first port of call in the mornings was the *charpie*. Now I could say that this was a loo, but I'm not sure it deserved such a description. The tiny, dark, stinking shelter with its concrete shoot and bucket of water provided an ideal habitat for millions of flies, wasps and enormous spiders. Not too pleasant. The next mission of the day was washing. Situated about two minutes from the house, was a trickle of water over a grooved stone. It had dried up to a mere drip and, to make matters worse, was set in a bamboo grove and was incredibly public. Washing meant donning a *lungi* (a tubular piece of material tucked up under the arms) and giving it your best shot without flashing a boob or exposing too much thigh to many an amused onlooker!

After all this trauma, my first meal, at 9am was very much appreciated. *Dal Bhat* (rice, lentils and vegetables) was our twice-daily ration for the duration of the placement, but was actually something of a rarity amongst the villagers. We were lucky to get such a tasty meal when the rest of the family lived off *dhedo* (a thick black millet paste), some lentil soup and vegetables.

Every day, we taught environmental classes in the school which was a half-hour hike up through the jungle over the ridge. Quite a walk, but I quickly became armed with calves of steel and was ready to take on any trek and in flip-flops! The school was well equipped according to the standards set by the average government-run institutions, but was still extremely basic and stark. Education consisted of a timetabled eight rudimentary classes per day, but in reality the kids received about five. If it wasn't them missing school, it was the teachers. The apathetic atmosphere made our work quite challenging, yet we were often rewarded by feeling like we'd brought a little life and extra-curricular activity to the place. On the whole the kids were very responsive and it was a joy to spend time with them.

The Green Club in Kshamawoti

Our Green Club (and the rest of the school), got involved in plenty of after-school events such as: paper recycling, painting a wonderful two-by-three metre wall mural, song competitions, drama, an excellent wall magazine, making of over 100 mud bricks and sports of all types. Having supplied a volleyball, the kids were inspired to develop an unbeatable team. Of course the older boys and a couple of very hard girls dominated the precious ball so the younger kids, in true Nepali style displayed their amazing innovative skills and made their own net from twine and a ball from an old plastic bag filled with dried leaves.

Towards the end of the school term, with just over one month left in the village, we turned our attention towards the community. A successful presentation to the most influential members of the area on the benefits of *chulos* (smokeless stoves) and charpies secured the village's support for these grassroots projects and we set about putting our theory into practice.

Firstly, we demonstrated the building of a chulo in one of the school buildings where the English teacher lived. Many people attended and excitedly demanded that we build one in their houses. This created certain problems. Our objective had been to pass on the technological know-how and our aim was for interested people to take their own initiative and build their own (with help from the local development organisation).

It was here that we encountered one of the problems development workers must face time and time again. Everyone enthused about our new idea, they nodded and agreed wholeheartedly about its benefits to their health, their environment and daily workload. Then they sat and waited for us to implement it. When we didn't, when they realised that actually they needed to contribute some of their own time and effort, the attitude of the vast majority of people was, 'Oh well, we've put up with smoke in our eyes, a high risk of bronchitis and runny noses for hundreds of years – *ke garne* (what to do)?' It was infuriating.

We ran into similar problems when rectifying the complete lack of toilet facilities in the village's two primary schools. With 150 children attending each school on a daily basis, the areas were in much need of some sanitary upgrading. It was unanimously decided that two charpies would be built. The difference between the two projects was startling and proved just how important it was to have the full support and backing of the local people. One of the projects ran smoothly from start to finish, was efficient in both time and money and was a delight to complete. The other, however, created problems right from the start. Its co-ordinator, our Green Club teacher, revealed a rather disturbing habit when he embarked on a ten-day drinking binge. He emerged from his den of iniquity only to abuse unfortunate passers-by into supplying him with more alcohol. This caused the labourers to fall into disarray and they started to make unreasonable ultimatums regarding their wages. Time was of the essence and unfortunately there was little we could do but meet their demands. Word soon spread that the foreigners were paying out, and over twenty people got to work, building the charpie in just one day. It had been a job for no more than five skilled labourers and one which required careful planning and masonry. The result was a shambles. With some remarkable negotiation skills from Sujit we managed to salvage the project.

Our farewell was a grand affair. Any doubts surrounding just how worthwhile our placement had been were quickly dispelled as we were invited from house to house to be bestowed with garlands of flowers, fruit and whey. Leaving our family was an emotional time – full of tears, presents and promises to write. We left the school on a similar melancholy note, but after three hours of speeches and dances, our emotions were slightly less heightened.

Back in Kathmandu, it was tough adjusting to the hectic pace of the brightly-lit city and I'm sure I was not the only one to feel the first pangs of nostalgia for the peacefully remote village with all its characters we had come to know and love.

It had been the most incredible experience. Whilst it was no easy ride and at times I felt I was more entertainment value than respected volunteer, I know in my heart that we did well. We left a small legacy of numerous grassroots projects and many happy memories for the kids. On top of that, I returned home with my eyes opened and my attitude humbled. The Nepalese might live in one of the poorest countries in the world, but out in the villages, it's hard to believe. Smiles complimenting an easy humour and simple celebration of life is Nepal's legacy for me, one which will no doubt, remain a part of me for as long as I live.

Lasti Borni's Firsti Communion
Jean Cooper (Tanzania)

A medical student and myself were invited to a friend's 'lasti borni's firsti communion'.

Very early in the morning, before the heat of the day, Sebastian and I walked the 3 km sandy track to the village, arriving in time for the full church service. It was crowded, drums were being drummed and there was plenty of chanting. There were comings and goings throughout the service, and the baby in the pew in front of me had a cold and was suckling and snuffling so loudly that the priest had to shout even more loudly.

When the service finished we walked to the *shamba* (smallholding) where the party was being held.

When everyone had finally trickled in the fun started. Frederick, the lasti borni, aged eleven, sat in the chair of honour and listened to amazingly long Kiswahili speeches, aimed at him. He looked so sweet, all his clothes were brand spanking new: with his bow tie set at a jaunty angle he looked as if he was just about to go to a dancing lesson. Then the chanting started and people danced up to the table in front of him with presents and money.

Following that, there were more speeches (much loved here), and then Frederick had to start the dancing. I felt sorry for him, but he turned out to be a little raver. Everyone has a go here, whether you have a partner or not, you just get up and jiggle a bit. There was lots of food – pilau, rice, beans, salad, chicken, etc. – and tea, juice, home-made wine and a very popular alcoholic beverage that smells like gangrene and injures the liver.

We danced, sang and laughed until it was beginning to get dark, then about seven of us started to walk back home. Several of the women had babies tied up in a *kanga* on their backs.

One little girl was holding her plastic box on her head with one hand – too young to balance it without support – but the older ones were carrying luggage of all shapes and sizes without any difficulty. As we walked along we all chatted and sang. Every time someone branched off the track to their home the rest made up a song about them.

I will always remember that day – it was such a happy time.

Time off: Travelling with Nana Rob
Rob Palmer (Ghana)

The modes of public transport in Ghana are legion, all leading to some culture-bound syndrome, complaint or psychological disorder.

Trotro-leg: most Ghanaians use a wild bush taxi called a *trotro*. Imagine something that resembles an over used VW camper van with no tyre treads packed full of sixteen seats, each with enough legroom for one of the forest's red, hairy dwarfs, the *mmoatia*. Cram in twenty-five adults, plus luggage, hens, chickens and bags of yam and plantain, throw in a couple of breast-feeding babies, and a free-standing goat on the roof. Mix all to the sounds of Ghanaian 'highlife' music played at deafening volume on the crunching old speakers. Add a bumpy pot-holed road and propel at high speed through the tropical forest region to a temperature of 35°C. These cramped conditions are the most common and induce pain in the leg and paranoia about getting a *trotro* version of deep vein thrombosis.

Trotro-prayer: everyone who travels this way for any time has their own trotro-story. Once, when in a trotro going up a hill, there was a loud bang and the back doors flew open. The luggage was sucked out and the whole scene smacked of the film *Alive,* where the plane hits a mountain and splits in two, luggage and people sucked out the back. A friend of mine, while travelling in a trotro with a live pig that was apparently making too much noise, found himself witness to an impromptu decapitation with a large machete, 'so that the driver was not disturbed'. At first I was puzzled as to why most trotros have some slogan written on them: 'In God We Trust', or 'Prayer is the answer'. After travelling by trotro for a while they soon lost their novelty and I too found myself believing that 'prayer is the master key'.

Trotro-paranoia: Trotro is the most widely used means of transport, but it was never possible to travel *incognito*, on the quiet. The movements of the *obruni* around the village and away from the village seemed to be carefully mentally noted by the community or their contacts in other villages, towns or the nearest city, Kumasi. Sometimes you'd get the feeling that you were being followed. You'd often get people coming up to you saying something like, 'Have you seen me?' meaning, do you recognise me? You look at them blankly and they continue, 'I was sitting three seats behind you to the right on the trotro going from Otaakrom to Nyinahin five weeks ago. You had two plastic bags of food with you.' You'd still look at them blankly, though this time in disbelief.

Shared-taxi shoulder: shared taxis are normal taxis that seem to be entering a Guinness World Record competition. They are simply not designed to have two in the passenger seat and four in the back, plus luggage and live animals. Yet it happens here with resulting dead-arm pain.

Dropping-taxi worry: a taxi to yourself? Luxury. You may think so until you realise that your driver seems to be doing everything possible to attempt suicide. One thing I could never get: Ghanaians walking are the most chilled-out ever (apart from when it rains and they run like headless chickens), but stick them behind a wheel and they become complete psychos.

Fast-car desperation: if you're in a hurry there's nothing quicker than a fast-car. Aptly named, these cars drive at insane speeds to reach their destination as quickly as possible. Should only be considered as a last resort or when in a serious rush.

State Transport Coach (STC) Arse: STC coaches are theoretically the safest means of transport when travelling any distance in Ghana, if for no other reason than their size means that any goats that the vehicle hits will be blasted clean away. Unfortunately the company saw little need to invest in comfortable seating for these journeys, that sometimes take twenty-four hours, resulting in severe dead arse pains. The counterpart coach company in Côte d'Ivoire at least recognises its downfalls, being aptly named STIF.

Travel around Ghana is amazing. It's also dirt cheap by 'our standards': you can travel the whole length of the country for about £6, so long as you can handle being covered in red dust and going through a combination of trotro-leg, shared taxi shoulder and STC arse. The coast west of Accra has some stunning beaches, many of which are very secluded, though some are used as public toilets.

On a trip into Côte d'Ivoire, some friends and I tried out what a guidebook describes as (and I quote) a 'budget paradise'. Actually, it was a 'maison de passage', more commonly known as a brothel. Unfortunately we didn't realise until it was too late, and we were too tired, to care. The tariff on the wall per hour was 50p. I choose to forget that night, and being woken up numerous times by someone banging on the next door and shouting what I'm sure translated as 'your time is up'.

Back in Ghana we took the overnight ferry up the Lake Volta. For £2.50 we got a seat on a bench with room enough on a table to slump your head forward to go to sleep. The boat was packed. There was one toilet. Unsurprisingly, children (and some adults) started to relieve themselves on the floor and as the boat rocked gently back and forth, things started to spread.

We were travelling at night and I did start to wonder about how exactly the boat was navigated though obstacles such as the phantom forests that were drowned as Lake Volta was created in the '60s. One of my friends had the answer – one that I really didn't want to hear. He went up to the bridge and saw the captain. Looking around, he saw what looked like a large navigation instrument so felt quite reassured, then the 'navigation equipment' started to play music. From what he could see, the navigation consisted of someone standing on the front of the boat with a large torch giving directions to the driver. I was just pleased you could buy beer on the boat.

When travelling in Ghana, particularly the north, you do have to be especially patient and accommodating to the local environment, situation and local customs. You have to be prepared to wait a day for a bus, and when you finally get it not be too upset if it breaks down after turning the first corner. You have to be prepared to eat street food and not think too much about exactly what meat you're eating. Above all, you have to be very accommodating with toilet facilities. Most places have maggot-pits to squat over, some being communal where the person next to you will want to greet you and perhaps strike up a conversation about England. Toilets are often not located close to houses so a 3am maggot dash through the village is not uncommon if your yam or shito is giving your stomach grief.

Once a cat in my village fell into the maggot pit. For three days every time you visited the pit you could hear her meowing, but there was no way to rescue her. It stopped after a while. In other places, like Larabanga in the north, they simply have 'free-range' toilets.

'Where is the toilet?' I ask in the early evening.

'Over there,' he says pointing to a grassy field.

'Where?' says I.

'Anywhere,' says he, 'by the way, do you have a torch so you can see where you are treading?'

'Right.'

* * *

After being in the village for ten months, we had managed to achieve a lot towards the development of the training centre and the village. One morning the village Chief came to talk to me in private, informing me that he and the village elders wanted to make me a sub-chief for the village. When a chief is made in Ghana they are given a special carved stool to sit on and a special name that they then take and are called by. I was informed

'Chief Nana Rob'

my new name was to be 'Nana Kwadwo Rob Mframa Ampafo Otaakrom Nkosouohene', which loosely translates as 'Rob, of Monday, Chief of Tree Wind, King of Development for Otaakrom traditional area'. Though I let my friends call me 'Nana Rob'.

When I asked the Chief Elder what 'Tree wind' was, he said something wise, 'wind is the bringer of many things, it shakes the leaves and carries seeds to grow, eh-heh'. Not a reference to groundnut soup and fish-head flatulence, I was told.

So it was that on 2 October 2001 I became an African Chief. I was presented with many traditional chief's articles: a carved wooden stool, two pairs of golden sandals, two Kente cloth togas (one to wear, one for the wash), two crowns, and a protective sash made by the village fetish priest. I had to undergo a ceremony involving drumming, dancing, meeting other Chiefs and drinking gin.

Back in the UK, I sometimes wake up in the early morning, my eyes darting around the room, and I have to ask myself if the whole eleven months in Ghana was just one long Lariam dream. But then I notice the small wooden stool in the corner of my room and realise that this is one dream that I'll never forget.

Nana Rob's top tip for volunteers in Ghana: don't get lost in the severed cow-head section of the Kumasi market.

VOLUNTEERING CHANGES

EVERYTHING –

NOW BACK HOME SEEMS WEIRD

TOO

Leaving is Hard
Holly Twiname (China)

My time here in Zhoukou is fast drawing to a close. I only have one day left before my career here as a teacher is over. It'll be strange to leave it all behind – people walking backwards early in the morning and late at night apparently exercising; the dog with the wig; the knitted ear covers, in the shape of your ear; people randomly singing to themselves on the street, loud and proud; sellers and food stalls always on the move; the bus that slows down but rarely stops. It's no wonder Zhoukou is pronounced *joke-o*. I wonder equally what people make of my quirky behaviour: saying thank you when I buy something; eating out and enjoying it; using chopsticks; walking slightly faster than the normal strolling pace; taking pictures of everyday scenes; saying *ni hao* (hello) instead of 'Where are you going?' or 'Have you eaten?'

I shall miss life here with cyclists weaving in and out of each other's way all day long; my happy chirpy neighbours; the restaurant I usually eat at, owned by a family that never want to take my money when I eat there. I will even miss random strangers wishing to know how much I earn, how old I am, what I am doing in Zhoukou, and whether we eat noodles or rice in Britain. I might even miss the novelty of being the only foreigner here. But most of all I shall miss my students. The way they greet me in the most enthusiastic way, the way they want to share their simple pleasures in life with me, the way they pour their kindness on me in all sorts of different ways – like bringing a bag of peanuts grown by their parents in their village.

I will end with a something one of my students wrote to me in a card, which I am yet to understand.

'Yearning is a quiet clear river which ripples with every spring wind of friendship.'

Last Six Weeks
Christopher Osborn (Thailand)

We have fully settled into our place. We have our own toaster, hot pot and sandwich maker. We buy regular clumps of food (noodles mostly, and bread). We found a place in town that sells peanut butter, and we have food carts to go to in the evening to have dinner. Our spoken Thai, while not exactly smooth, at least now gives way to sparks of recognition in the vendors when we inquire how much their tigers cost ('tiger' and 'shirt' are close words), or whether there is any more news left to eat ('news'/'rice'). At least now they don't stare at us blankly waiting for some hint of intelligence to emerge from our mouths, or via our wild hand signals. At moments of rare adjustment I look around and say 'I could live here.' Then someone asks me if I'd like some chicken to go with my news and, not understanding a single word, I nod politely and ask, 'Is there any sand I can eat with my radio?' and realise that, in addition to providing comic relief, I have some distance to go before I can really fit in.

Four weeks to go. My days are spent tracking down money to send Sompop to New York City for the September 19th UN conference (cancelled on September 12th), to send him to Washington DC for the 40th anniversary celebration of the Peace Corps, and acquire four bags of rice to feed 150 children for two months. Oddly, I find it easier to send a delegation to New York, DC and Tokyo than to find anyone willing to buy four bags of rice. (I never did find anyone willing to fund rice and cooking oil purchases – anyone with a spare $50 could make a really huge difference.)

Two weeks to go. I go for my first walk up the mountain to the village where the children come from. A new recruit has discovered our website and asked if we are looking for volunteers. Sylvia and I climb up the road and check out a village cock fight, then wander into the border village where we run into one of the Daughters. All these months I have worked and sweated at the base of the hill and this is the first exploration I have made into our local populations' homes. We sit on a platform perched on the side of a house overlooking the entire Mae Sai river valley, a panoramic spread of forty miles, ringed by distant mountains. It is breathtaking and serene. The Daughter introduces her father and he sits with us while we drink some water and talks about the day, his daughter, and the incredibly detailed Burmese script tattoos on his arms. Of course our Thai is limited to direct noun commands (Where is the bathroom? . . . How much for the tiger? . . .) so the discussion is torturous and rife with misunderstanding, but somehow the exchange matches the incredible vista in serenity and no-one is impatient to make the conversation achieve anything more than four folks hanging out on a porch on a lazy summer afternoon. Sylvia and I go down the road to an abandoned bridge trestle that spans a river going nowhere. She teaches me some German and tells me about a bunny she found lying on the stairs to the fifth floor of her apartment in Bangkok.

Last week. One by one deadlines loom for reports, grants and newsletters. With each passing week, I get less efficient and the new volunteer smoothly picks up the reins and keeps everything working. We prepare to gracefully slip off during the school holiday with Sompop's family and see the land of his childhood. But, before we can make our exit, the school has a going-away event planned whereby the school can make the volunteers feel extremely self-conscious by saying all sorts of nice things about them, and giving hand-drawn cards, hand-made scarves and hugs from the school population (rare in Thailand). Two hours of music and spectacle leave Christian and me feeling unworthy and nostalgic.

Our trip with Sompop's family is every bit as well planned as you can imagine. The six of us take up our positions in the car for our ten-day, 2,000-mile journey into the not quite specified. Sompop's house is a pastoral two acres in the suburbs of Chiang Rai. The family pet bounds up to meet us when we pull in the driveway. 'Haw', the water buffalo's eyes plead us to pet her. Of course, at 700 lbs, it is a little hard to ignore Montagh's 'requests' for petting, especially as her eyes are just about level with mine. She is cute and it is impossible to believe that something so massive could have such a tiny little voice. 'Hoo wah.'

Sompop has a delicious house nestled into the middle of his plot of land. In a completely atypical approach to Thai construction, he has been planning the construction of his house for ten years or so and is not rushing the physical building. He should be done in another ten years or so and easily have the most well thought-out and beautiful house in the entire neighbourhood. It already exceeds most of what I have seen elsewhere and he has only completed the walls and roof so far.

Our parting is sudden, somewhat unplanned and emotional. Sompop and his family decide to turn back a little early and focus the remaining portion of the trip with their relatives and training for the swimming competition that is coming up. We are left standing in the early morning of Krabi city, our bags leaning against the building and a job offer and invitation to return to be a part of Sompop's family floating on the early morning zephyrs, as their family car weaves into the motorcycles and wobbles out of sight.

The return to the West is now a looming event. I have always had a mental picture of air travel as being projected by a giant slingshot. It starts with the mental preparation to go abroad, becomes fully cocked on the last day of your 'regular' routine. Then as you board the bus to go to the airport, or sell your house to leave the country there is a huge 'whoosh' as events travel past propelling one onto an aeroplane and into the sky. We step up into our giant slingshot, and begin the slow backstep to cock the rubber bands. It begins with going out to find a restaurant to have Mexican food and sitting at a bar to watch 'Shrek' the movie on a tiny island in the Andaman Sea.

Little things are starting to get on our nerves: no-one ever yields the right of way; people don't smile at one another in queues. Everyone wants to help us, give us rides, do anything but let us explore (a person without any friends clustered around them must be lonely, right?) In this way we have already left Thailand – it just remains for our bodies to catch up.

November. We spend our last two weeks staring at fish underwater and staring at rain from our beach bungalow. Then, **Bangkok.** The city we saved for the very last. The slingshot is whooshing along nicely now. We do all of the tourist things, see the king's palace and his other palace. Ride the water buses up the river. Eat at little kitchens, perched precipitously over the water for $1 per meal. The city is full of traffic, noise, pollution, people. It is everything one expects in a thriving capital city of a developing nation – but it seems different now to me than Chiang Mai did six long months ago. The smells are still strange to my nose, but I know how to use the buses, the money. I know how to order food, and find a place to sleep. The phones are annoying as hell, but I *could* get one to work if I really needed to. . . . In short I could live in Bangkok, or Thonburi or Krabi or Chiang Rai or Mae Sai. The job offer from Sompop echoes in the back of my mind and is comforting.

I walk through the restaurant that our guest house is connected to, clutching the guidebook that we used to get around Thailand. I scan the restaurant looking for English-speaking newcomers that I can gift the book to.

'Hello. I don't mean to interrupt but would you like my guidebook?'

'Thanks, but we already have one. We are on a trip around the world, and just landed here today. Any places in Thailand you can recommend. . . ?'

The Volunteers – Parental Postscript
William Grant

The Volunteers. We all know where they go to – from Albania to Zambia – but have you ever thought about where they come from? People who are perhaps work-weary or aspirational or want to make a contribution above and beyond the normal confines of day-to-day existence or who feel they have something special to give to others or people who are just evangelical.

These people are stimulated and enthused by the possibility of making a difference. By a desire to contribute; to make an effort, albeit in a small way, to the improvement in the conditions of those who are less fortunate.

And very laudable aspirations they are. However, you will note that the common feature of the all these characteristics is that they are ego driven. That is there is a lot of *I* would like to do this, *I* will be able to improve the lot of others, *I* can make a difference if *I* really try.

This finally results in a statement that *I* will now push-off to some hostile territory for up to two years exposed to some hostile environment where disease is rife and the local populace a very unknown quantity.

Some of these people are what is, in polite society, termed mature and there are many reasons that they might want to volunteer. They could have had a 'jolly good life' and feel that to restore the balance of nature within themselves they want to put something back; or else they may have just gone through a major personal trauma and are seeking to expunge the results by directing the focus of their lives away from anything familiar. They may just have retired and are looking for something meaningful to occupy the gap between work and mental and physical incapacity. In all of these cases it is perfectly legitimate to presume that they have discharged any responsibilities to their nearest and dearest.

But there is another category of volunteers who are driven to become involved at an earlier age, and as a result a particular group of people become impacted significantly. I speak about the parents of those departed these shores who, given the territories where most of the volunteers end up, do not even have the opportunity to use their offspring as a reason to enjoy a carefree holiday in a tropical paradise. Parents who, having brought up their little Bridget or Hugh to contribute to society from the nice safe haven of a merchant bank, school staffroom, surgical operating theatre or a high profile job in the media, suddenly find them jetting off to a place where the normal mode of transport is a dugout canoe in a crocodile-infested river.

They are not ecstatic over the idea that their child (who may by this time be well into his/her thirties) is off to some hostile territory for up to two years with not a thought for those who remain in the homeland. They dare not show it for fear of being thought too constraining or not allowing the necessary freedom which is an essential part of engendering flexibility in the parent-child relationship. But they are fraught with worry and concern about exposure to goodness knows what in some hostile environment where disease is rife and the hazard of avoiding passing traffic as well as the occasional possibility of coming off second best in a confrontation with snakes, lions, crocodiles or hippos.

Now there may be some parents who would be delighted to have the opportunity to give their teenaged children an opportunity to try out their natural boisterousness and vituperation on a passing hippopotamus. But by the time they are eligible to join an overseas voluntary organisation they have passed the age where such a solution is in any way attractive.

And so they go, these courageous, clear-sighted, motivated people to 'do good' in foreign lands and we, parents, sit at home, looking at the statistics of the numbers of people dying of AIDS precisely where they are located. We see from photographs and videos the appalling conditions under which some of the volunteers work and think about the positive impact that they can have in improving them. We marvel at, delight in and are amazed at the fact that we have created someone who seems to have the ability to take our own relatively modest achievements and, using them as a foundation, build upon them to limits which are usually way beyond our own aspirations.

Airports are normally buzzing with activity and appear almost alive. Suited businessmen moving purposefully through the crowds with a confident familiarity of the procedures mixed together with vast numbers of holidaymakers enjoying the once a year novelty of being part of the great travelling and looking wide-eyed at who might be there. But late at night when the last aircraft is departing and the place is closing down for the night, it becomes virtually deserted. It appears to be waiting, with ill-concealed impatience, for the flight to depart and the public to go home so it too can slumber before the arrival of the first aircraft, early the following morning.

Against this background, my youngest daughter departed for two years to

Zambia. My wife and I said all the right things as we had dinner and we all tried to act in a light-hearted way. We not wanting to show concern, she, I suspect, not wishing to expose any doubts or fears.

Communications are not easy from the far-flung outposts to which the volunteers are sent and the eagerly-awaited first letter seems to take forever to arrive. We heave a joint sigh of relief when it eventually does, containing, as it inevitably will, a very positive report of their arrival and initial settling in. But we had the enormous benefit of technological development with the use of email enabling us to keep in relatively close contact, given the vicissitudes of sporadic electrical supplies, poor or occasionally non-existent telephone services and local computer problems.

And there were of course other upsides. Conversation at dinner tables was skilfully brought around to the topic of children or Africa so we could, with appropriate demure pride, retell the latest story from the daughter in great (and sometimes mildly-embellished) detail. Friends became interested in developments and we sometimes glowed in the reflection of her achievements abroad. And as the years progressed we became impressed at her ability to deal with a variety of extremely difficult circumstances and consequently a the concern about her well-being gradually lessened.

But that did not detract from the mixture of emotions on her eventual return home. Pride on realising the size of the task she had taken and successfully completed. Pleasure that we had come through a period of vicarious involvement in a project that would be very beneficial to the development of people we had never met. Delighted that the experience had given to our daughter a breadth of expertise, understanding and knowledge of that area which, if applied properly, could continue to benefit the people of that area. But most of all – and selfishly – an enormous relief that she had returned safe and sound. And I think she is going to stay, though recently she did say that she has been considering . . . no I don't even want to think about it.

Reflections on Fiji
Laura Smith (Fiji)

A year ago, I hadn't been to Fiji, the Cooks, French Polynesia, Tonga,
New Zealand or Vanuatu.
I had never taught a class,
Swum in a waterfall,
Sat on a bus without windows,
Danced in a tropical rainstorm,
Kept a house on my own.
I couldn't open a coconut except with a hammer.
I hated bargaining.
I took tap water for granted.
I spoke more loudly.

It was important for me to go out a lot.
I was in the dark about colonialism and globalisation,
Secure in my ideas of 'home', 'self' and 'culture',
Convinced democracy was the only viable way,
And much more 'sure' of the future.

Before, I didn't know the difference between Melanesia, Polynesia and
    Micronesia.
No longer – because I have friends from each of these regions.
I had never heard of Kiribati and certainly didn't know how to pronounce it.
No longer – I can spot an I-Kiribati and tell her apart from a Tongan.
I couldn't say 'hello' in Fijian.
No longer – I can have a whole conversation and sometimes fool people on the
    phone.
I could happily stand to talk with a sitting person.
No longer – I feel odd if I don't stoop, crawl and mutter 'tilou'.

A year ago, I might have joked about men wearing skirts.
Now I would notice more if a man were wearing something else.
A year ago, I wore shoes and socks every day.
Now anything but mud on my feet feels restrictive.
A year ago, I thought 'cold' was when you got the scarf and gloves out.
Now I feel cold at 24 degrees!

Once, the people I considered friends were all of my own generation.
Today, some of those closest to me are three times my age.
Once, I could talk freely with an unmarried man.
Today, it feels odd for a man even to look me in the eye.
Once, I had never met these people.
Today, they are some of my best friends.

Then, I may have taken a surreptitious look at a person whose skin was a
    different colour to my own.
But now, I stare at white people because they look odd and incomplete.
I believed racism was when dark-skinned people were less likely to get a job.
But now, my definition and my eyes have widened through my experience of
    racism directed at me.
My understanding was that humans are individual things responsible mainly
    for themselves.
But now, I have seen that one can represent many and many can act as one.
Poverty and development seemed strictly economic categories.
But now, I understand that the poor in GDP can be richer than the poor in spirit.
I believed that the law and the police force had superhuman objectivity and
    fairness.
But now, I think all things can be manipulated.
I thought of the earth as a dead, passive thing.
But now, it is vital to my spirituality.

I had never seriously talked theology with someone of another faith.
But now, I do so most days, even with shopkeepers and taxi drivers.
I knew many things in my head that I didn't understand in my heart.
But now, I have found more balance.

A year – an eternity.
A year – the blink of an eye.

Can't Wait to Go Back
Carol Hawthorne (Zambia)

Well, how was it in Africa? Temporarily stunned by this interested inquiry I took a breath and . . . but by then the conversation had passed on to the latest events on reality TV.

Well, everyone knows what Africa is like, don't they? Hot, dangerous, famine, drought, floods, refugee camps, shortages of everything, megalomaniac dictators, endemic corruption, internecine violence and apathetic people. We see it on the box and in the newspapers. A mish-mash of hopeless basket cases. An occasional ray on sunshine that is quickly blotted out. Power corrupts and absolute power corrupts absolutely – a truism demonstrated more vividly in many African countries which are without the checks and restraints that characterise older democracies.

These were the preconceptions that I took to Zambia. I was completely unprepared for the stark beauty and simplicity that surges into the heart like a tidal wave and leaves an undying affection in its wake. No matter the many petty annoyances of day-to-day living – well, some matter at the time but they do teach the wonderful patience and stoicism with which most of the Africans I met seem endowed. Life moves at a slower pace despite its greater brevity. Staying alive is a time-consuming activity.

I found a society shaped by customs and behaviour alien to me. An extended family support system that is both sustaining and draining. Differing 'family values'. The generally inferior position of women. The struggle going on to temper existing customs in the light of modern problems. The sad sight of high levels of literacy and education in rapid decline. I also found a vibrancy, a joy and happiness in small pleasures, an acceptance which somehow seems patronising to describe. An open friendliness that was a delight.

What was my greatest disappointment? The discovery that 'development' is a business with all the associated motivations and rivalries. I had always understood that government aid is given for political ends but did not comprehend the level of strings attached. Yes, we will give aid to update your tele-communications system – but you must buy our hardware and software (appropriateness not an issue), employ our experts . . . . The appearance of a giving and concerned nation on the global stage.

I had not fully realised the jockeying for position that goes on even (or perhaps that should be especially) among the Christian agencies. The degree

'Who could forget the slaughter-house?'

that fashion is a factor in funding aid programmes. So I lost my naivety. Nevertheless, there are many individuals out there for whom helping the less fortunate is a main concern and I was also lucky to meet some of them.

What did I bring back? A preference for simpler living. A less hurried view of life. Sights, smells and scenes. Who could forget the fragrance of frangipani? Or a long drop toilet? A busy rural market with its piles of tomatoes, vociferous marketeers and slaughter-house. Fresh produce *par excellence*. Women carrying water at sunrise. At midday. And at sunset. Long dusty roads, spare of vehicles but peopled by walkers and heavily-laden bicycles. The broken and deforested landscapes. Music everywhere. And coffin makers. The buses with their complement of livestock. A greater appreciation of the mores and traditions of another culture and how they shape society. To view things from a wider perspective. That there are no universal answers.

Oh – and an intolerance for so many things previously tolerated. The sheer volume of choice so seductively displayed. The waste, the blatant consumerism. Perhaps in time I will once again become an obedient first world minion doing my bit for world trade. But the tomatoes will never taste as good as the misshapen, off-colour rejects of the EU.

Meanwhile, I can't wait to go back.

Sell-By Dates?
Jean Hales (Guyana)

Back here in Britain I now have to adjust to avoiding eye contact with strangers as I pass by them in the street and resist the urge to say 'Hello'. I have to remember that shopping is a functional occupation and not a social activity. Oh, how I missed my beloved Sainsbury's when I first arrived in Guyana, where I could get everything from the same place. Oh, how I missed everything neatly packaged, labelled and presented. In Linden it seemed such a chore at first to have to trail around different shops and market stalls to get everything I needed.

Why, for example, couldn't I get bread from the supermarket? Yes, there were a couple of loaves, but it was a bit of a lottery as to what they stocked.

It took a while to get used to the pungent smells – no, let's be honest, 'stench' is a more appropriate word – of meat and fish, and to see them openly exposed to the elements and flies and, horror of horrors, happily nestling next to each other, not to mention huge slabs of cheese unrefrigerated, sweating in polythene. Why don't people get food poisoning, I wondered. You would see eggs and shrimps on stalls out in the sun all day. Sell-by dates are for wimps in Guyana.

And so my Saturday shopping became a social event which took up most of the day, what with stopping and having a gaff and a laugh with friends, shopkeepers, market stallholders, mini bus and taxi drivers. What an ego boost it was to get into a taxi and not to have to tell them my address.

Whenever I was feeling down and lonely, and I often did (living and working in another country you really do pass through the loneliness pain barrier), I would just go and take a stroll down the market and soon the cries of 'Sister Jean' or 'Miss' (from school students) or even 'Baby' or 'Darling' would lift my spirits. Yes, political correctness has yet to reach Guyana. It took me some time to get used to the sucking sound that Guyanese men make with their teeth when a woman passes by, accompanied by cries of 'Hello baby, I love you, why don't you marry me?'

Subtlety is not a Guyanese trait. 'You're getting fat, girl', was a regular comment from friends, and a compliment, as in many poorer countries. None of your mealy-mouthed euphemisms either such as 'stout' or 'big' or 'large' or 'well-made'. If you are fat you are fat and that's it.

There is a similar directness and lack of negative connotations in naming people according to their racial origin. I cringed when I first heard Black people referred to as 'negro' or Indians as 'coolie' Chinese as 'chinee' or Amerindians as 'buck'. I got referred to as 'whitey' or 'white meat'. I was assured that no negative connotations were attached to these labels, but I must admit I never really got used to them.

Back Home for the Holidays
Eva Corral (Angola)

Angola is a country whose mention evokes landmines, amputees and war. My family was waiting anxiously for my return home for the holidays after having spent three months working as a volunteer agronomist in Kuito, Angola. They expected to see me emaciated, worn and sick.

During the first two months I spent in Angola my mother used to phone me every week to know how I was and to write me mountains of two-line emails, saying, 'How are you? Please eat well and look after yourself.' My father, on the other hand, would sometimes say in our telephone conversations, 'You don't have to stay there if you don't like it. You can come back whenever you want.'

When my father and I arrived home from Madrid airport my mother was waiting behind the door and opened it before we even put the key in the lock. She gave me a hug and afterwards she looked me up and down. 'Let me see you.' She looked me over in front and behind and when she had assured herself my health was fine and the colour in my cheeks was adequate, we went into the living room and sat down to talk about my job and life in Angola.

I was feeling very excited and could not remain seated on the sofa. I stood and continued talking with them while I wandered through the house and saw everything afresh. The living room with its bookshelf full of books, the bathroom with its huge mirror covering the whole wall over the sink, the cat lying on the floor in the middle of the corridor. My words were tripping over themselves, I had so many things to say that I jumped from one to another without finishing explaining any of them, throwing in comments on how beautiful the house was and that the vase on the table was new or that they had removed the carpet. The house seemed enormous and luxurious compared to the one in Kuito.

Suddenly I remembered my suitcase and the presents I bought for the family. I grabbed it from the hall and dumped it in the middle of the living room. I opened it and started to take things out. Handicrafts in Kuito are very poor, the only things I could find to take home as gifts were some wood-carved birds and a couple of tin cars made by children in Kuito from empty cans of humanitarian aid oil.

I suddenly felt hungry and went into the kitchen. I opened the fridge. It was full, my mother had gone shopping and had bought all that I liked to eat. There were golden apples, big, round and appetising. I picked one up and without washing it, bit into it while I continued scanning the contents of the different containers in the fridge.

The vegetables were all huge, perfectly shaped and enticingly coloured. There were things whose existence I had almost forgotten, like yoghurts, liquid (not powdered) milk and red meat. But the thing I missed most in Angola was cheese – of which there were plenty of different types in the fridge. I looked at the time. It was only eleven. Eleven in Spain is twelve o'clock in Angola and we used to have lunch at twelve-thirty. But in Spain we would have lunch at half past two or three in the afternoon. I decided to give the cheese a go.

Next morning I woke up early, at six o'clock, as I used to do in Angola. At home nobody woke up until a couple of hours later. By that time I was tired of looking at the ceiling, I had read and I had written a couple of letters. I had lots of plans. Two weeks before going home I had dreamed of it and I had made a mental list of the things I wanted to do on arrival. The list included taking a bath: to fill up the bath with hot water and to submerge myself in it until the fingers of my feet and my hands became wrinkled. It included having a cappuccino with a lot of foam that I would eat with the spoon before drinking the coffee, and covered with grated chocolate. It also included having a Rioja before Sunday lunch on a terraza in Madrid while reading the newspaper.

At noon, after having a bath and having enjoyed spending my time doing nothing, I went to buy the newspaper. I opened it on the kitchen table by my cup of coffee. Real coffee, made with an Italian coffee machine, with liquid milk, and sugar without ants – the ones that are so small that it is difficult to separate them. There were six films and two exhibitions I wanted to see. I also wanted to meet friends and relatives. It seemed difficult to achieve considering I only had two weeks in Spain.

But apart from doing all these things, I wanted to stay at home, to rest, to do nothing. Just before flying to Spain I had lain down on the bed in my room in Kuito and imagined with closed eyes my house in Madrid; the hall with its pictures, the living room with its glass doors. I was going through the house slowly, opening the doors of the different rooms and going into them. The last room I entered was mine. I stood in the middle looking at everything very carefully and then I lay down on the bed with my eyes open.

The next day I met some friends. We went for dinner and they asked me about Angola. Once again I had to repeat the same things. During the second course they started talking about the trip they had made to Portugal when I was away. I realised there were many things I had not been able to share with them; life had gone on normally without me. I also realised, while telling them about Angola, that they could not understand what I had lived, what I felt the first time I took a malnourished child in my arms or when I was woken up in the middle of the night by gunshots. I could not share that with them. I felt alone.

The first days back at home I found myself at a loss, lost, I didn't know where to go or what to do, I had the impression of being in a cloud or in a dream. Walking the streets I looked at everything with a certain bewilderment, what I saw was alien to me, as if I were in a film and I wasn't participating in it.

I remember seeing a boy with crutches and a plaster on his leg and feeling a strange solidarity with him. It was rare for me not to see people with crutches in the street. In Kuito there are many amputees.

Nevertheless, I soon got used again to life in Madrid and things stopped surprising me so much. My house was not huge and luxurious, the fridge emptied very quickly and my diet moved on from being based almost exclusively on apples and cheese. My family did not pay me the attention of the first days and went back to their everyday activities and I started creating new memories to share with my friends. Nevertheless I still had the feeling, sometimes, of not belonging there any more.

Dinner with my college friends was especially strange to me. One of them had got married while I was away and two others planned to do so in the near future. Almost all had bought cars and many were paying the mortgages on houses they were moving into with their girlfriend or boyfriend. Towards the end of the dinner in the group to my left at the table, the men started discussing different designs of tie to wear the day of the wedding. The group to my right, the women, were discussing which venues were cheaper for hosting the wedding reception. I had the impression of being in a surrealist film. What was I doing there? What had happened to my old friends from university? What had happened to me?

After dinner we went to a bar. We had to squeeze in, shoulder to shoulder. Inside the music was so loud that we could hardly speak and the blue neon lights gave the people a space-like appearance so that they seemed to move like robots. It was not my first time in this bar but this time I didn't feel comfortable.

It was very hot, people were pushing me constantly, the music was deafening. I asked a friend to take me home.

In Kuito there are very few bars so we normally meet at somebody's house for dinner, to have a beer or to watch a film. Choosing the film we are going to watch is not easy: most Angolans prefer action films like Stallone or Van Damme ones, while the expatriates prefer something completely different.

Due to problems getting my visa for Angola renewed, I had to stay in Spain two weeks longer than planned. I had time to go and see eight films, as well as two exhibitions and to visit the Prado Museum. From my third week in Spain I started wanting to go back to Angola, to Kuito. That feeling surprised me, but it was real. I missed it. I had already seen my family and friends, brought myself up to date on the cinema, had real coffee, drunk good wine, stuffed myself with cheese and I had taken so many baths that I had practically developed scales. Now I wanted to go back and, as time went by, this feeling was growing stronger.

When at last I got my visa and flew back to Angola I carried with me, as well as some packages of Spanish ham and two bottles of wine, some photos of family and friends to put on the walls of my room in Kuito, and a coffee mug. My coffee mug.

Development Studies
Catherine Gee (Ghana)

Before leaving Ghana, we prepared ourselves to answer the inevitable string of questions about what we had been doing as volunteers there. We had the short and long answers to 'what was it like' all mapped out. Unfortunately, when I actually got home, the one question that I was asked most was one for which I was least prepared: 'So what next?' I apologise now to all those people whose heads I bit off, but it was so painful to be asked that over and over again as if everything I had done and experienced in the past two and a half years was not at all interesting and best moved on from . . . and I just didn't know the answer.

The question of what to do next is one of the most difficult ones that a returned volunteer faces. Do you go back to what you were doing before? Some do, in the expectation that their experience will add to their skills and approach in their chosen field. Some do because they have rent to pay and it seems like the route of least resistance. Do you try and find something different? For many this was part of the reason for volunteering, the opportunity to change direction, but that means deciding where you are going next. A lot of teachers, it seems, find themselves in this position. Finally, some of us had hoped that the volunteer experience would somehow point the way or open new doors we had not perceived before. In other words, we had no real idea.

While in placement the issue has a rather surreal quality, a distant and non-urgent nature. The first time I considered it was about a year before I was due to return. I was in the category of changing careers or finding a new avenue. I had thought my time as a volunteer would point me in the right direction, as well as give me more time to make up my mind. I was enjoying the volunteer experience. Development work seemed to be something I could do. Exactly what that would entail, however, I was not very sure, so I decided whatever it was I probably needed some training in it. It seemed from what I had read in the advertisements in the international editions of papers that to work in the development field some kind of postgraduate qualification was a useful asset, so I set off to the British Council in Accra which had most of the postgraduate prospectuses and sat down to find a course.

The language of the development courses seemed very distant from teaching in Damongo: international development targets, multilaterals, the international economy, industrialisation, technology policy, environment, gender relations all seemed to bear little relation to my normal life as a volunteer teacher. I knew going back to essay writing and reading would be hard after so long out of the academic world. Since I was leaving Ghana in August, I thought it might be better to wait until the next academic year before starting, give myself time to make up my mind and resettle. Plus, there was a small matter of paying for a course, so time to earn some money seemed a good thing.

The reality of my return was a lot harder than I had expected. I found at the last moment that I really didn't want to leave after all, but my flight was booked, my replacement selected and so I found myself back in Britain. That post-volunteering slump was a pretty awful few months, and I still had no clear idea of what was next. Based on the experience of my fellow volunteers, I know now that getting on with something is a good plan. With my confidence low, I wavered over whether to go ahead with development studies and looked at other options, including teaching in the UK.

In the course of browsing the web I came across the Institute of Development Studies and their course on governance and development, which sounded interesting and seemed to be practically focused, with the possibility of going back overseas.

I applied and was lucky enough to be offered a place on the course. I still had misgivings – the course was *very* expensive and Brighton is not the cheapest place to live. During my time as a volunteer I had been having too much fun to worry about my financial situation afterwards and had used a lot of my savings to pay for touring the region, something I certainly do not regret. My post-return resettlement grant had supported me through my period of unsuccessfully sitting around waiting to feel resettled. By this time I had little left to put towards the tuition fees. Cost is one of the biggest deterrents to doing postgraduate study. I chose a career development loan which I didn't have to start paying until the course was over, in the hope that the course would open doors to a 'good job' afterwards and enable me to pay it.

Waiting the year after my return was a good idea in hindsight, preparing me for the hard work involved in a one-year Masters course. Two and a half years as a teacher in Ghana seemed very poor experience compared with that of the rest of the course members who had an impressive total of years in 'real' development work between them. But it was exciting too. I was finally going to find out what this development thing was all about.

To my surprise, I knew a lot of it already. The language and concepts of the course made sense of a whole range of things I had been aware of in Ghana. Using my own experiences, I was able to understand and even challenge the theory I was learning. There were a lot of new things to learn, not least from the other students, but I found I too had knowledge to offer. Not surprisingly, for most of my assignments I considered Ghanaian case studies.

Armed with my MA I still have to answer the 'What's next?' question, but it doesn't make me run away screaming any more. There are specific paths available in place of the abyss of post-volunteering options. And aside from the job prospects, I now have a much clearer idea of where my work in Ghana fitted into the larger development picture and can use all sorts of clever jargon to describe it. It's great to know that I was engaged in capacity building, developing social and human capital and providing the tools for integration into the globalised international economy, when I thought I was just teaching English . . . .

Home
Karen Harmatuk (Mongolia)

A lot of volunteers leave a country, to be re-implanted into a life they once held back in Britain or Canada or wherever. I had heard of such experiences. Many expatriates got a taste of reintegration by visiting their former home for a holiday.

'My mother sent me off to the shop to buy some toilet paper. What a shock! One-ply, two-ply, pink, recycled, cushy soft. So many choices,' one volunteer recounted after visiting Scotland at Christmas. In Mongolia, there's one kind of toilet paper, if you're lucky.

I, however, took a different route home: the ease-into-the-idea-of-going-back method. I went from Mongolia to China, Nepal, India, Thailand, Laos, Cambodia, Malaysia, Indonesia, with a final flight that took nine stops through places like Bangkok, Seoul, and Alaska before landing in Toronto, nearly a year after I finished in Mongolia. I had had the techno shock of an ultra-modern movie theatre in Bangkok, the delight of coconut curries and fresh seafood far from the mutton and milk tea of Mongolia, and the interaction with travellers fresh from Western thought.

Best of all, I had gotten together with my best friend without having to head to Canada. Spending time with her again felt more like home than any physical place. She had just finished a volunteer stint herself, a three-month experience in an Indian orphanage. We met in Nepal and drank lemon sodas at Sunny's café in Baktapur, as monsoon rain hit. Some people orient themselves in the world through geography. Yet in the exotic ornate city of Baktapur, I felt centred, which is perhaps what one is really searching for in going home. The comfort in no longer feeling lost.

While travelling, I compared everything around me with Mongolia:
'In Mongolia, they pass drinks like this, and social rules say that you do

that . . . .' People around me got sick of it.

Boy, did I have fun focusing on the present back in Canada . . . all my favourite things were indulged: canoe camping in Algonquin Park, my favourite café in Montreal, the Danforth in Toronto. Then you have to face the need to earn money. So I reverted back to a job I had done six summers before at a summer camp in Ontario's near north. Sure, I learned to lead climbing activities on a ropes course in the forest instead of merely fulfilling my former position as counsellor. Technically that meant I was learning something new. Only I know now I was doing what was comfortable, known.

The unknown jumped me in the autumn. I lamented being so lost and unhappy during one of my favourite seasons in Ontario, the maple leaves reddening, the skies crisp and blue. I found myself in a town of 100,000 called Guelph, about an hour from Toronto.

'Why Guelph?' all kinds of people asked me. I shrugged unhappily. The reality was I clung to the few people I knew at the time. Two friends were getting a place in Guelph, and I would be close enough to Toronto to visit my best friend and my family. I was like a child on apron strings. I couldn't venture far from the people I knew. Life was dismal and I was unemployed. Slowly, I picked up jobs to tide me over as I awaited the bureaucracy of school boards and teacher's colleges.

In six months, BOOM! A full-time contract teaching, a car, a cell-phone, a gym membership, a CD player and the latest music. I had cursed western culture, with its reliance on technology, its overuse of automobiles, its advertising, and its heaps of garbage that magically disappear when the garbage people take them away. My hypersensitivity to socially conscious issues fizzled in the face of Canadian routines, habits that fool you into believing you are home. I slipped into cruise control.

That is how I coped this year. I had wanted to do bigger things, take bigger risks and make new lifestyle choices. Ironically, this is more difficult in one's own culture than overseas. Going to Mongolia, life was supposed to be different and hard. You're far from home. You and other volunteers willingly take the risk to live in a new country. Canada is a place where I am supposed to feel at home, where life is supposed to be easy. However, approaching it from three years overseas made it just as foreign as the Mongolian steppe or Indian side streets. Like feeling odd in your own skin.

It has taken me this year to re-gather my strength and self-assurance, to be ready to take risks in following my dreams, to *choose* my path instead of easing back into the old armchair. I have chosen a town in the Rocky Mountains of western Canada to move to, where I have never visited, where I know no-one and have no job set up. Doing this is harder than it was to leave for Mongolia. I am searching for a new sense of home.

INDEX

Contributors (Country of Origin/Destination)

Countries

Volunteer Organisations

Volunteer Organisations

A list of volunteer organisations, many of whom our contributors volunteered with. This list is not comprehensive – please email us on info@volunteertales.org for any more organisations you know of. Also note that the views expressed in this book are solely of the authors and do not reflect those of the agencies mentioned. At no point have we been asked to represent the agencies either.

AFS	http://www.afs.org/
Aga Khan Foundation	http://www.akdn.org/
Amigos de las Americas	http://www.amigoslink.org/
Amizade	http://amizade.org/
L'Arche	http://www.larche.org/
AusAid	http://www.ausaid.gov.au/
British Trust for Conservation Volunteers	http://www.btcv.org.uk/
BUNAC	http://www.bunac.org/
Concern	http://www.concern.ie/
Concordia	http://www.concordia-iye.org.uk/
Coral Cay	http://www.coralcay.org/
Cross Cultural Solutions	http://www.crossculturalsolutions.org/
EarthWatch	http://www.earthwatch.org/
EarthWise Journeys	http://home.teleport.com/~earthwyz/
Frontier Projects	http://www.frontierprojects.ac.uk/
GAP	http://www.gap.org.uk/
German Development Agency	http://www.gtz.de/english/
Geekcorps	http://www.geekcorps.org/
Global Service Corps	http://www.globalservicecorps.org/
Global Volunteers	http://www.globalvolunteers.org/
Go M.A.D. (Make a Difference)	http://www.go-mad.org/
Green Volunteers	http://www.greenvol.com/
International Volunteer Programs Association	http://www.volunteerinternational.org/
JICA	http://www.jica.go.jp/
NetAid Online Volunteering	http://app.netaid.org/OV/
Peace Corps	http://www.peacecorps.gov/
Raleigh International	http://www.raleighinternational.org/
Student Action India	http://www.studentactionindia.org.uk/
Students Partnership Worldwide (SPW)	http://www.spw.org/
Take action in Africa	http://www.lindersvold.dk/
Tearfund	http://www.tearfund.org/
Teaching Abroad	http://www.teaching-abroad.co.uk/
UNAIS	http://www.internationalservice.org.uk/
UN Volunteers	http://www.unv.org/
UN Information Technology Service (UNITeS)	http://www.unites.org/
VolunteerAbroad	http://www.volunteerabroad.com/
Volunteers in Technical Assistance (VITA)	http://www.vita.org/
VSO	http://www.vso.org.uk/
WorldVision	http://www.worldvision.org/